THE DNA OF DISASTER /
CATASTROPHE BY DESIGN

Copyright © 2025 by Devin Savage. Published by Karlier LLC

Author: devinsavageauthor.com | DNA of Disaster: dnaofdisaster.com

All rights reserved. No part of this publication may be reproduced, stored in a retrieval system, or transmitted in any form or by any means, electronic, mechanical, photocopying, recording, scanning, or otherwise, except as permitted under Section 107 or 108 of the 1976 International Copyright Act, without the prior written permission except in brief quotations embodied in critical articles and reviews. Every effort has been made to ensure that all the information in this book is accurate at the time of publication; however, the author neither endorses nor guarantees the content of external links referenced in this book.

ISBN 979-8-9918829

Cover, design and layout: Studio Eyal &

THE DNA OF DISASTER / CATASTROPHE BY DESIGN

/ DEVIN SAVAGE

TABLE OF CONTENTS

- - - - - - - - - -

OPENING	8
ON LUCK	14
THE HOUR ON THE STAGE	25
INTELLIGENT DESIGN IN THE MARKETPLACE	26
DESIGNED SYSTEMS REST ON PREDICTABLE ASSUMPTIONS	33
THE FOUR BASIC HUMAN FOLLIES AND THEIR NICKNAMES	34
CASSANDRAS	44
NO PEN, PAPER, AND SCISSORS? A ROCK WILL DO!	52
THE SACRED AND THE SACRILEGIOUS:	
UPON WHOSE SACRED TURF DO WE TREAD?	57
ABORIGINAL ORIGIN STORIES:	
THE CHAIN OF AUTHENTICITY BEGINS WITH THE ANCESTORS	62
THE ELEMENTS OF A DESIGNED DISASTER	70
HUMAN INTELLIGENT DESIGN:	
NEED GIVES RISE TO DESIGN, DESIGN ENABLES FUNCTION	71
CATASTROPHIC POTENTIAL OF A SYSTEM – WHETHER DESIGNED	
BY NATURE OR BY HUMANS	73
CASE STUDY OF A DISASTER: CLIMATE CHANGE	75
THE FOLLIES	78
THE ARCHETYPAL DISASTER:	
THE SINKING OF RMS TITANIC	80
A STOVE BOAT AND DAVY JONES	83
THE AGE OF THE SUPERLINER	87

SELLING SUPERLINERS	88
BULKHEADS, LIFEBOATS, AND GIANT SHIPS:	
PROTOTYPING DESIGNS ON ACTUAL PASSENGER VESSELS	89
BULKHEADS OR LIFEBOATS? THE BOARD OF TRADE'S COZY	
RELATIONSHIP WITH SHIPOWNERS	91
THE CALL FOR COMPULSORY BULKHEADING	93
RENDERING A SHIP UNSINKABLE:	
THE STONE–LLOYD AUTOMATIC BULKHEAD DOORS	95
THE SS SUEVIC: PROOF OF UNSINKABILITY	98
THE BLUE-SKY MONUMENT BUILDING OF THE TITANIC ERA	100
A PUSHED NARRATIVE BECOMES THE BANDWAGON	105
CASSANDRA WEIGHS IN:	
THE JOHN BULL NEWSWEEKLY AND HORATIO BOTTOMLEY	107
PART II: HISTORY'S MOST FAMOUS 'UNSINKABLE VESSEL' VS. ICEBERG	112
THE TIMELINE OF THE SINKING OF THE TITANIC	113
HOW THE MIGHTY FELL	125
THE REGULATORY ENVIRONMENT OF THE TITANIC DISASTER	
REFLECTED IN THE PRESS	129
INTELLIGENT, SEMI-INTELLIGENT AND BLIND	132
DIAGNOSING THE SINKING OF TITANIC	136
THE DNA OF DISASTER RULES APPLIED TO THE SINKING	
OF THE TITANIC	141

THE NASA SPACE SHUTTLE CHALLENGER DISASTER ---- 146

THE SHOCK OF SPUTNIK AND THE BIRTH OF NASA	150
A FAINT SIGNAL EMERGES FROM THE NOISE	151
RED FLAGS IN THE FAMILY	153
TWO CASSANDRAS: ROGER BOISJOLY AND ALLAN MCDONALD	155
THE CASSANDRAS' UNSUCCESSFUL ATTEMPT TO PREVENT THE DISASTER	159
THE OPPORTUNITY TO WRITE THE HISTORY THAT FOLLOWS	164
THE ROGERS COMMISSION INVESTIGATES	166
COMMISSIONER DR. RICHARD FEYNMAN'S FAMOUS O-RING	
C-CLAMP EXPERIMENT	170
THE DNA OF DISASTER DIAGNOSIS	172
MONUMENTS & PRIORITIES	177

PILOTING A [FLAWED] NATIONAL MONUMENT: THE CONCORDE DISASTER — 182

CONCORDE: FAR MORE THAN AN AEROPLANE	184
DID THE WORLD NEED CONCORDE?	185
A STAR IS BORNE	187
THE 'CONCORDE EFFECT'	190
BUILD IT, AND CONCORDE WILL COME	191
AN ACE IN THE ATOL	193
CONCORDE DESIGN AND OPERATION: ADAPTING UNUSUAL CHARACTERISTICS TO TYPICAL CONDITIONS	195
A RED FLAG EMERGES	198
A CASSANDRA APPEARS	200
THE CRASH AND THE FIRST CLUES	201
THE DNA OF DISASTER DIAGNOSIS	202
THE ENVIRONMENT OF THE 'FACTORY FLOOR'	205
CRASH ANALYSIS	211
A COMMERCIAL FLIGHT: A QUALITY PRODUCT PRODUCED IN A TIGHTLY CONTROLLED ENVIRONMENT?	213
LESSONS FROM DESIGNED SYSTEMS PRODUCING UNEXPECTED OUTCOMES (AKA NOISE)	217

THE WORLD'S ONLY CARBON-FIBRE SUBMERSIBLE — 224

IN SEARCH OF STOCKTON RUSH	227
'THIS IS NOT YOUR GRANDFATHER'S SUBMERSIBLE'	234
'IT'S A NEW TYPE OF TRAVEL'	236
TITAN'S CASSANDRA	238
THE TITAN DISASTER	243
THE FOLLIES	246
NOISE GIVEN OFF BY THE DESIGNED SYSTEM	249
INNOVATION: CARBON FIBRE	253

CONCLUSION: CATASTROPHE BY DESIGN — 260
DESIGN ENABLES FUNCTION — 261
APPLYING WHAT WE HAVE LEARNED: HOW A DEATH FROM
  A SEPTIC MISCARRIAGE IN IRELAND PARALLELS THE SPACE
  SHUTTLE CHALLENGER DISASTER — 266
NATURAL DISASTERS — 273
CLIMATE NOISE — 275
FUTURE CATASTROPHES — 277
MY BIGGEST WORRIES — 278
SUMMARY OF WHAT WE HAVE LEARNED — 280
CLIMATE CHANGE — 289
THE CULTURAL MONUMENTS OF THE HOME TEAM — 291

BIBLIOGRAPHY — 296

INDEX — 316

OPENING

According to the seventeenth-century English philosopher Thomas Hobbes, life for early humans was practically a disaster. His description of the primitive condition of man is still oft-quoted: life before society formed was 'solitary, poor, nasty, brutish, and short.' This description may lack detail, but he had an implied point: disasters, natural and otherwise, have been with us since the dawn of man. Human beings have been subject to and shaped by the forces of nature since *Homo sapiens* first appeared 300,000 years ago. For the vast majority of the time humans have walked the Earth, they have lived in small groups and been limited to the knowledge and know-how present within these small groups. Compared to modern societies, those small tribes were next to helpless against the forces that produce disaster. The natural disasters that effectively capped the lifespans of those early humans are still with us. Earthquakes, volcanoes, hurricanes, tornadoes, floods, and tsunamis, as well as drought, famine, and pandemics will probably never completely disappear. But there have been two major changes since those early, pre-societal days that Hobbes was referring to: humans have vastly increased their accumulated knowledge of the environment and therefore become good at building systems that function to separate and insulate themselves from that environment. The other major change is that vast populations have arisen that depend on these human-designed systems, and flaws in those systems may inadvertently cause a disaster or worsen a natural disaster as unintended consequences of some well-intentioned but inadvisable policy choices come home to roost. These larger populations impact their environment in ways the hunter-gatherers would not recognise; populations so vast and resource-intensive that not only do they tax the natural systems they reside within, but a certain brittleness forms that almost eliminates the resilience inherent in natural systems. These large populations cannot simply move when disaster strikes; the adjacent lands may not be habitable, and if they are habitable, they are likely already populated, and the newcomers may not be welcome. Humanity has made an almost Faustian pact: the designed systems allow much larger populations than possible in the past, but when disaster strikes, the number of deaths and the destruction of property can be truly immense.

As I tease apart the following disasters, both large and small, examining those in power, those who control the generally accepted narratives, and the systems humans build and those who build them, it seems in hindsight that these disasters were fully preventable. But as we examine human motivation and judgement, we may begin to ask ourselves — are disasters really preventable?

As human knowledge expanded, mankind made considerable progress in the ability to insulate individuals from their environment. This knowledge accumulated gradually within family and tribal units and was passed down through the generations as stories and rituals, sometimes passed on again to outsiders. The stored knowledge contained everything needed to understand the world through the eyes of the ancestors, and this increased the chances the family and tribe would know where and how to find what was needed to survive and continue to produce subsequent generations. The supply of necessities for hunter-gatherers was, to borrow a phrase from modern supply chain terminology, just-in-time. The means of survival for the tribe were hand-to-mouth, and these supplies mostly came from their immediate surroundings. If supplies ran low, it was time to move camp or face hunger. But as knowledge and know-how increased for those early humans, just-in-time gave way to just-in-case; over thousands of years humans learned to build durable shelters and to organise and categorise certain aspects of their environment, which eventually produced such comforts as permanent settlements, domestication and animal husbandry, horticulture, food preservation and storage. But there was a trade-off: those inhabitants of settlements were increasingly at the mercy of the success or failure of the human-designed fabrications providing those comforts.

As an example, one could consider the possibilities for crossing a river. If the river isn't very wide or deep, you might be able to cross it with your horse, or you could swim across. But people are designers – they can design and build boats to get across a body of water. The person swimming is in direct contact with the watery environment, as, mostly, is the person on horseback. But the ingenious person who designs and builds a boat can pass over the water completely dry, and with a payload to boot. The swimmer is almost completely unprotected and must rely on knowledge, strength, and skill to cross the water, all the while subject to any risks present. Is there a strong undertow? Are there any crocodiles lurking under the surface, a risk of sudden flooding, or very cold water? Are there mainly naturally occurring hazards, or are there man-made barriers or traps present? The traveller in the boat may be above all of those risks, but is instead subject to the embedded design and operation of that boat. If that fails, he must then face the water. The boat passenger must put his or her faith in those who built the vessel, as well as those who operate the vessel, which could have been constructed with embedded design flaws. The operational design of the vessel is also subject to error: the boat may have been steered incorrectly or maintained poorly, or could strike an underwater obstacle or be blown off-course by a passing storm. Whether embedded design or operational design, when the boat sinks, there is a component of human design involved.

Similarly, a weakness in the hull of an oceangoing vessel can give way and cause the vessel to sink, but a navigational error which causes the same vessel to encounter a reef can also lead to a hull breach and a sunken vessel, and perhaps an oil spill in addition. A large dam that holds back millions of gallons of water could, in the right conditions, be weakened by heavy rains from a passing storm and suddenly burst, leading to a huge catastrophe. The fundamental flaw in this hypothetical dam could have been a design error, the use of the wrong building material in key areas, cost-cutting by the builder, or it could have been due to sabotage in a conflict zone. A number of factors can play a part in this type of modern disaster, but a commonality is that the designed components must be able to account for the environment in which they must function.

These hypothetical examples involve designed components. Even the swimmer must design her swim: what to take, whether to throw her clothes across to the other side or pile them up on her head. She must assess the swiftness of the current and so on. Because there is a component of design to human decision-making, it is possible to identify and predict many disasters, sometimes many years prior to their occurrence: for example, it is no surprise that Japan experiences earthquakes. Almost everyone knows that in Japan, it is highly likely that a powerful earthquake will occur, since Japan is in one of the world's most seismically-active regions. Exactly when and exactly where may not be precisely known, but what is known is that the structures built upon that seismically active land should be, at the very minimum, built to withstand all but the most unimaginably severe earthquakes and tsunamis. An understanding of the environment is required to make this determination: the catastrophic potential of the environment and of the design itself must be identified in order to minimise the risk of disaster. We can likewise predict the catastrophic potential inherent in the building of a city on the slopes of a sleeping volcano. To assess the risk, you need to know something about the volcano. Building structures that cannot withstand major catastrophic events that are practically inevitable is a breach of the implicit agreement between the members of a society: when you are entrusted with the design and construction of an office tower in downtown Tokyo, where thousands of people will work daily, it is an implicit obligation to Japanese society that the designers and builders take necessary precautions to produce a final product that can withstand the most violent earthquake that has been known to exist. To do otherwise is folly. In the same way, if you're building a large television-transmitting station in the middle of a field, the catastrophic potential for loss of life is low if it topples over during a storm or earthquake, but things may change dramatically if you change the environment of that same television tower and build it somewhere else. Native Americans have lived near the mighty Mississippi River for thousands of years. They had undoubtedly seen the river flood many, many times over that period, and it was probably reflected in their shared cultural memory, the stories and rituals passed down through the generations. But they probably had few permanent structures that were vulnerable and could pick up and move out of the way of the floodwaters. Catastrophe averted, but only temporarily. European settlers would soon have designs on the rich bottomland of the Mississippi River Valley...

Mother Nature will always be throwing storms, floods, earthquakes, and volcanoes in our paths with less-than-certain predictability. In contrast, the human-designed disasters or components of disasters are, to a large extent, more predictable. As long as humans have existed, naturally occurring events have thwarted their best-laid plans. But human activity has become such a growing component of disasters which take a toll on human lives that we must seek to understand the intentions of those activities. Human error is often predictable, and so are human intentions, and these errors and intentions manifest themselves in human-designed systems, displaying recurring patterns and resting on well-accepted assumptions. I have lived long enough to have witnessed some of these designed disasters myself, and to have seen some of the best-laid plans, articulated intentions, and assumptions turn out to be completely wrong, the exact opposite of what was sold. I have also had my share of little personal disasters as I have travelled through this life and have sought to understand them and objectively learn from them. But I have also ventured outside my comfort zone and stepped through the streets of others' disasters, and I have arrived back home to tell you the story. It's a very human story, a story of hubris and a desire for power over nature and control over others, a story of greed, and often a story of unintended consequences.

ON LUCK

/ LUCK IS THE RESIDUE OF DESIGN.

Branch Rickey, *American baseball executive, 1881–1965.*

It's all about design: some succeed, others fail. Almost all fail eventually.

While the success or failure of an intelligent design is determined chiefly by the cleverness, industry, and foresight of its human designer, evolutionary design has a large component of randomness contributing to its success or failure.

Most people have had at least one lucky break in life. Some people claim they make their own luck by hard work, while others assert they know how to make the best of a bad situation. Call it what you want: chance, luck, fortune, serendipity, and even blessings – random events are a part of life, and chance does indeed favour the prepared mind. The ability to make up one's own luck may be obvious, but that only holds true until that same person's luck runs out. The ability to make the best of a bad situation depends on judgement, and judgement depends on knowledge and intelligence. One must take the rocks along with the rest of the farm, and intelligence, along with industriousness, helps one determine what to do with those rocks. Culture, the passage of information from the older generations to the newest generation, makes up a large part of this knowledge. The prior generations remembered notable events from their daily activities and passed along their observations to their children with legends and rituals, a transfer of information we can think of as Cultural DNA. Human beings worldwide have similar concerns about the necessities of life, and a similar cultural information transfer to their youngest citizens. This cultural knowledge transfer consists of designed solutions – solutions to cope with a known environment. But this brings up a key point: one cannot design an effective solution to account for an environment in which the hazards are unknown. In that case, you must take your chances and try to survive despite the curveballs the new environment throws at you. We could say the same of our ancestors. Wise as they were, they could not design solutions for a world they did not know. Thus, there is a continuous need for thinking individuals in any society, a place for those who do not simply rely on received information; that old, established knowledge that many conservatives regard as sacred and unchangeable. The human brain capable of judgement, capable of questioning the status quo, a single organ able to account for a multitude of physical limitations of the human body, is utterly the most important tool for survival in a changing world. Make no mistake, this same tool can also be a powerful undoing in the hands of the inflexible; old systems, hierarchies, and algorithms appear in the place of judgement. Consider the millions of species that do not possess the ability to make judgements about their environment – they live purely by chance. When they die, they never knew what hit them. But when intelligent beings enter a new, unknown environment, some may survive by chance when bad luck strikes, living to tell the tale of what happened, and they in turn learn something about the event: what went wrong and why, to the best of their judgement. This is the process of intelligent design: the designer learns from his or her mistakes, as long as the designer survives the mistake. But those countless species that were unable to make those same observations were not lucky, and they simply disappeared. Throughout Earth's history, many of those disappearances also coincided with abrupt changes in the environment. These species could not make the same abrupt adaptations to the new environmental conditions. This begs the question: what about Cultural DNA which cannot be changed due to the conservative nature of tribal elders and preexisting systems and biases? Is it possible that this enduring Cultural DNA can contribute to a failure or some catastrophe? In other words, can old, outdated world views that no longer satisfactorily explain our environment and our place in it actually contribute to a catastrophe? An extinction?

If you look up extinct species on the National Geographic website, you find that 'more than 99 percent of all organisms that have ever lived on Earth are extinct. As new species evolve to fit ever changing ecological niches, older species fade away. But the rate of extinction is far from constant.'

Does this mean that more than 99% of species failed or that disaster struck 99% of species that ever existed? Perhaps it is better to consider the time a particular species was present on Earth. The dinosaurs dominated the Earth for 165 million years. Was their nearly complete extinction an ultimate failure? It seems like that amount of time is a good run. Humans have a long way to go to get that far out from our beginnings as a species. Will we be the root cause of our own demise? Or will there be a cosmic event that wipes us out, too? I consider a 165-million-year span for human existence to be unlikely.

For most of the Earth's history, human beings were not present, but there were many other species that were. These species occupied their niche in the environment until that niche was no longer able to sustain the species. If that species were to survive, it would need to change to keep up with the changes in the niche – that little space in the environment it occupied. We think of this as design by evolution; that is, species change, but ever so slightly as they adapt to small changes in their niche. When things change abruptly, those species which no longer fit their niche are unfit for continuation as a species unless they can adapt to occupy another niche. Animals cannot store food for long periods of time, with a few exceptions, and plants cannot 'store' sunshine for an extended period of darkness. Hibernation and dormancy are adaptations to the environment: of course, seeds do not need sunshine, but living plants, with few exceptions, need regular sunshine. This is the just-in-time basis of naturally evolved systems.

For humans in the modern world, just-in-time has given way to just-in-case, as I pointed out above. This switch has required a change in thinking: human thinking about the future scarcity of resources must design a method to store that resource to act as a buffer against the brutal forces of design by evolution – which, as we know, involves deaths, sometimes a complete wipeout of entire species with abrupt changes that exceed that species' ability to adapt. The human designing the buffer against these evolutionary forces of nature must understand the environment to predict what will be lacking in the future. For example, the stored food must be protected against spoilage, foraging animals such as rodents and bears, insect infestation, or even marauding plunderers. We can regard this thinking as intelligent design – designed solutions which must be informed of the hazards of the immediate environment. What did the designers of early boats or bridges learn about their designs when there was a storm or a load that was too heavy to place upon their boat or bridge? How were limits determined? The designers needed to incorporate their new knowledge into their next design to avoid catastrophe. We can think of this as design by intelligence – or intelligent design, as opposed to evolutionary design.

With both evolutionary and intelligent design, success or failure is determined to a large degree by the environment. The stakes are huge with both. With evolution, a species' adaptability to its environment will determine nothing less than its continued existence. For intelligent designs – be they for technology, machines, travel, or the laws, structures, and covenants of different societies – success is concomitant not only to adapting to a changing environment, but to how well a design will serve the purposes and needs of both the designer and the end user.

Time is the ultimate proving ground in both, measured at times over millions of years, even aeons with evolutionary design, and with intelligent design in units ranging from split-seconds to centuries, or even millennia. With both, each iteration must prove its worth on the savannah, plains, forest, desert, alpine meadow, ocean, skies, or marketplace as the environment changes. Perhaps the most extreme example of the disruption of an evolved system was the mass extinction event of 252 million years ago, the End-Permian Event, when up to 96% of all marine species and 70% of land species went extinct. Those lost products of evolutionary design, optimised over millennia to succeed in their native environments, were not equipped to deal with sudden cataclysmic changes. The exact geologic or cosmic event that delivered the knockout punch to so many species is unknown, but it is thought that unusually large volcanic eruptions in Siberia were the cause.

Compare that time frame to its rough equivalent in intelligent design, at least the advent of intelligent design associated with the appearance of *Homo sapiens*, a species whose success is linked by anthropological findings precisely to its capacity and desire for design. Our presence as a species represents only a tenth of the 2.5 million years of the Stone Age, and in our current form we are but the latest iteration of a natural selection process begun in South and East Africa in the distant past. Past versions include *Homo habilis* ('handy man'), the first of the genus *Homo* to fashion stone tools, which evolved into a bigger, smarter, and faster species some 500,000 years later, *Homo erectus* ('upright man'), and ultimately *Homo sapiens* ('wise man'). We shared the Earth with Neanderthals for all but the last 40,000 of our estimated 200–300,000-year existence, and it was not until roughly 12,000 years ago that our greatest accomplishments in intelligent design, i.e., horticulture, farming, and food storage, came about in the Mesolithic and then the Neolithic eras. Even with such dramatic temporal differences separating the two forms of design, i.e., evolutionary vs. intelligent design, their true divider is not time but rather chance, or the less precise but more common term, luck. That component of dumb luck was first identified in Charles Darwin's ground-breaking 1859 work, *On the Origin of Species*. The culmination of almost thirty years of geological, zoological, and botanical observations that had begun on a five-year voyage from England to Patagonia, the study was strongly supported by observations, data, and evidence. So much so that its principal concept, revolutionary as it was, gained much wider acceptance within a decade or two: that nature moves forward not by fate, destiny, or divine will, but the gradual evolution of some species and not others.

What would remain unacceptable to the bulk of Darwin's readers, scientists, and laymen alike was the corollary concept of 'natural selection': that successful species carried an inheritable set of genes that affected adaptation to a changing environment. Darwin had first come to the concept while studying the breeding practices of animal husbandry, but it was a population study by a political economist, Robert Malthus, that solidified the idea. Malthus argued that societies increase until their numbers outstrip available food supplies, and then consequently fail, in what has since become known as a 'Malthusian catastrophe.'

That theory, advanced half a century before Darwin's work, was also highly controversial, as it argued against popular beliefs that society was a God-given construct, and thus capable of perfection. Similarly, the lack of any start-to-finish control of an all-seeing divinity helped make natural selection or 'survival of the fittest' unacceptable in Darwin's time. Life and death or existential competition of species in nature came with an understanding that it was not a repeatable and easily communicated set of laws and morals that dictated success and failure, right and wrong, but rather luck or chance. The precept that randomness exerted such a controlling force offended even the greatest and most progressive minds of both Malthus' and Darwin's day. In Darwin's time, there was so much said of men and apes that little focus was paid to the failure of species, the focus rather on the evolutionary success, which we would later learn that an adaptable genome (a changeable genetic blueprint) made possible. What can we learn from Darwin's ideas about those individuals who do not survive, and can that information shed light on the causes of the demise of not only a species, but of something designed by a human being or groups of human thinkers, i.e., an intelligent design?

Answering this question is what I explore in its various guises throughout this book. For both intelligent design and evolutionary design, a blueprint is helpful. An intact instruction set or genome seems to be required for successful evolutionary design, dependent as it is on nucleic acids to store the information necessary for the continuation of a species. Viruses also share this in common with actual living entities, but viruses exist mainly as packets of information and they depend on actual living cells to carry out the instruction set contained within their genetic code. With intelligent design, I am, of course, discussing 'DNA' in its increasingly popular metaphorical sense: 'the DNA of an idea, of a company,' or as the reader will see in the chapters to come, of a set of laws or a pervasive ideology.

The success or failure of an evolutionary design – in short, its ongoingness in successive genetic variations – is determined by a single advantage: the ability to reproduce. When individuals are unable to do so, genes are simply not passed along. Each individual of a species can thus be thought of as an experiment by nature, though as Darwin was first to observe, there is no judgement of its success or failure, simply living or not living, passing along genes or not passing along genes. It is important to understand this experiment by nature is a success regardless of whether a particular individual passes along its genes or dies without reproducing, for over successive generations, the failure of such individuals functions to clear out the deselected instruction set, i.e., those genes unable to successfully contribute to the next generation. In that way, DNA is self-cleansing. Any new gene variants that impart some advantage become fixed in the species' genome. Whether or not that individual survives, thrives, and reproduces on the world's stage does not depend on external cognitive agency: there is no grand plan. What is at stake is not right or wrong, good or evil, but merely the genetic feedstock of the next generation: to seed or not to seed.

It is possible and likely quite common that a very fit and completely adapted individual is unable to pass along its genes. This could be the result of a freak accident or some other cause. In any case, that individual is a biological dead-end. Again, there is no judgement and no reward or punishment implied: success or failure, thriving or ending in disaster, the passing along of genes is the ultimate test of life, one that makes each individual an iteration of the cosmos. Indeed, one could say each life, each iteration, is, in a way, an experiment of the cosmos – without cognitive judgement of its success or failure.

That lack of judgement can hardly be said to apply to intelligent design. Humans have been conducting experiments throughout our existence, most likely begun as very simple testing of a design – the making and use of spears, for example, and later of arrowheads, axes, and the other tools and traps needed to obtain sustenance. Such experiments have continued throughout human existence. Human existence has been a long story of experimental design, from the viability of various shelters to the health effects of certain foods, to the friendliness or hostility of surrounding tribes, and strategies to cope with the vagaries of environmental conditions. Those humans designed their daily activities and passed along their observations to their children with stories as Cultural DNA.

We can assume that an early experiment conducted by humans could have been a simple pit trap to catch an unsuspecting woolly mammoth or other large game. Digging a pit large enough to injure and trap a large mammal could have been substantial work, depending on the soil type and tools available at the time. Undoubtedly, any large animal falling in would have been butchered in the trap, and the scent of the decaying carcass and blood would likely have rendered the trap unusable for a certain time – the unmistakable smell of death a signal for other animals to stay away. Perhaps these early humans thus learned to bait their traps and mask smells with fragrant flowers, hay, or fruit. Without a doubt, they came to know their environment very well and were quite observant of the effects of their hunting and trapping endeavours. They intuitively understood the concept of cause and effect, and this became the basis for the manipulation of small parts of their environment to suit their purposes.

Humans also cultivated and domesticated wild plants through careful selection and testing, and were able, over time and many successive generations of selection, to successfully eliminate toxins that occur in certain wild plants. Perhaps more germane than any other in human history is the potato, its adaptability and versatility noted by Darwin some two hundred years after its importation to Europe by the Spanish. 'It is remarkable,' he noted in the log of his journey to Patagonia, 'that the same plant should be found on the sterile mountains of Central Chile, where a drop of rain does not fall for more than six months, and within the damp forests of the southern islands.' It is a nightshade, along with tomatoes, peppers, aubergines, and tobacco, a family of plants that can contain substantial amounts of alkaloid toxins. These naturally occurring irritants served to ward off pests, and thus enabled these plants to flourish and reproduce over millennia: the earliest known edible potato has been dated to about 10,900 years ago based on potato starch found on stone-grinding tools. All potatoes contain alkaloids, even the edible variety. But the wild version contains the highest amount of toxin, which makes it quite resistant to the typical agricultural pests, including the potato blight fungus. Humans modified wild potato plants to reduce the amount of toxins present in different strains, the toxins being almost completely eliminated through continuous breeding and testing. Undoubtedly, observational testing was employed during the selective-breeding process: potatoes that were toxic likely had a bitter taste, for example, and it is now known that toxins in plants often impart a bitter taste. It is quite possible that ancient humans used nothing more than taste and appearance to cultivate potato variants and that the same methods could have been used for many of the edible plants we take for granted today.

So where exactly do these similarities and differences between evolutionary and intelligent design place us in the grand scheme of things?

Carl Sagan began his best-selling book, *Cosmos*, with an almost biblical first line: 'The Cosmos is all that is or ever was or ever will be.' The vastness thus envisioned affected me and many in my generation deeply as we wondered about ourselves, our world, and our place in it. Is there a guiding hand of a supreme being that moves us about like pieces in a chess game, according to some divine whim or wish? For me, there was something mediaeval in that doctrine which I could not accept. With new information, I felt even as a young man, we need new explanations. Twisting old, limited world views from our past to fit our ever-expanding knowledge of the universe will never be fully satisfactory for thinking individuals.

The substance of the cosmos in our immediate vicinity is what influences the Earth directly. The proximity of the Earth to the sun keeps our climate safely wedged between freezing and burning up, while the moon exerts a gravitational pull on the Earth, as seen in the changing of the tides. Other influences from the cosmos, including cosmic radiation and an occasional comet or asteroid, have almost certainly impacted life on Earth in its 4.5-billion-year existence. Aside from those bombardments, the sun, moon, Earth, and the life upon it have self-organised into a stable system, within what's become known as 'the Goldilocks zone.'

That term, originating in a 1953 study, would later become central to a theory that, like Darwin's roughly a century earlier, began with a voyage from England to the polar south. This idea had begun formulating several years prior to the 1953 study in the mind of James Lovelock. A radically brilliant British chemist, he had begun a consultancy at NASA, designing life-detection instruments at a Pasadena, California lab that would be used a decade later in the first probes of Mars. A colleague brought in an armful of data with infrared analysis of the atmospheres of Mars and Venus, and it was clear that both planets were 'dead' — nothing but trace gases and carbon dioxide held in static equilibrium, as opposed to the dynamism of Earth's atmosphere. Lovejoy turned to his colleague, Carl Sagan, and vented his confusion. Why this success on Planet Earth? Free oxygen here accounts for only 20% of our atmosphere, and all the laws of chemistry dictate that this highly reactive gas would combine and settle down, and not therefore help support precisely that which is needed to keep the planet growing, i.e., life, in its many forms.

Sagan was only able to suggest that the sun had been much cooler in the past, but it was all Lovejoy needed to concretise his theory five years later on his lengthy voyage south: it was life itself that caused Earth's atmosphere to remain continuously alive: microbes, plants, and animals metabolising matter into energy, the conversion of sunlight into nutrients, emitting and absorbing gas. In short, Earth and the life upon it had coevolved into a durable feedback loop over billions of years. On the advice of his neighbour back in England, the Nobel Prize–winning author William Golding (of *Lord of the Flies* fame), Lovelock named his theory the Gaia Hypothesis — after Gaea, the Earth Mother of Greek mythology. In the equilibrium granted the planet by its advantageous position within the Goldilocks zone, life on Earth had become so pervasive it stabilised a hostile environment that otherwise would have dictated its conditions upon life, and, over the course of aeons, stabilised it to a point where the entire system is self-perpetuating. A planet in the Goldilocks zone, with the right atmospheric chemistry, ocean chemistry, and soil chemistry, showered with photons from the sun for billions of years, transforms into a life-sustaining oasis in a vast, seemingly lifeless universe.

Imagine yourself standing on the moon, the Earth before you, against the backdrop of the Milky Way. With binoculars or a small telescope, you may be able to vaguely trace the Great Wall of China, but the only products of the human brain you can easily see are those binoculars or the telescope, the spacecraft that brought you to the moon, and the spacesuit adapting you to the harsh environment of lunar space. With radio equipment sensitive enough, you might be able to tune into broadcasts emanating from Earth, but everything else you can hear is the product of the universe. Think of those radio broadcasts from Earth as intelligent design, like the work of those early humans who began to change their environment, one woolly mammoth at a time: a tiny, insignificant speck in an enormous universe.

THE HOUR ON THE STAGE

As we saw from National Geographic, more than 99% of the estimated five billion or so species that ever existed on Earth are now extinct. Many died off in the five great mass-extinction events throughout the Earth's history; additional species have come and gone as the environment changed and competition for a niche occupied by an old species was won by a new and more fit variant. In this way, all species are interrelated, and they in turn are interrelated to the environment. As soon as one component is removed or changed, the system shifts as some species gain an advantage whilst others suffer disadvantages. The disadvantaged species may be forced to adapt or die off, while the advantaged species has the opportunity to thrive and proliferate. The abrupt removal or change of a component of the system in equilibrium can be thought of as an evolutionary force. The simplest life forms are the most durable through time. The more complex and evolved the life form, the shorter its time on the stage. Lowly bacteria have been around for billions of years, while the vast majority of the higher life forms have come and gone.

Likewise, many human inventions have come and gone. But some essential components to human existence have been in use since they were invented – one could consider the wheel to be such a component. Cups, plates, knives, shoes, hats, steel and concrete, institutions and corporations: these are the basics that will be with us throughout our hour on the stage. Out of this limited list, perhaps corporations may not be with us for our entire future existence, but they certainly can outlive their human operators. Our history is also littered with designs that had their day, useful and even widespread intelligent designs, but which ultimately went the way of the dinosaurs. I am confident that no matter how technologically advanced humans become – lowly bacteria will still be with us. They are the ultimate survivors.

INTELLIGENT DESIGN IN THE MARKETPLACE

A company can be thought of as very similar to an organism surviving in its niche. That organism must continually scan its environment for threats and opportunities, a task that falls to the company's directors. Will the C-suite have the necessary judgement for the company to survive?

Intelligent design must follow the same rules as the products of evolutionary design, i.e., life forms. Consider the struggle in the cell phone industry between a newcomer, Apple, and the well-established Nokia. The world's dominant producer of cell phones and cell phone operating systems for more than a decade before the arrival of Apple's iPhone in 2007, Nokia was valued at its peak that year at $1.52 billion, on sales of more than 45 million units, accounting for 38% of a booming market that had expanded 16% that year alone. But after Apple's phenomenally successful rollout, that hegemony was lost. Not overnight, but thoroughly. By 2014, Nokia's global brand value had fallen from an overwhelming 1st to 98th place and its market value declined by nearly 90%, whereas Apple sold a record 231.22 million units that year. That same year, the Finnish company abandoned its business model and sold its handset device business to Microsoft. The stakes could not have been higher, for these devices would lead in very short order to paradigm shifts in human behaviour in the order of the domestication of animals and the invention of the wheel.

In the marketplace, a company that loses value like this is like a species deselected from passing its genes on to the next generation. How did this failure come to pass? In the early to mid-1980s, Nokia took its first steps to transform a multi-platform business model to concentrate on the manufacture and sale of mobile devices, beginning with an early digital car phone, and in 1984, the first 'portable' cell phone, weighing in at almost two pounds. Transforming in the early 1990s to what would later be known as smartphones, these 'feature phones' would come to have capacities such as digital media players, cameras, and personal organisers, and, increasingly important, access to a new global communication network, the internet.

Sales were phenomenal, with Nokia's profits increasing fourfold from $1–4 billion in the decade. As the dawn of the New Millennium approached, Symbian, an operating system (OS) that Nokia and other phone manufacturers had acquired from Psion, an early telephony pioneer, became the industry standard. All the major manufacturers began introducing proprietary software to run on it: two-thirds of all smartphones were using Symbian as an OS by the time of the iPhone's introduction in 2007. It was clear to all that, while not claimed outright, the OS was Nokia's property, with plans to possibly launch an App Store and extend Symbian beyond mobiles to other devices, such as games consoles, a market that began to explode in the twenty-first century.

However, the Symbian OS that ran on Nokia feature phones was limited in many ways. It was particularly weak in its support for third-party app developers and fees were charged for consultation and assistance with app development. Nokia deliberately blocked the inclusion of standard consumer interfaces (APIs) in the toolkit, insisting on its support for Nokia-controlled hardware to the exclusion of established industry standards such as Qualcomm. After unit sales of Nokia phones peaked in 2007, the decline was not long in coming – Apple launched its App Store a year later, helping to win the race to link their smartphone with other technologies.

It would prove a classic case of the failure of intelligent design, a failure of a company to institute the correct changes at the correct time to account for the environment. After more than a decade of global control, the end of the line was in sight and the Nokia C-suite at the top just could not see it until it was too late to prevent it: days before Apple introduced the iPhone, prototypes arrived at Nokia's headquarters. A top executive brought one home and bemusedly gave it to his four-year-old daughter, as he would any toy. The little girl learned how to use the iPhone immediately. Somehow, he knew his company was in trouble when the girl begged him to let her bring her new 'magic phone' to bed with her.

Nokia bought Symbian outright the next year, but it was again too late. The Symbian OS, legacy software designed to run on low-powered mobile devices, was unable to change quickly enough to compete with the major smartphone ecosystem Apple soon came to embody, with many third-party app developers and its well-stocked App Store. Rather, time revealed Symbian's limitations: a quirky proprietary system that third-party app developers and end-users found hard to work with. Nokia never learned to exploit the value of the software running on its devices. In contrast to the inaccessible and inflexible Symbian OS, Apple tapped into a marketplace of ideas, leveraging the huge existing developer base from its personal computer business, experience with its existing iTunes store, and a quarter-century of expertise in software behind it. The public was ready, thirsty even, for an easy-to-use platform, and Nokia was unable to deliver a similar satisfactory customer experience. Nokia's directors did not understand the origin and the nature of the value of products to their customers: seamless integration of hardware and software, with no roadblocks or barriers that could interfere with the production of value or the consumption of value.

Where, exactly, did the fault lie? Put simply, Nokia failed to recognise that they were competing in two marketplace environments, the device marketplace and the software marketplace. While they had years of experience in the device marketplace, their ability to compete in the software marketplace was hamstrung by one-way technology with limited environmental (user) feedback and incomplete control over the operating system. A great way to think of one-way technology is to imagine an eighteenth-century playwright, used to the immediate, rich information available to him with the feedback of the audience – applause, laughter, revulsion. But when he tries his hand at writing novels, his only feedback information might be sales numbers, and perhaps a mention by a book critic. Nokia was blind in the same way as the playwright-turned-novelist with its limited, one-way technology.

Apple, in contrast, had an effective content delivery system well before it attempted to enter the smartphone market, opening its iTunes Store on 28 April 2003 because of Steve Jobs' push for a digital marketplace for music. In 1999, Napster showed the music industry there was a demand for easily downloadable-to-desktop music, a fact noticed by Jobs, who in 2002 had an agreement with the five major record labels to offer their content on the iTunes Store. By the time its App Store was launched on 10 July 2008, Apple had considerable experience offering content created by others on its platform. Apple was already royalty in the hardware and software side of the digital music Value Chain: it had cracked the code of the content Value Chain and was able to get out of the way so that consumers could consume what they value: music. Five years later they were poised to crack the code of another Value Chain: applications.

When Nokia's hastily cobbled together Ovi Store finally opened in May 2009, it was riddled with bugs, and users were unable to redownload purchased apps, meaning they would thus lose purchased apps if they ever needed to reset their devices. The Ovi Store was supposed to ensure that apps purchased would be compatible with the user's connected device, but the software simply could not function in this manner. Users often bought software their devices could not use, and considered the Ovi Store an utter failure. Apple, in contrast, had years of experience with using desktop software to authenticate and load music onto its iPod devices. Each time an iPod connects to its host computer, iTunes can synchronise entire music libraries or music playlists. The majority of iPod devices could not be used to browse the iTunes Store and make purchases since they did not have their own internet or cell phone data connections. This feature allowed users to store and backup content on their main computer and bypass the slow cellular data connection speeds prevalent at that time by browsing exclusively on their desktop software, iTunes. This software was easily ported to the iPod Touch and then the very similar iPhone when it was launched in 2007, and further, these more advanced handsets were poised to make the most of the faster cellular data networks that had become available. In contrast, Nokia device users complained that there was no integrated desktop software to work with the Ovi Store, forcing them to navigate the store via their handsets, an almost unbearably slow and cumbersome experience. Users were also forced through a time-consuming merry-go-round of authentication procedures involving SMS messages and identity confirmation, all while looking over their shoulders at Apple device users with envy. With its desktop iTunes software, Apple successfully accounted for the slow cellular data connection speeds at the time, while Nokia was hamstrung by those same slow connection speeds.

Obtaining direct feedback from the environment provides a basis for making judgements on what changes are necessary so a designer can alter a product or service to better accommodate the pressures of that environment. With this information, the designer must use cognition to adapt the design for a better product–environment fit, i.e., a product–market fit, or the intended purpose may be better fulfilled by another product or service. It is possible that a previous design could find an unintended purpose within the environment, but that is not quite the same as fulfilling the needs of the market by design. Nature accomplishes this task through the iteration of new individuals that must adapt to survive and pass on their genes. Designers must accomplish this task through continuous sampling of the environment: through customer feedback, through careful observation, or by trial and error, sometimes called iteration and delivery, followed by seeking feedback from product testers and sales, especially early adopters. The quantity, quality, and continuity of the information obtained must be correctly interpreted, so that the implementation of solutions and the timeliness of the introduction of the amended design will have the best chances of success. Applying changes to the design too soon or too late may condemn that design to the museum, as would applying unhelpful, misdirected, or non-functional features or changes.

The results of the battle in the marketplace between Apple and Nokia show that Nokia's one-way design was somewhat deficient in the gathering of market information. To compete with Apple, Nokia's management would have to have made timely, detailed observations about the marketplace and would have had to act appropriately. It would require information about the marketplace other than from surveys of customers or from sales data. Nokia would have had to recognise that the slow cellular data environment was unsuitable for content consumption, and a bridge, like iTunes, was necessary for success. Looking back at their decisions, we can see that the Nokia C-suite was completely unaware of the need for such a bridge. By opening up a marketplace for music and later the same for apps, Apple created an entire platform where users interacted both with the company and with app developers and content creators. Apple and iOS developers quickly understood the value of this interaction; sales data became available not only on the devices, but also on the apps and App Store. Popular apps were shared on social media and elsewhere, sharing was immediate, and apps could thus gain popularity exponentially (attaining virality). The timing was perfect, given the mass expansion of social media platforms like Instagram that followed faster cellular connection speeds and could enable the frequent updates which were required to keep the apps current and allow notifications. Apple's mobile devices provided the fertile ground for the apps, which in turn provided fertile ground for social media users. It all became a self-perpetuating feedback loop. Was it a masterstroke, or was it luck? Perhaps a little of both, but Apple was uniquely poised to benefit from the new high-speed cellular data and the advent of wifi. By the time Nokia had a platform, Apple, Samsung, and Google had already cemented their positions in the marketplace, leaving little room for latecomers. Interestingly, after a 15 year partnership with Intel, Apple recently abandoned Intel processors in favour of its own designs, which are being manufactured by Apple's partner in Taiwan, TSMC. Apple claims its new products incorporating Apple-designed silicon are superior in battery life and speed than what was possible on intel chips. Is Intel going the way of Nokia?

A C-Suite is a kind of brain, a nerve centre of sorts which must constantly adapt to its environment to maintain its existence. This brain is dependent on cognition, which is in turn dependent on the transmission of sensory information to the brain and the flow of information within it. This C-Suite must be continually fed with market information coming in from a sensory apparatus, which can be a branch or division of that company tasked with collecting market information. Clearly, this essential information about the environment must flow freely within the entire enterprise for company leadership to make timely decisions and to account for changes in the market or regulatory environment. If there are interruptions in that flow of information, such as broken or faulty connections, cognitive biases interfering with the interpretation of that information, or even nodes along this network capable of voluntarily interrupting the free flow of information, the company leadership risks biases in their decision making and deficiencies in execution.

Like a tribe, a company must scout territory, monitor competition, nurture relationships, identify strengths and weaknesses, and remain poised to take advantage of opportunity as well as effectively interpret warning signs from the environment. Any interruption or deficiency in the ability to carry out these functions can spell disaster for a tribe or company alike.

DESIGNED SYSTEMS REST ON PREDICTABLE ASSUMPTIONS

Humans build systems. The design of these systems, as we will establish, must account for all aspects of their respective environments to be considered perfect intelligent design. However, a perfect system is more myth than reality since some aspect of the environment nearly always goes unaccounted for. Perfection is something people strive for, a shining city on a hill that we can never fully attain, always more theoretical than practical. But as the system must fit the environment to some degree, that degree of fit determines the degree of intelligent design. When we consider evolutionary design, the forces doing the design work originate with the environment and can be traced back to the origin of the universe. Humans have shaped a few of the life forms on Earth with selective breeding, a form of intelligent design, and they have been implicated in the extinction of a number of life forms. But humans had nothing to do with the evolution of the life forms on Earth (climate change and pollution effects notwithstanding), just as they have nothing to do with volcanoes, the majority of earthquakes, or of course asteroid strikes. Humans make judgements and assumptions when they design and carry out an action or design and build a system. When part of their design leaves something unaccounted for, they could be leaving their system open to chance or to manipulation by others, or they could be making an error caused by a built-in bias. In order to understand the root cause of a disaster, we must understand the nature of the assumptions made by the builders of the systems we are considering, as well as the assumptions of those who observe that system or can be affected by it. I have these common assumptions and misunderstandings categorised into Four Basic Human Follies to enhance legibility. These categories are helpful for any observer or designer to identify weaknesses in a system- by revealing components of the system at risk or somehow exposed to one or more aspects of the environment that system will operate within. Designs that account for their environment(s) are considered intelligent designs, while those more poorly adapted to their intended environment(s) are considered 'semi-intelligent design.' Most designs suffer from a compromise which leaves one or more aspects of their environment(s) unaccounted for, which means that the vast majority of human-created designs are 'semi-intelligent.' We must also consider the future environment of an intelligent design: outdated designs may be marginally useful, but at some point they make their way to the museum or the history books. On this basis, with a nod to the resignation that perfection is ultimately unattainable, in reality a design need not be anywhere near perfect to be useful. Categorising the Four Basic Human Follies helps us understand the origins of the assumptions upon which intelligent designs are based, and further allows us to peer into the assumptions and mechanisms by which designs that display even very deep flaws are continually pressed into service.

THE FOUR BASIC HUMAN FOLLIES AND THEIR NICKNAMES:

1. Assuming the presence of intelligent design when merely semi-intelligent design or no intelligent design is present.
(The Divine Intervention Folly).

2. Assuming the absence of intelligent design where it is present.
(The Propaganda Folly).

3. Misunderstanding the true nature of an intelligent design.
(The Trojan Horse Folly).

4. Misunderstanding of the true nature of the universe, randomness, and evolutionary forces. (The Marie and Pierre Curie Folly).

Let us now clarify the Follies in preparation for applying them to disasters. The Four Basic Human Follies describe the relationship between intelligent design and evolutionary design. Intelligent design is a product of a brain or multiple brains. Evolutionary design results directly from that force which produced the components of the universe. Ultimately, the universe also gave rise to intelligent design, but since man uses intelligent design to maintain a buffer between himself and his environment or himself and other humans, intelligent design must be characterised in relation to the universe. The Follies are assigned names to facilitate recall, but are by no means limited to the events or entities they are named for. Further, the Follies can be mixed and interdependent in a disaster. Therefore we need a memorable rule of thumb to keep handy, something like: any system or event can have as many diseases as it pleases. This is borrowed and modified slightly from wisdom I encountered during my medical education: A patient can have as many diseases as he or she pleases. It's a reminder for clinicians to look for all possibilities and not to become complacent by outward appearances, or perhaps even worse, to be blinded or distracted by the first problem that comes into view. Of course the more formal wording would be something like this: 'any poor outcome can have many causal maladies'. I changed it slightly for ease-of-use as the DNA of Disaster rule of thumb: catastrophes can have as many maladies as they please.

Human Folly #1:
Assuming the presence of intelligent design when only semi-intelligent or no intelligent design is present.
The Divine Intervention Folly.

This is, simply put, the human mind's propensity to assign an intelligence – a will, for example – to certain phenomena, such as fate. It is even baked into our language: 'It was meant to be,' 'It wanted to rain today.' In these expressions, it is as if some natural event were caused by an entity that had agency, a goal to be accomplished. This folly is the assumption of an agency where there is none. There are cases where semi-intelligent design can be categorised as Human Folly #1 as well. Again, most intelligent design is characterised by an imperfect fit to its environment. Designs, both physical iterations of design and those which have no physical form and are particularly maladapted to their respective environments, are termed 'semi-intelligent design' for emphasis. A case of semi-intelligent design could act simply as an annoyance: Imagine a law still in effect in modern Germany which states that horses are not allowed in the Biergarten and must be tied up on the street outside. We can consider this law to be harmless, but is nonetheless obsolete and maladapted for most of modern Germany. Could there be cases where outdated laws or regulations actually cause problems or even lead to disasters? In the upcoming chapters, we will examine outdated laws and regulations which actually do harm.

When Mount Vesuvius erupted in 79 AD, undoubtedly there were witnesses who assumed a supernatural force was responsible, such as a god or gods who caused the eruption through their own agency; gods who had created the world and its myriad threats to human life for their own use. But modern science has revealed that the eruption was actually caused by geologic forces whose chain of events can be traced back to the beginning of the universe. This was largely unknown at the time of the eruption of Mt. Vesuvius, and therefore, Human Folly #4 applies as well: a misunderstanding of the true nature of the universe, randomness, and evolutionary forces (The Marie and Pierre Curie Folly).

This is simply intelligent design vs. the forces which arose with the beginning of the universe. For the purposes of clarity, I call these forces evolutionary design or simply evolution. So we get intelligent design vs. evolution when distilled down to their rudimentary components, therefore Human Folly #1 is the assumption or belief in the existence of an intelligent design where none exists. Imagine a scene from 2,000 years ago: a farmer with his fields on the banks of a great river. The god(s) have sent unusually heavy rains this season, and the river is swollen and rushing with huge white-water waves, threatening to overflow its banks and flood the farmer's fields and farmhouse, drown the family, and wash away everything, perhaps even the whole village. The farmer imagines or remembers from his Cultural DNA that this means the god(s) are angry with him and that he needs a sacrifice to atone for disappointing them with his perceived wrongful actions or inactions. The farmer remembers a spell from his ancestors that requires him to command his youngest daughter to jump into the raging river to appease the god(s). Everyone agrees this spell and sacrifice worked many years ago, the last time the gods were very angry, and again, a farmer's sacrifice saved everyone, except for the daughter, who died for a good cause. This scene, in one iteration or another, has repeated itself throughout human history and has formed the basis of religions.

Human Folly #2:
Assuming the absence of intelligent design where it is present.
The Propaganda Folly.

This folly results from a withholding of information or a misrepresentation of events as they actually occurred. It is best to think of this folly as constituting a type of fraud. An unsuspecting person sees what appears to be an untouched nature preserve, and while walking across it, encounters a buried landmine. The simplest example of this type of folly would be intentional poisoning. The victim or bystanders might interpret the symptoms as an illness with natural causation. Factitious disorder imposed on another (previously called Munchausen syndrome by proxy) is another example. A further example is gaslighting, where the perpetrator conspires to manipulate the victim's perception of self, environment, and relationships. The introduction of an engineered pathogen into a population, whether deliberate or not, is another example. The folly arises from the assumption that the pathogen is naturally occurring, since the introduction of the pathogen can be deliberate or accidental. If an engineered pathogen was introduced into the population deliberately, the intelligent design lies within both the engineering of the pathogen, constituting embedded design, as well as the mechanics of the introduction: the method of introduction could be intentional, constituting a deliberate action (intelligent design), or unintentional, constituting a failure of an intelligent design to account for its environment. This folly can also be thought of as the revisionist folly, where history has been deliberately manipulated. History occurred in the past and cannot directly be changed. It is not subject to agency, but the understanding of it can be manipulated so as to change the meaning of past events as they are understood.

Human Folly #2 occurs when the viewer or receiver of the account assumes he or she has been given accurate information or a true narrative about an event as it actually occurred or about an entity as it actually stands and does not detect that the historical account has been manipulated. This folly will become more common in the future as we deal with non-human intelligence, most likely AI. As AI gains the ability to manipulate information in real-time, we may be left wondering if we were given an account that has a basis in reality, or a fabricated account of past actions, or more disturbingly, active manipulation of actual events or reality in the present for some end goal. The question of manipulation will always arise, giving rise to another question: whether the manipulation was intentional or accidental. In the future, we may be dealing with very sophisticated AI that can fool us into believing something is naturally occurring, but is, in reality, a fabrication of that AI. This is presently referred to as a deepfake, but the manipulator is, at this time, human. In the future, as today, we may not be able to trust what we see.

Another example of this folly is the confusion or debate over the original meaning of a ritual or a law that was handed down from the past via semantic changes in word usage. For example, the Second Amendment begins with a statement about 'A well regulated Militia, being necessary to the security of a free State.' It is well established that Thomas Jefferson, among others, felt that standing armies and navies increased the chances of going to war, and that militias, consisting of armed citizens, were all that was necessary to protect the homeland. Over two centuries later, it appears the American people have become the target of a self-serving, capitalistic swindle, as this antique statement about militias has been deliberately turned into a constitutional right to own personal firearms, while the industry supplying those firearms has prospered.

Human Folly #3:
Misunderstanding of the true nature of an intelligent design.
The Trojan Horse Folly.

Whether fact or fiction, the story of the Trojan Horse illustrates how expectations and outward appearances can lead someone astray, ensnaring them in a trap. The inhabitants of Troy misinterpreted the giant wooden horse as an offering to the goddess Athena, but the Greeks' design and intent for the horse were quite different from what was expected or assumed by their enemies.

Human Folly #3 is quite common. An example that comes quickly to mind is Alec Baldwin's unintentional shooting of Halyna Hutchins on the *Rust* movie set in 2021. Baldwin was handling a revolver on set when it fired. The single bullet killed Hutchins, the cinematographer, and wounded a director. Baldwin misunderstood the true nature of an intelligent design: the revolver had a live round in it. When a designer hands an operator a designed system, what are the designer's obligations? What are the operator's obligations? If the designed system has catastrophic potential, it appears that the designer must inform the operator of that catastrophic potential, and the operator must also seek to evaluate the design for any catastrophic potential and take the necessary precautions. Operators are obligated to fully understand the designs they are implementing. Any designer who intentionally misleads an operator is committing an egregious fraud.

Human Folly #3 can be illustrated by the present state (2024) of Tesla's self-driving software. The many instances of crashes in bizarre circumstances underscore the difference between true intelligence and embedded intelligent design. With true intelligence, a system (a brain) can read the available environmental information and can predict the correct actions at the correct time to bring about the most favourable outcome in a sequence of events with novel complexity. This assumes that the system has enough sensory input at all times to correctly and predictively read the environment, and it also implies a form of judgement in that system. A semi-intelligent system must be trained on available data, which means the intelligent design is embedded by the designers of the system. Thus the true intelligence lies in the designers, not in the system.

The truly intelligent system will be able to recognise the correct action at the correct time to account for the environment, making quick sense of the events as they happen and will not need to rely on pre-programmed, embedded scenarios to make sense of the environment in real time. The folly lies in the perception that the system will be able to account for the environment at all times, the same way the lazy or distracted Tesla driver assumes his or her Tesla knows what to do in each situation while on what Elon Musk refers to as 'Full Self-Driving' mode. There have been numerous crashes involving the Tesla Autopilot Systems, and Tesla and Musk have been criticised by other manufacturers for refusing to drop the term. For a designed system to be able to drive a car, not only must the sensors feeding information about the environment provide continuous, accurate information to the decision-making system, but the system must be intelligent enough to make a decision and safely guide the vehicle through traffic and road obstacles and situations. That system needs judgement and must be able to read the environment in real time, and predict the outcomes of each of the available options at the precise moment they are considered.

As for the misplaced assumptions regarding the true intent of the Athenians, the inhabitants of Troy also were not able to account for the new intelligent design suddenly in their city, since their 'training data' included only limited scenarios such as 'offering to Athena' and did not include 'giant wooden horse containing Athenian soldiers.'

Another real-world example is demonstrated by the whole stolen election narrative repeated during the 2020 US election season. When President Donald Trump began to say that Democrats were plotting to steal the 2020 election, those who believed him were subject to the folly. He told his supporters that Democrats and co-conspirators, using a designed process, i.e., the mail-in ballot electoral machinery, were planning to impose their own intelligent design (their will) upon it to hijack the election. Of course, this was a false narrative, but Trump had pushed a Trojan Horse upon the people. The Trojan Horse set the stage for Trump to push Human Folly #2 upon his followers and the rest of the Nation, a revisionist fabrication put forth to explain why he lost the election in 2020. Simply, Stop the Steal is a manipulation of past events. The intelligent design in this case was not what Trump said it was, instead, he was fabricating a shell (the Trojan Horse) to house his real intention: revisionist lies designed to create indignation in his base and harness the ensuing rage, which caused a backlash against the US Government on 6 January 2021, intending to keep him in power. Stop the Steal, like so many of Trump's stunts, became a propaganda tool to motivate Trump's 'righteous' MAGA warriors.

Human Folly #4:
Misunderstanding of the true nature of the universe, randomness, and evolutionary forces. The Marie and Pierre Curie Folly.

One could describe this folly as the failure to understand nature and its intricacies and hazards. Again, our definition of evolution within the scope of this book is: what matter does when left to self-organise by chance. It is the product of matter, energy, and time coming together to produce an event. On the timescale of the universe, these events produce the features of the universe itself: stars, black holes, planets, asteroids, earthquakes, volcanoes, life in our biosphere. On the timescale of human beings, evolution looks like chance. The forces which produced evolution are the overwhelming forces of the universe. Those unfortunate enough to be in the shadow of Vesuvius when it erupted in 79 AD were likely displaying both Follies #1 and #4, then perhaps hiding in a corner of a house in Pompeii, Folly #3, not necessarily in that order.

While the Curies were conducting their laboratory experiments, they were handling highly radioactive materials in large quantities. They suffered red, inflamed hands from the continual handling of the radioactive material and began to feel too sick to go to the lab and even physically exhausted. Both Curies were resistant to the idea that the materials they handled daily were responsible for their ailments, but ultimately the true nature of radioactivity became known: we understand today that the Curies were showing signs of radiation sickness. In 1902, Marie isolated radium and determined its atomic weight as 225.93. In 1903, Marie and Pierre were awarded the Nobel Prize for Physics jointly with Henri Becquerel for their combined, though separate, work on radioactivity. Pierre Curie died in 1906 in a street accident, but Marie persevered with her research, at first unaware of the risks to her physical health. In 1920, Marie became visually impaired and had to be led around by her daughters. She learned that she suffered from double cataracts, which we know now can be caused by exposure to radiation. Marie died in 1934 at the age of 66 from aplastic anaemia after working unprotected with radioactive materials over a long period of time. Aplastic anaemia is a blood disorder in which the body's bone marrow does not make enough new blood cells to replenish older blood cells. The Curies' notebooks, belongings, and remains are so radioactive that they are now stored in lead-lined containment. The suburban south Paris laboratory is popularly known as 'Chernobyl on the Seine' due to the high levels of radioactive contamination on the site. The most common isotope of uranium, uranium-238, has a half-life of 4.5 billion years, which means over that immense period of time only half the nuclei in a sample of uranium-238 will decay. This discovery led to the understanding that radioactive elements decay in a predictable fashion, which gave rise to radiometric dating of substances found in the environment. The best-known radiometric dating method involves the isotope carbon-14, with a half-life of 5,730 years.

The Curies' discovery led to products that contained radioactive substances, often touted as having healthful benefits, or which had unusual properties. Doramad Radioactive toothpaste from Germany was sold from around 1920 until around 1945. It contained radioactive Thorium, which was claimed to increase circulation in the gums, destroying germs and increasing the 'life force' in the tissues of the mouth.

Human Folly #4 is not limited to radiation. Instead, it covers any ignorance or misunderstanding of nature, by which I mean natural phenomena that can trace its chain of events to the universe's origins. This could be any disease or event with an unknown cause, for example, the bubonic plagues of the distant past. The hypothetical farmer mentioned above, who commanded his youngest daughter to plunge into the raging river, not only displayed Human Folly #1 but also Folly #4, in that he did not understand the true nature (the cause) of the raging, swollen river. As we shall learn, multiple follies often interact synergistically to precipitate disasters.

Most intelligent design is not purely intelligent design. That is, it is often composed of material that originated from the universe. For example, an apple that we have today is a product of the universe but augmented by the intelligent design of hundreds of generations of humans who bred and hybridised the apples until they became what they are today. An apple is an example of embedded intelligent design complementing and augmenting what was, before human manipulation, just another product of the universe. Another example of embedded intelligent design: with its short, stubby legs, long droopy ears, and sorrowful appearance, a Bassett Hound is a far cry from the ancient wild stock from which it descended. Manipulated by generations of human designers, a Bassett, or a typical toy breed like a Chihuahua, simply could never survive in the wild. However, one could not say it is a pure intelligent design since it started with a wild ancestor that humans had no hand in. An example of a pure intelligent design is a rule or a law. The US Constitution is an example of embedded intelligent design, embedded in a system that uses its algorithms as an operating system. As we look into the causes of disasters, a good place to start is to look for noise thrown off by a system. Using the term 'noise' brings into the picture a phenomenon that is common to both naturally occurring systems and intelligent design. While the universe can throw an occasional meteor or asteroid at our planet, a volcanic eruption or earthquake can cause significant destruction as well, and human-designed systems can and often do produce unexpected results, which I call noise. Noise is indicative of a designed system that allowed chance to play a part in the outcome of an event. Noise often goes unnoticed until it is recognised as a component of a disaster. We will discuss unexpected outputs in the coming chapters.

CASSANDRAS

In many cases, disasters were foretold by a Cassandra who had a platform and a position to warn but was not in a position of power to prevent the disaster; paralleling the Cassandra of Greek mythology, who bore Apollo's curse that although she could peer into future events, nobody would believe her.

Not every disaster produces a hero or has had a Cassandra's forewarning, but while Cassandras have been proved correct many times in the past, they have also been quite often incorrect. We need only look to examples of prophecies of doom from the days of pre-telescopic astronomy. Halley's Comet, easily observed with the unaided eye, appears every seventy-six years, about the length of a human lifespan, allowing most humans to observe it once in a lifetime. When it appeared in 1066, Harold Godwinson, the last Saxon King of England, was said to have interpreted it as a bad omen, while the invading Duke William of Normandy was certain it was the opposite – his success at the Battle of Hastings no doubt confirmed to him his skill in prophesying the future. There may have been a Cassandra, an elderly monk by the name of Elmer, who knelt in terror at the sight of the comet in May 1066. It is thought that he had witnessed either Halley's Comet in 989, or another comet in 1009, both of which were associated with prior invasions of England. One can see the depictions of the scene on the Bayeux Tapestry, commissioned by the Duke's brother, Odo, to commemorate the conquest, of a populace alarmed at the sight of the comet. But now we know which of the Human Follies applies: Human Folly #4: Misunderstanding of the true nature of the universe, randomness, and evolutionary forces (The Marie and Pierre Curie Folly) and Human Folly #1: Assuming the presence of intelligent design when no intelligent design is present (The Divine Intervention Folly). If the story of Elmer is true, it's not because he had any scientific understanding of the real nature of the comet; it would have been based only on the historical association of the prior invasions or just straightforward superstition. I think the aged monk may have known something about human nature and the likelihood that someone like the Duke of Normandy would have used the appearance of the comet as a basis to generate the support he needed to invade Anglo-Saxon England.

Scientific knowledge is a continually limited resource, but it is expanding. A continuous problem is that scientists must exhaustively test their hypotheses about natural phenomena to arrive at a consensus. A complete consensus amongst all scientists is relatively rare, but as knowledge increases, some areas of enquiry have fewer challengers. But scientists understand that as new information becomes available, the explanations of the now-better-understood phenomenon must be updated. Sometimes, longstanding ideas need to be thrown out in light of a preponderance of new evidence. Therefore, scientific knowledge consists of the best understanding of the truth as it is known based on the best evidence available to arrive at a consensus. It's not always uncontroversial and it's often inconvenient, but science is ignored at the peril of humanity. But it is just as risky to ignore human nature and the intentions behind pushed narratives when those narratives can advocate for or affect something with high catastrophic potential. Consider, for example, something like 'Drill Baby Drill.' Just two years after the slogan was introduced at the 2008 Republican Convention, the Deepwater Horizon disaster occurred in the Gulf of Mexico, which caused extensive environmental damage and cost an estimated several billion dollars. Republicans were mocked by alternate slogans of 'Spill Baby Spill.' If we are to have any hope of understanding the intentions of these initiatives – which may end in disaster, or at a minimum contribute directly or indirectly to a suboptimal outcome for the masses or the environment – it's illuminating to look at past design failures and disasters. When such an event is identified, it's also instructive to look for a Cassandra, someone who may have had an insight or very intimate knowledge of the natural or designed system headed for catastrophe that disrupt a Cassandra's warnings from preventing predictable disasters.

I studied chemistry and biological sciences in college as well as liberal arts. I was always a science enthusiast, always looking to science for explanations of the physical world. Carl Sagan loomed large in my thinking – I was exposed to him early on through the *Cosmos* television programme and his books. Sagan mixed scientific explanations and philosophy to explain the origins of knowledge. With Sagan's words swirling in my head, it became more difficult for me to ignore others who were so beholden to superstition. I remember well when walking with a high school classmate on an ordinary garden path, we happened to see a small snake going by, minding its own business. My friend exclaimed: 'Kill it! It's evil!' Even as a youth, I was always looking for the simple explanation, the one without judgement, without evil spirits, and without the Loch Ness Monster. The intersection of politics and science has always been fascinating to me. While I was a grad student in Pittsburgh, we students had the good luck to be able to slip out of the laboratory and walk downtown for a Clinton rally on Friday, 30 October 1992. I had prepared a sign in response to President H. W. Bush's prior mocking of Al Gore, Clinton's running mate, as the 'Ozone Man.' My spouse, who worked in diagnostics in one of the many Pittsburgh hospitals, met us and we all made our way to the rally area. Holding up a homemade sign saying 'We Love the Ozone Man,' I was able to get Clinton's attention and even a comment during the speech. Bush derided Gore's warnings about chlorofluorocarbons (CFCs), a major component of refrigeration technologies at the time that were, according to scientists, degrading the Earth's ozone layer and diminishing the atmosphere's filtration effect of harmful UV radiation. As someone studying the sciences, I understood the importance of atmospheric chemistry and the concept that changing the composition of the gases in Earth's atmosphere can affect the physical properties of the atmosphere. There had been general discussion in the department, and I recall in particular talking with fellow students and faculty on the subject. We came to the conclusion that the current President, who had earned a Bachelor of Arts degree in economics in 1948, had little to no understanding of gas chemistry and was just bloviating. It was such a bro-thing for a president to say. In contrast, Al Gore had taken a class from renowned oceanographer Roger Revelle in the 1968–69 academic year, who later became president of the American Association for the Advancement of Science, and in 1979 was the founding chairman of the original Committee on Climate Change. Revelle's enthusiasm and his research into the human effect on the Earth's climate impacted Gore as a young student. Climate researchers did not have the advantages of satellite observation and data collection of the oceans when Gore was his student, but Revelle and his colleagues arrived at their opinions with knowledge derived from simpler methods such as measuring the carbon dioxide in the atmosphere or the temperature of the ocean water.

Vice President Al Gore has always been the Cassandra of the Climate Crisis. However, in a twist of irony, he played a part in a disaster for the American working class, and unfortunately his part was not as a Cassandra. This part was played by another presidential candidate, the independent candidate in 1992, Ross Perot. 1992 happened to be the year business interests chose to push their agenda upon the American people: to completely remove trade barriers that exist between Canada, the United States, and Mexico. The North American Free Trade Agreement (NAFTA) entered into force on 1 January 1994. The agreement was negotiated by the Bush Administration and signed by President H. W. Bush on 17 December 1992. The main assumption sold to the American public: free trade creates jobs. Additional assumptions were that free trade enhances the development of supply chains and will lead to greater efficiency, which in turn provides the basis for the increase in productivity, which will undoubtedly show up in workers' paycheques.

I remember well a long telephone conversation with my father about Mr. Perot, his favourite candidate, who was against NAFTA. My father almost begged me to support Mr. Perot, who warned the other candidates: 'You implement that NAFTA, the Mexican trade agreement, where they pay people a dollar an hour, have no health care, no retirement, no pollution controls, and you're going to hear a giant sucking sound of jobs being pulled out of this country.' The second part particularly struck a chord with the American people during the second presidential debate in October 1992. I liked Ross Perot quite a lot as well, but I remember telling my father that due to the design of the American political system, a vote for Mr. Perot was a wasted vote and that his real purpose as a third-party candidate was to get the truth out there. The mainstream narrative we were being sold over and over again was that free trade creates jobs. What was often omitted, though, is exactly where those jobs would be created. Both my father and I were sceptical of this accepted mainstream and oft-repeated narrative, and he was captivated by Mr. Perot just like I was. With his Texas drawl, Ross Perot looked and sounded unlike any contemporary national politician we knew of, especially those who were pushing so hard for free trade. The NAFTA sales pitch came with a sudden concern for the welfare of workers and the environment in Mexico, and this struck us as disingenuous at best. Bush, Clinton, and Gore told us there were two side agreements to NAFTA, one to protect labour, and the other to protect the environment, and it was sold as a 'good deal' for America. But we had become accustomed to American companies fighting wage increases and lobbying against organised labour, blocking single payer healthcare, even fighting against the improvements in fuel efficiency, safety equipment, and pollution controls of the cars on our own streets. Who could have forgotten the huge battle for the forty-hour work week and to remove lead from automotive fuel, the 1969 Cuyahoga River Fire, and the appalling corporate pollution that led to the creation of the EPA? We're supposed to believe these same players will voluntarily adhere to the spirit of the brand new American environmental and labour standards in Mexico when nobody is watching? What are the chances that employers based in Mexico, already accustomed to rock-bottom wages without benefits and without pollution controls, would suddenly have a change of heart and play by the new rules? In 1992, the minimum US wage was a paltry $3.80 per hour and did not include health insurance. But in the US, factory workers could earn $12 per hour or a little better, with benefits. How much lower did American companies want their labour costs to be? Much lower, as we would find out.

A feedback loop exists in the issuance of a report card immediately after the semester, but geopolitical events sometimes take decades to play out. Mexico has historically had an abundance of cheap labour. In my opinion, this simple disparity was the driving factor in the push for NAFTA; all the other factors in play were just window dressing. In 2024, over thirty years later, we have the benefit of hindsight, allowing us to peer into the facts to see who was right and issue a verdict. In 1993 the US–Mexico trade balance was $1.7 billion, a US surplus. Predictably, after two decades of NAFTA policy, that number had swung sharply out of favouring the American worker: by 2014, that surplus was gone and the US had a

$54 billion trade deficit with Mexico. By 2022, that number had reached $131.1 billion in Mexico's favour. Between 1993 and 2016, Mexico's automotive manufacturing sector had gained more than 500,000 jobs. So, the assertion that free trade does indeed create jobs is correct, but those jobs were in Mexico, not the USA. Further, an unintended consequence of NAFTA was that American manufacturing bosses could use plant closure as a stick to take the wind out of the sails of union collective bargaining. NAFTA gave corporations the upper hand; any attempt at unionisation or striking for better pay or benefits would produce threats to close down plants and move the operations to Mexico. According to the Economic Policy Institute, between 1993 and 2000, the US manufacturing sector lost 544,750 jobs (72% of all jobs lost); the states with the highest manufacturing job losses were California (82,354), Michigan (46,817), New York (46,210), Texas (41,067), and Ohio (37,694). Changes in trade policy predictably produce winners and losers. The American factory worker, a stalwart of the middle class, lost the battle, but the Mexican worker has inherited the conditions present in American sweatshops of the 1890s, now perhaps the most exploited labourers in North America. At the time of writing, workers in Mexico are fighting to get what Americans had won during the Franklin D. Roosevelt presidency: a five-day workweek. In 1990, about a fifth of Mexican workers earned at or below $4 per day. Across Mexico today the minimum wage has been increased to about $1.80 per hour, and the average Mexican factory worker earns under $4 per hour. The maths is simple here, and it is very revealing: if your constituents possess political power and are simultaneously opposed to the plantation economic model, simply move the plantations offshore, and call it 'Free Trade.' Alas, the yin and the yang of a two-party duopoly allows the calculating populist to save face and pose as an honest broker. Nonchalantly, they drive the nail deeper and then do them one better: beat the drum and call your opponent 'Protectionist.' Oh, the power of words!

Thirty years on, a glaring flaw in the design of the American electoral system, which produced an outcome unfavourable to American workers, has not yet been remedied. President Clinton adopted the Republican agenda which reflected the interests of those wielding economic power. This Republican free trade fantasy was widely sold; it was the sequel to

"It's morning again in America" and the trickle-down economics the cat dragged in with it. In the new, revised story, those workers who were about to lose their livelihoods in manufacturing would get both better jobs and lower prices as their dollars would surely go further in a Walmart full of cheap imported goods from Mexico and China. But the real wages American blue-collar workers take home has barely budged since NAFTA came into force, while CEO pay has increased to over 350 times that of the average worker. After three decades we can now answer the question of who has benefitted the most from free trade. It certainly wasn't the protectionists, and both American blue-collar workers and their Mexican counterparts have gained little ground, leaving them ripe for the picking by a populist social entrepreneur: a divider who would descend upon the political scene, perhaps years in the future, wrapped in the flag and pointing fingers. Mr. Perot, a Texas billionaire, was able to articulate to the American public what he thought was wrong about the mainstream narrative being sold to us, but he did not possess the power by design to actually prevent this pending disaster from descending upon the American worker. That should have been the job of the elected officials, those who had actual power. Where was the social contract, that set of obligations that we have to each other as Americans? These are the same obligations that prevent a poorly designed and built skyscraper from being located in Tokyo or Taipei. When we hand power to politicians, do we not assume they will use that power in our best interests? Or are we doomed to be subject to the wishes of those who have the politician's ear?

RIP, Mr. Perot. You were absolutely right, as many of us suspected.

NO PEN, PAPER, AND SCISSORS? A ROCK WILL DO!

/ SOCIETY IS INDEED A CONTRACT ... BUT THE STATE OUGHT NOT TO BE CONSIDERED AS NOTHING BETTER THAN A PARTNERSHIP AGREEMENT IN A TRADE ... TO BE TAKEN UP FOR A LITTLE TEMPORARY INTEREST, AND TO BE DISSOLVED BY THE FANCY OF THE PARTIES. IT IS TO BE LOOKED ON WITH OTHER REVERENCE ... A PARTNERSHIP IN ALL SCIENCE; A PARTNERSHIP IN ALL ART; A PARTNERSHIP IN EVERY VIRTUE, AND IN ALL PERFECTION ... A PARTNERSHIP NOT ONLY BETWEEN THOSE WHO ARE LIVING, BUT BETWEEN THOSE WHO ARE LIVING, THOSE WHO ARE DEAD, AND THOSE WHO ARE TO BE BORN.

Edmund Burke, *'Reflections on the Revolution in France,'* 1790.

How did ancient societies pass along their accumulated knowledge about the world?

Knowledge is indeed power, and early societies had an information management problem. Those early groups of humans had very basic needs and those needs were nothing new; they were encountered and solved by scores of generations of ancestors. These tribes had to survive and thrive- passing the torch to a new generation, averting the 'disaster' of tribal extinction. They had to solve problems such as avoiding inbreeding, resource allocation, how to deal with encroaching threats and how to fend off danger in a world indifferent to their survival. These early peoples needed landmarks that could survive the ages, being passed down intact through vast stretches of time, so that each succeeding generation could benefit from the survival and accumulated knowledge of their ancestors. If these landmarks were unchanging and durable features of the human environment, they were especially useful as the centres of an ongoing culture and could function as a written history-sans-writing: the history, tribal law and the algorithms from the ancestors could be embedded within the cultural landmark itself as stories. Those cultural landmarks became a kind of 'superpower' for early groups of humans.

As we go about our daily lives in our modern world, we can scarcely wake up in our beds without immediately encountering a product of the human mind: whether the bed and the blanket, the roof over our head, our alarm clock or smartphone, or our mass-produced clothing. We wake up to newspapers and news websites, cable television programming, social and streaming media, and other components of public discourse that keep us all informed of the latest items that work their way to the surface, that which is served up by algorithms and achieves virality or otherwise captures our attention. Let us step back in time and explore a culture in which the products of intelligent design were much less palpable, more intangible, or even imperceptible to outsiders. Ancient cultures relied on stories and traditions to pass along accumulated knowledge between the generations. Cultural Monuments, which are culturally significant constructs, have been and continue to be landmarks or beacons which are capable of passing along this information over many generations and thousands of years in the absence of written information storage. Large, ever-present, naturally occurring objects have been readily available for these purposes, with enormous size and observability being key to making these features available for inclusion in cultural stories.

The sun, Earth, moon, a few observable planets in our solar system, and the stars comprised the entirety of what humans considered the universe for almost our entire lineage on Earth. Prehistoric renderings of the solar system provided the foundation for later models, beginning with cave markings, drawings, and structures such as passage tombs that would align with the rising sun on the mornings around the solstices and equinoxes. Henges built as monuments to ancestors also aligned with the sun, as did immense ancient structures such as the Great Pyramid of Giza. As giant luminescent orbs in the sky, the sun or moon could be seen from anywhere on Earth inhabited by humans and, ever-present and old as time itself, were worshipped by most ancient civilisations as deities in one form or another. They became monuments, the loci of the most sacred rituals, from the burial of leaders to the assignments of crop plantings and harvests to the issuing of prophecy, as with the Oracle at Delphi. Celestial objects have been integrated into cultural narratives and world-views as well as providing navigational aids in both ancient and modern cultures.

These celestial monuments are pivotal to our understanding of the six cultures cited by various authorities as the 'first human civilisation': in Mesopotamia, Mesoamerica, Ancient Egypt, India, China, and Peru. But a different and naturally occurring geographic feature – and its accompanying culture – predates all six by dozens of millennia: the sandstone formation in the centre of Australia known today as Ayers Rock, or Uluru by the Aboriginals who have walked the continent for over 50,000 years – recognised only lately as 'Indigenous Australians.'

The oldest known society and the first formed by the human emigrations off the African continent, Aboriginal Australian cultures have been continuous and largely intact since their arrival in Australia. Though the land offered no domesticable flora other than the macadamia nut, recent studies indicate they had tried their hand at farming far earlier than traditionally thought. They appear to have been largely hunter-gatherers, their prey originally including a range of large animals (or megafauna) inhabiting the ancient Australian landscape. Flightless birds that stood as high as three metres, goanna lizards reaching six metres in length, and among mammals, kangaroos twice the size of humans, various other marsupials, a giant buck-toothed wombat, and massive crocodiles were known to have existed at the same time as those early Australians.

Several of these animals made their way into the myths and origin stories of many of the tribespeople who were gifted, as per the Australian anthropologist Inga Clendinnen, with a capacity for:

> steepling thought-structures – intellectual edifices so comprehensive that every creature and plant had its place within it. They travelled light, but they were walking atlases, and walking encyclopaedias of natural history. ... Detailed observations of nature were elevated into drama by the development of multiple and multi-level narratives: narratives which made the intricate relationships between these observed phenomena memorable.

As with most cultures, the Aboriginals maintained these origin myths through communication from elders to the young, narratives that formed what has become known as the 'Dreamtime.' These stories explain how 'Creation Beings' created the landscape, the people, and the environment. To this day, Aboriginal peoples see dreams as glimpses of events that happened during the creation period. There are also deities called 'Ancestral Beings' who are considered distant ancestors to those currently living. These Ancestral Beings are the source of the tribal laws prescribing the roles of members by gender regarding marriage and childbirth, laws pertaining to all aspects of life, and the day-to-day knowledge the living need to make tools and weapons and in order to hunt and survive.

These cultures withstood the test of time, and even two centuries or so of European arrivals, beginning with the dawn of the seventeenth century – Spanish navigators at first, then the Dutch, who named the continent 'New Holland.' The Australian continent's forbidding reaches dissuaded further incursions inland until the English arrivals in 1770 on the eastern coast. These explorers claimed the land for Great Britain, later spreading word that the continent, inhabited by peaceful tribes, was ripe for colonisation. Australia's colonial period began as a dumping ground: a penal colony was founded there in 1788. Other Europeans began arriving soon after, and made their way further and further inland: their presence, specifically their viruses, would soon threaten the oldest surviving intact human culture – and a population estimated at the time variously between a half-million and a million lives. What their pathogens did not destroy, their firearms and religions would threaten.

THE SACRED AND THE SACRILEGIOUS: UPON WHOSE SACRED TURF DO WE TREAD?

The difficult terrain of Australia demanded adaptation by its inhabitants. The extreme nature of the climate meant that the environment yielded almost no material even for very simple technologies to produce paper records or written laws, clay tablets, or to collect a written cultural history. Australian Aboriginal cultures relied out of necessity on oral traditions and, for the creation myths of Aboriginal tribes in central Australia, such as the Pitjantjatjara, upon the oldest sacred monument known to man, the sandstone formation Uluru, their word for 'Earth Mother.'

Elevating the culture and its monuments to sanctified status has been a key part of the survival of these indigenous tribes. Indigenous cultural preservation projects help to understand how tribal law and other Cultural Monuments enabled the continuation of those cultures:

> *Ananguku Tjukurpa kunpu pulka alatjitu ngaranyi. Inma pulka ngaranyi munu Tjukurpa pulka ngaranyi ka palula tjana-languru kulini munu uti nganana kunpu mulapa kanyinma. Miil-miilpa ngaranyi munu Ananguku Tjukurpa nyanga pulka mulapa. Tjukurpa panya tjamulu, kamilu, mamalu, ngunytjulu nganananya ungu, kurunpangka munu katangka kanyintjaku.*
>
> There is strong and powerful Aboriginal Law in this Place. There are important songs and stories that we hear from our elders, and we must protect and support this important Law. There are sacred things here, and this sacred Law is very important. It was given to us by our grandfathers and grandmothers, our fathers and mothers, to hold onto in our heads and in our hearts.
>
> **Tony Tjamiwa,** *one of the traditional owners of Uluru.*

Nintiringkula kamila tjamula tjanalanguru. Wirurala nintiringu munula watarkurinytja wiya. Nintiringkula tjilpi munu pampa nguraritja tjutanguru, munula rawangku tjukurpa kututungka munu katangka kanyilku. Ngura nyangakula ninti – nganana ninti.

We learned from our grandmothers and grandfathers and their generation. We learned well and we have not forgotten. We have learned from the old people of this place, and we'll always keep the Tjukurpa in our hearts and minds. We know this place – we are *ninti*, knowledgeable.

Barbara Tjikatu, *traditional artist and senior Pitjantjatjara woman.*

Uluru is Australia's heart, emotionally and spatially – located pretty much in the dead-centre of the continent, 335 kilometres from the nearest major population centre, Alice Springs. A sandstone formation 348 metres in height and with a girth of 9.4 kilometres, it is particularly spectacular at dawn and sunset, when it glows an almost luminescent red: the result of millions of years of sun and water oxidising the stone's high mineral content, particularly iron.

All Australians have come to revere the Rock. But Uluru is far more significant for Aboriginal and Indigenous Australians and its traditional custodians, the Anangu people. A collection of several Central Australian tribes, they oversee the more than three dozen sites within and around Uluru that are deemed sacred – several of which are still exclusive to the Anangu and have never been seen by outside eyes.

In 1920, Uluru and nearby Kata-Tjuta (Mt Olga National Park) were set aside as sanctuaries for Aboriginal people, but by 1940, the Anangu had lost their full traditional pattern of land use as tourists began to arrive to visit Uluru and Kata-Tjuta. By 1958, both Uluru and Kata-Tjuta were removed from the Aboriginal Reserve and declared a tourist and wildlife reserve. During this period of time, tourist buildings were erected and a well was drilled for water at the site. Local Aboriginals continued to lay claim to the Ayers Rock–Mt Olga National Park and were finally recognised as the park's traditional owners in 1980, and the Anangu finally regained control of the land in 1985, as well as other long-denied rights, but only after a great deal of political work.

One Anangu man told reporters that Uluru was a 'very sacred place, like our church.' The rock was finally closed to climbing in 2019. In a last-minute frenzy of climbing before the ban was officially enacted, hundreds of people climbed the rock, to the disappointment of the locals. 'Get off the rock!' a group of indigenous women yelled at tourists as they were coming back down after a climb to the top. The locals have been more assertive towards those who visit their ancestral home and climb the rock since a push to improve the representation of Australian Aboriginal people in the Australian Constitution has garnered more support. For the Aboriginal and Indigenous peoples of Australia, there are no separate deities; the people, landscape, and Uluru itself fulfil that function. The people have custodial duties and are fundamental in keeping the lore and law alive. The country is cared for with song, ceremony, stories, and art, the concept known as Tjukurpa (discussed in greater detail below). It is a word difficult to translate into English as it encompasses deep and complex religious meanings that link the people to the environment, ancestors, and, most crucially, the landscape. Australian Aboriginal people focus on the preservation of their culture and their cultural homeland; for them, there is no separation of church and state since their church is a feature of the land itself, and is also integral to their culture. The church is not only the school; it's also the law clerk, the judge, and the jury.

Whilst Westerners have the concept of land ownership, the Aboriginal peoples are land custodians. From the Western perspective, if you own land, you can do what you want, including climbing all over it and exploiting it for monetary gain, regardless of the damage caused. Aboriginal peoples see their relationship to the land in the past and present, and themselves as custodians of its future. A custodian looks after something; they care for it to pass it on in the best condition possible to the forthcoming generations. Exploitation is impossible, and would be considered a crime against the past, present, and future. When non-Aboriginal Australians clamoured to climb the Rock, for example, it was seen as a statement of ownership and conquest. This act deeply saddened Aboriginal people and was seen as a sign of the utmost disrespect. These differences of ownership versus custodial duties are clear when one compares Uluru and its creation myths to the Garden of Eden of the Abrahamic religions. There the first man seems almost an afterthought as a creation of a monotheistic God, and woman yet more so; issuing from a spare rib, she and all descendants of her sex were made as companions to the males, to be lower in the hierarchy, while man has been given explicit dominion over all of God's earthly creation. In contrast, the Aboriginals see themselves as the descendants of the ten creative spirits of the Dreamtime and thus part of the Rock itself: 'The entire land and seascape is named and the cultural memory of our people is written here.'

Geologists tell us that Uluru was formed during the shifting of tectonic plates, millions of years before even the Himalayas were formed. Aboriginal peoples will tell you roughly the same thing, though their tectonic plates are the ten Dreamtime Ancestors moving around the land, creating the landscape, and Uluru is the place where they came to rest. Both geologists and Aboriginal peoples assert that Uluru was not formed by a single geologic (or spiritual) event, but by several, separated by vast scales of time and caused by enormous forces. For geologists, Uluru became a rock around 550 million years ago and has been eroding for over 300 million years, a grey rock turned rusty red, baking in the heat of millions of summers: Uluru is literally the original Aussie baking in the sun.

All of these conditions and inclemencies made their way into the Dreamtime narratives. Each part of the Rock was created by one or more of ten different ancestors, and the Anangu believe that they can communicate with and receive blessings from their ancestors by touching parts of the Rock. The caves and fissures around the base of the Rock are sacred and filled with art that tells the stories of the ancestors.

The Dreamtime stories available to us are a fraction of the whole, for no one, even the Anangu elders, the traditional custodians of Uluru, is entitled to the full narrative. Although there is much more to it than this simple description, people who are not Anangu are only allowed the legend told to children, who have no entitlement to the sacred and profound greater versions told in song, dance, and art. As Tony Tjamiwa put it, in order 'to understand the significance of Uluru for the Anangu, you have either to be an Anangu person yourself or to have lived with them for a considerable time.'

The Rock is the resting place of ten different Dreamtime Ancestral Beings who travelled across the land at different times, forming the landscape. They did not disappear, and according to the tribal lore, still exist as a fundamental part of Uluru and the surrounding landscape. The word the Anangu use for this knowledge – and its evidence in the landscape of the Ancestral Dreamtime Beings – is Tjukuritja, a wisdom that, like the gendered social organisation metaphorically begun in the Garden of Eden, is both shared and separated by men and women, both sexes having knowledge the other is not entitled to.

Tjukuritia knowledge is gendered, which means the knowledge and skills held by men differ from those held by the women of the tribal unit. Knowledge and tasks are passed to the tribal children who accompany their parents and relatives to the Bush to search for food. Boys spend their time with the women and girls, later becoming familiar with the men's tasks, songs, stories, and sacred sites. The wisdom is hereditary, totemic, and age-specific; as a person matures, he or she is entitled to more knowledge. A person's identity, including a spiritual animal and that of their parents, where they were born, and what 'skin' they have, entitles them to specific knowledge. A person's 'skin' is their spiritual identity, part of a unique social structure that divides all of Australian Aboriginal society into a number of groups, each of which combines particular sets of kin. Essentially, Aboriginal customary law, it governs a person's life in fundamental ways, including who they can marry. 'Skin' divisions are passed down from parents to children, and the system ensures that inbreeding in a small population spread over the country does not occur and maintains the genetic diversity of the small groups.

ABORIGINAL ORIGIN STORIES: THE CHAIN OF AUTHENTICITY BEGINS WITH THE ANCESTORS

Every culture reveres its forbears. When cultural stories and knowledge originate from the ancestors and 'living' supernatural beings, there is a naturally embedded reverence for that Cultural DNA, a kind of built-in authenticity that is folded in with identity, land, and tribal belonging.

For the Anangu, the landscape was created at the beginning of time by Ancestral Beings who are their direct ancestors. Kata Tjuta, another natural stone formation less than 20 km away, is also part of the same ancestral dreaming landscape and Tjukuritja. The Dreamtime stories are more than explanations of origins; they are moral codes, land management guides, biological texts of flora and fauna, an academic encyclopaedia of knowledge, history, law, and much more. But as outsiders looking in, we can only access the children's version, the oversimplified extract of a much larger body of knowledge.

The story of Lungkata, for example, explains the black streaks on the rock and why it should not be climbed. The black streaks on the Rock are Lungkata's flesh singed by fire. Lungkata's story teaches the dangers of climbing the Rock, the morals of hunting, not to steal, tracking methods for emus and lizards, emu butchery, and how to manage land. The children's version of this story is quite simple; the more detailed lessons and knowledge in the fuller versions of the story are reserved for the more mature tribe members.

Other Dreamtime stories tell how certain features in the Rock, such as cracks, holes, and stones, came to be there. The southern face of the Rock, for example, was formed by the battle between the Liru (venomous brown snakes) and the Kunia (Woma pythons). The holes on this side of the Rock are the scars left by the spears thrown in that battle. The northern face of the Rock was formed when another group (the Mala) arrived.

There seems to be an explanation for just about every outwardly visible feature of the rock in the Dreamtime stories, which teach people to finish what they start, listen to warnings of dangers, explain features in the Rock, and contain a map of the area and a songline to South Australia.

Songlines, or dreaming tracks, are paths across land or sky in Aboriginal Australian belief systems. They trace routes of creator-beings from the Dreaming and connect people to ancestral lands. Songlines serve as navigation aids, cultural knowledge repositories, mythological narratives and geographical guides that interconnect groups. They provide a framework for social interaction by acting as a kind of cultural passport between these groups, facilitating the preservation of cultural knowledge by transcending language barriers that exist between the widely scattered groups in the Australian outback. Songlines are known to be central to Aboriginal identity and culture, and are key to preserving ancient knowledge across vast stretches of time and over hundreds of generations.

— — — —

The significance of Uluru to Aboriginal and Indigenous Australians cannot be overstated and is difficult for others to grasp. Every part of the monolith is a living entity that connects people to their past and the thousands of generations who have lived there before. Uluru is more than a sacred site; it is the embodiment of the survival of the oldest culture in the world on the harshest continent with the least resources.

As with Native Americans, the creation stories often included natural phenomena such as flora and fauna from the local environment and invented or long-dead actors, and have incorporated local landmarks in the tribal narrative. In the case of Uluru, a massive geologic formation has, over time, become a Cultural Monument central to the people who inhabit the area surrounding the massive stone. It is clear that even a naturally occurring object such as Uluru can acquire sacred status. Elevating a Cultural Monument to sacred status, also known as consecration, appears to be an excellent way of ensuring such a monument has a steady supply of devotees ready to defend it. Sacred status is thus a way of future-proofing a monument, thereby preventing the natural obsolescence over time common to everyday designs, traditions, and lesser Cultural Monuments, rules, and laws. The durability of the sacredness of such an entity, or indeed of any monument, depends greatly upon the number of people who acknowledge its cultural import and, in the case of religion, its sacredness.

A great deal can be learned from this culture, which has been surviving and thriving in such a landscape for aeons. In the very simplest sense, this indigenous culture has embedded within it all the knowledge necessary to account for the harsh environment, lack of resources, and the limited gene pool over some 2,600 generations.

As we know, something from the distant past can have a certain authenticity about it, while new things are admired more for their utility and inventiveness, or judged based upon an aesthetic ideal or standard. But will a new idea stand the test of time?

The Anangu and other cultures with similar celestial object deities show us that at a very basic level, humans can project a sense of reverence upon a naturally occurring feature of the Earth or the solar system, elevating that object to sacred monument status. The monuments are embedded within the narrative framework that a given culture uses to explain its origin and/or existence. The Aboriginal cultural narratives contain the heritable cultural knowledge necessary for the survival of that culture, Cultural DNA. This idea was touched on by Richard Dawkins, who coined the term 'meme,' which is described as a unit of cultural transmission. Such culturally embedded knowledge and monuments such as Uluru comprise a collective cognition or accumulated wisdom gathered and filtered through the ages and a set of algorithms that are communicated between generations, time-tested, and capable of continuously safeguarding new generations in wildly fluctuating environmental conditions over dozens upon dozens of millennia. Unlike biological DNA, which changes very slowly over time and many generations, Cultural DNA can be quickly adapted simply by changing the narrative. Tribal elders can see changes over time and quickly adapt the stories to account for those changes.

This is in contrast with the cultural mores of the European colonialists who would subjugate them. In the instances involving the colonisation of the Americas and Australia, the European newcomers slowly became the dominant culture through resource extraction and systematic exploitation, oppression, assimilation and, in some cases, eradication, enabled by higher-yield intensive farming methods, weapons technology, population growth, and embedded communicable diseases imported from Europe. Indigenous cultures relied on sustainable subsistence through horticulture and farming methods which were not capable of sustaining large populations. These methods of living from the land and within the bounds of traditional land custodianship were characterised by a light footprint on the land, sustainable relationships between humans and the natural environment, and the elevation of the land and the tribe's ancestors within that land to a sacred status. This sacred status ensured that the land would be passed on to succeeding generations intact and unexploited. One could describe this cultural adaptation as spiritual ecology.

The capacity to hold an entity sacred is as old as humanity itself, occurs spontaneously in human cultures, and is a very durable feature of the function of the human mind. This sacredness is part of a social contract between generations, that is, between the dead, the now-living, and the yet-unborn. The social contract consists of the Cultural DNA embedded within the cultural monument which is elevated and protected by the sacred status of that cultural monument. Thus, the sacred social contract contains the Cultural DNA and future-proofs Cultural Monuments, thus improving the odds that important information required for survival will indeed be passed along to successive generations intact.

If we acknowledge that these Cultural Monuments have the durability to be passed on from generation to generation, the ability to instruct future generations on what is to be considered bad is also necessary. The original dichotomy – that of good and evil – is the most enduring Cultural DNA that we have accumulated in our collective knowledge. It does our progeny no service to teach them what is good without also including what is bad for an individual, a tribe, and a society. But for that information to 'stick' and become an actual Cultural Monument of the negative type- it must become a building block of societal worldviews and decision-making processes. 'Dark-Sky Monument Building' is my term to help better understand how one man's freedom fighter can become another man's terrorist. I found no adequate preexisting terms available to describe this, or at least as I understand it. The term 'demagogue' describes a politician who engages in Dark-Sky Monument Building. Donald Trump fits the definition of a demagogue like a glove, but the term does not adequately explain the nuts and bolts of monument building, positive or negative, which is done by willing participants, most of whom are not politicians.

Dark-Sky Monument Building is an activity common in both religious and political endeavours and has had a long history, but curiously it has heretofore lacked a uniform label, at least outside of religious contexts. For example, the term 'borking' was popularised by the *Wall Street Journal* after the Senate rejected the nomination of Robert Bork to the US Supreme Court in 1987. 'Borking' means to systematically attack or defeat a nominee or candidate for public office unfairly through an organised campaign of harsh public criticism or vilification. A scapegoat, one who is blamed for another's actions, is similar, but it is not the same meaning. The biblical terminology is perhaps closer: there are two young goats in the ceremony, and upon the head of one of the goats is placed the weight of all that is bad. One of the goats is sacrificed while the other (the scapegoat) is set free to carry away the sins of the community that were laid upon his head, all under the watchful eyes of an all-seeing God. The Abrahamic idea of the sacrificial lamb is also close, where a lamb (which could also be a person such as a martyr or, simply, Jesus) of high value is sacrificed for the public good. 'Whipping boy' is also similar, but its whimsical overtone does not do the notion justice. For a very good example of ongoing, never-ending Dark-Sky Monument Building, consider the life and career of Satan. The traditional adversary of all that is good, Satan began his very, very long career with a mention in the Old Testament. The original meaning was rooted in the Hebrew language, the term for "accuser" or "adversary" and as a common noun, was applicable to both human and mythical entities. However the term has gradually changed in meaning from being a common adversary to what may be more aptly described today as the Devil. Today they appear to be interpreted as one and the same, at once an angel, possessing wings, but also imagined with human-like attributes, augmented with supernatural powers such as immortality and the ability to become completely invisible at will. Santa, who also has a notable career spanning hundreds of years, ostensibly needs his reindeer to get around, but the Devil's angelic origins gave him wings, which impart a sense of being everywhere at all times. Unlike Santa, who must perform actual work by climbing down the chimney, Satan is unaffected by physical barriers or by the wishes of those who would rather not be tempted by such a cunning and powerful adversary. He is also capable of taking the physical form — such as a serpent, or as a humanlike figure but with vampire-like teeth, a tail, horns, and cloven hooves; depictions which seem to be invented especially to invoke revulsion in any person who casts his or her eyes upon his beastly presence. While Satan is indeed in the realm of the imagination, the utility of such a career to function as a living cautionary tale for any individual at any time or place is the ultimate in convenience. Satan began his career in the lap of luxury — literally the ankles of divine power. After a disagreement that caused a ruckus in the celestial C-suite, he was reassigned for what amounts to insubordination: a combination of pride and hubris, considered the mother of all vices. His new job description, according to the high priests of religions everywhere, is to visit upon the scenes of the crimes of humanity itself, collect evidence, and expose the obvious flaws of mere mortals for public display. But in modern times, technology has allowed most of Satan's work to be done remotely, and he needs only to be named to inspire fear and loathing to those within earshot of his mention. Satan may be powerful, and his career may be long and prosperous, but it has had a tinge of Charlie Brown after all. Grace and goodness are always there to swipe the ball away at the exact moment of his swing, sending him skidding down the field — to his constant torment; the implied message being that there is to be no reward for wickedness. Further, Satan's pride has mirrored that of the nonbeliever in that he wished the other angels to adore and worship him as a self-created god. Satan has played his role well, pleasing his own accusers every Sunday by sticking to the plot in absolutely every single instance. Never out of character, he always was and still is the villain who could be counted on to show up for every sermon just by being named – or by reciting his job description in front of practically any wretched sinner and willing believer alike. Of course this Dark-Sky Monument must be compatible with the existing, embedded Blue-Sky and Dark-Sky Monuments of a social group to be taken seriously. As an example, would-be monument builders may have trouble convincing a group of followers that the 'Flying Spaghetti Monster' is something to be taken seriously – the FSM has neither a chain of authenticity tying it to an existing, well-accepted deity, nor any real, plausible links to any other existing, culturally-embedded Dark-Sky Monuments such as Nazis, the Devil, Satan, or Deep State.

Monument building takes diligence and a demonstrable chain of authenticity; it requires the consent of those in whose presence the monument is being erected. But that consent can be manufactured within a captive audience. Just as Trump steadily repeated the term 'deep state' to demonise federal institutions, the term 'woke' has been transformed from its origins in social justice awareness into a dark-sky monument – a catch-all pejorative that conservative politicians deploy against any progressive ideas that challenge existing power structures, even as the underlying concept simply acknowledges systemic inequalities that persist in society. This type of monument building takes persistence, repetition and enough time for the concept to take hold within the susceptible group. Other instances require no manufacturing, only the seizing of the opportunity. With acts of terrorism, for example, on 9/11, a moment of so-called moral clarity occurred where the United States was clearly under attack from a foreign hostile group. Seizing his opportunity, President George W. Bush exclaimed: 'You're either with us or with the terrorists.' With this one sentence, the President lumped together anyone who opposed his policies with the perpetrators who had attacked the US. This was a case where dissent was almost completely removed by the 'moral clarity' of the obviously hostile act of terrorism, and little to no active Dark-Sky Monument Building was thought necessary to identify that particular 'devil' and prove that he is, indeed, bad. As we all now know, this terrorist act allowed the Bush Administration almost undisputed authority to go to war in Afghanistan and Iraq. A similar event is occurring as I write this: the invasion of Ukraine by Russia. It is interesting that the pretence being used by Russia, the sovereign power, is a preexisting, culturally-embedded Dark-Sky Monument that everyone understands: Nazis.

THE ELEMENTS OF A DESIGNED DISASTER

Human activity has become such a growing component of disasters that take a toll on human lives that we must seek to understand the intentions of those activities.

When a human being or group of humans design an object or a system for a purpose, there are many aspects to consider with respect to how that design operates within its environment. In general, a perfectly designed system is neither affected by nor affects its environment. But we know that real-world systems are both affected by their environment, and can affect their environment in some way. A designed object or system which is completely hermetically sealed off and isolated from its intended operational environment is the stuff of museums.

HUMAN INTELLIGENT DESIGN: NEED GIVES RISE TO DESIGN, DESIGN ENABLES FUNCTION

Human-designed objects or systems have a purpose or function, and they have embedded design to enable that function. Therefore, the object or system displays two types of design: basic embedded design and operational design. This designed object or system contains features which constitute embedded design, and the manner in which the object or system is used constitutes the operational design. When a human designer creates a design, we can call that intelligent design. Therefore, the designed objects or systems have been designed according to function; the assumptions held by the designer are, in a way, frozen in time. In contrast, the operator of that design must use decision-making in real-time during the function or use of that intelligent design. However, the embedded design assumptions made by a designer are not always completely understood by the operator of that system or object or those who could be affected by it.

The embedded design enables the function of that design. Designed systems display inherent and predictable assumptions and understandings of the physical, cultural, and legal environments within which the designed system is intended to operate. When these designed systems fail to produce a predictable output, it is possible to understand and categorise the faulty assumption(s) and misunderstanding(s) that led to the failure. An example of a simple system designed to produce an output is making coffee.

The inputs are:

- electricity or a heat source
- water
- ground coffee
- a coffee filter
- a functional coffee maker

Expected output:

- hot coffee
- a used filter
- spent coffee grounds

If there was an unexpected output – for example, the coffee tasted bad – among the possibilities for a cause would be stale coffee grounds. The person running the operation would be expected to look backwards into the process to find the source of the bad coffee. Perhaps the coffee company or supermarket has a poor system for rotating stock – if the coffee used was sitting in a corner for months and was then discovered and put on the display shelf in the store. This spurious result is an indication that the systems in place are not fully designed and implemented, allowing chance to enter the system, i.e., the chance that a package of coffee was ignored for a period and then was suddenly noticed and put on the shelf. The assumption was made by someone in the coffee supply chain that the coffee sold was fresh – or, perhaps more likely, it was bought and then forgotten by the customer, only being discovered months later in the back of the pantry, or it could have been placed in a damp area where it became slightly rancid. Either way, a faulty assumption combined with a chancy supply chain produced an unexpected output, not an intended output, not an expected output but a designed output nonetheless.

CATASTROPHIC POTENTIAL OF A SYSTEM – WHETHER DESIGNED BY NATURE OR BY HUMANS

1. The first question to ask is whether or not the designed object or system has the potential for disaster. On a very basic level, different designs possess differences in catastrophic potential depending on speed, quantity, toxicity, or vulnerability to potential uncontrolled energy or substance transfer. The potential for disaster occurs when lives, property, or nature are threatened by a design's speed, quantity, toxicity, or vulnerability to potential uncontrolled energy or substance transfer. For designed or natural systems we can add in potential pathogenicity of one or more component(s) of that designed or natural system, now that humans possess the ability to manipulate the pathogenicity of infectious agents. We should also include both intentional and unintentional privation in our assessment of the catastrophic potential of a system. For example a suburb built on the edge of a fire-prone natural environment- if the resources for controlling the seasonal wildfires are not present by design, this is considered a form of unintentional privation by design. Climate change will stress our embedded designs- those seasonal wildfires may become year-round or even much more intense, requiring constant vigilance and ample resources to avert catastrophe.

2. The next question to ask is whether the system which possesses the catastrophic potential places human lives, property, or nature at risk. For the catastrophic potential to pose a risk to human lives, the system producing the risk does not necessarily need to be in proximity to the affected system, but often the greatest risk is borne by human lives, property, or nature that is closest to the system containing the catastrophic potential. For example – a nuclear power plant stands

to affect the areas located nearest to the power plant, but the fallout from a nuclear accident or detonation can be carried worldwide by wind currents. Sea-level rise affects the entire planet, even though the polar ice caps and Greenland ice sheets are a great distance from the coastal low-lying and vulnerable areas of Western Africa, for example.

3. A human design must account for the environment in which the design is purposed to function. The design must fulfil its function with a minimum of damage to either lives, property, or nature. When a design cannot adequately account for its environment, the seeds of disaster are sown. Disasters are about loss; we can measure some losses, but there are other losses that we cannot measure, such as a loss of life or health that leads to a loss of reproductive capacity or the ability of natural systems to replenish themselves.

    A disaster at the scale of that of the *Titanic* can lead to the losses of generations of progeny to those who were lost in the disaster itself, but one cannot measure the exact number of future individuals of would-be children and grandchildren of those who were lost. In a similar fashion, genetic disturbances caused by bioaccumulation of radioactive substances which were formed in the core of a nuclear reactor can be passed to and burden future generations, or have the capability of perturbing the emergence of a future generation – not just of future human generations, but that of all life forms within the biosphere.

4. Designed systems which are unable to fully account for their environments often produce outcomes which are unplanned and seemingly unpredictable. A system that consistently produces outputs which the system was not designed to produce is a red flag that the system is producing noise. These unplanned outputs often appear over and over again prior to a larger, more disastrous event. As an example, near-miss incidents that have become common involving US commercial airlines are examples of a system which cannot control all components of the system at all times, an indication that parts of this designed system are leaving something to chance.

Let's apply this equation to a real-world potential disaster scenario.

CASE STUDY OF A DISASTER: CLIMATE CHANGE

Global warming or climate change threatens our environment itself. The catastrophic potential derives from human lives, property, and nature being threatened by an uncontrolled energy transfer from the sun to our global climate: the accumulation of greenhouse gases in our environment traps solar radiation output from the sun leading to an excess of heat energy within the Earth's atmosphere and oceans. The resulting increase in average global temperature will ultimately cause uncontrolled substance transfer: polar ice melting and ocean level rise will reduce the available habitable land and cause perturbations to the climate in the form of higher energy storms.

Catastrophic potential: The huge quantity of polar ice threatens human lives with encroachment of the sea onto inhabited arable land, and the excess heat trapped in the oceans can power ever more violent storms and atmospheric disturbances. Further, the great weight of the ice keeps a lid on the over 100 of volcanoes in Antarctica. A polar ice melt could reduce or remove this pressure on the magma chambers, likely triggering eruptions. Due to the number and size of these volcanoes, the earth's environment could be catastrophically impacted through eruptions which could last for many years.

The human component of this disaster includes the release of greenhouse gases into the environment mainly from heat engines which burn fossil fuel. The large-scale release of carbon from human activity into the atmosphere has the unintended consequence of trapping excess heat in the atmosphere and oceans. The source of this heat energy is, of course, solar radiation.

The people who designed the Otto cycle engine and began automobile production were unaware of this design's catastrophic potential as a consequence of wide scale adoption. The designed system involves groups of people who routinely extract carbon from the Earth and place it in the hands of those who burn it and release it into the atmosphere.

Sketching out the impending disaster, we must assess the catastrophic potential of the relevant systems.

Questions:

Does the weather system have catastrophic potential, i.e., potential for catastrophic speed, quantity, toxicity, or vulnerability to potential uncontrolled energy or substance transfer?

Yes, currently, water covers 71% of the Earth's surface, with around 2% of the total water on Earth in a frozen state in glaciers and ice caps.

Does this catastrophic potential place human lives, property or nature at risk?

Yes, via the potential for higher-energy storms and the rise in sea level from the melting of the ice caps.

We can then say this catastrophic potential is built into the Earth's present natural state (polar ice caps).

Does the human-designed system account for this feature of the environment?

No, humans continue to pump carbon from under the Earth's surface and move it to the atmosphere, placing water in the frozen state at risk of melting (uncontrolled substance transfer) and increasing the power of storms (uncontrolled energy transfer).

Is the Earth's climate producing noise – red flags that signal a disturbance in the balance of the system?

Yes, we are witnessing an increase in global average temperature, increases in the heat content of ocean water which is powering rapid increases in the energy of storms. We are also experiencing sea-level rise, which began around 1863. Prior to the Industrial Revolution, the sea level was actually decreasing, but since the mid-1860s, the sea levels have reversed and started to climb. Melting of the ice caps will have an additional effect on climate change. According to the Scripps Institution of Oceanography in San Diego, 'losing the remaining Arctic sea ice and its ability to reflect incoming solar energy back to space would be equivalent to adding one trillion tons of CO_2 to the atmosphere, on top of the 2.4 trillion tons emitted' since the beginning of the Industrial Age.

THE FOLLIES

At the start of the Industrial Revolution, there was very limited knowledge of the intricacies and workings of the Earth's climate systems. There was little observation of the state of the climate and climate science was primitive: Human Folly #4, a misunderstanding of the true nature of a system or object of natural origin.

The industrial machinery, transportation systems, and other fossil fuel burning devices which pump carbon from under the Earth's surface into the atmosphere constitute a Trojan Horse, Human Folly #3: at the outset of the Industrial Revolution, there was a complete lack of knowledge and a misunderstanding of this aspect of a human-designed object or system. We did not understand basic Earth science, that changing the Earth's gas chemistry could change its climate. In modern times, we possess a much greater understanding of the basic sciences, but we are ignoring the knock-on effects of changing the Earth's atmosphere.

Any assumptions that a divine power will save humanity — Human Folly #1: The audience or observer assumes the existence of a will or agency where there is none.

Human activity component to this unfolding disaster: human self-interest and a disregard of the wider effects of human activities. Humans participate in this unfolding disaster as cogs in a system: at present, these activities pose no immediate threats to the same humans who participate in the system, and therefore they will continue until they are presented with a catastrophic or economic event that causes those activities to cease or to be altered.

Bottom line: Human activities which put carbon into the atmosphere are leaving the future of the climate and environment to chance; the potential for cataclysmic change is very high.

— — — —

As the largest manmade moveable object in the world in its time, the *Titanic* had at least one thing in common with Uluru, that of sheer size. We humans all understand that with immense size comes a degree of impact, a certain sense of awe at first glimpse. As a business enterprise, the *Titanic* needed to be sold to the travelling public. We can predict there was a temptation to milk the aspect of immense size for all it was worth in the press. In the next chapter, we will discover how a dominant narrative was deliberately constructed in the public discourse and contributed to the legendary disaster. If we consider Uluru to be a Cultural Monument designed to pass along Cultural DNA to hundreds or thousands of future generations, is it possible that monument building can also be used to promote an agenda?

THE ARCHETYPAL DISASTER: THE SINKING OF RMS TITANIC

/ SHE SHOULD HAVE DIED HEREAFTER; THERE WOULD HAVE BEEN A TIME FOR SUCH A WORD.

William Shakespeare, *Macbeth, Act V Scene V*

The Titanic wasn't just a ship — it was the physical embodiment of an entire era's overconfidence. It was the ultimate expression of the belief that human technology could trump the forces of nature. The period between 1860 and 1910 was a time of continuous innovation; inventors were popping out world-changing gadgets. It was a time when seemingly intractable problems could be solved by man's ingenuity and sheer will. In 1861, Elisha Graves Otis patented his elevator safety brakes, creating a safer elevator and paving the way to more convenient and user friendly tall buildings. The 1870s saw George Westinghouse's air brakes, an ingenious system that greatly reduced rail accidents and transformed passenger rail into a safe, predictable form of transportation. In 1876 Bell invented the world's first telephone, and in 1880 Edison's "Electric Lamp" changed people's lives for the better, allowing the safety of electric illumination to supplant gas lamps. In the 1890s Marconi developed the wireless transmitter capable of sending messages over short distances, and by 1901, he had sent a wireless message across the Atlantic. Eventually his technology was installed in oceangoing vessels. Inventors like Marconi and Thomas Edison showed the world that innovation itself was a business, and those innovations were turning ideas into gold. It was a time when a bright idea could make you a millionaire. Innovations were also powering the race to the top: to build the biggest skyscraper or the biggest ships.

At 145 metres tall, the Great Pyramid of Giza was the tallest man made structure for nearly 4,000 years. In Europe during the Middle Ages up until the end of the 19th century, Christian churches dominated the skyline. But modern skyscrapers with a steel framework could be much taller than buildings supported by heavy masonry. These giants changed the landscape of city centres, creating a skyline for the first time in history, entering the scene in the 1880s with the Home Insurance Building in Chicago in 1884. At 180 feet (55 meters), it was the world's very first skyscraper. The Eiffel Tower was completed in 1889, and it reached 1,083 ft (330 m) at its tip. This kicked off a building spree – we were building in a way that fundamentally changed how our cities looked. For the first time in history, urban skylines became a thing.

The maritime industry had long been in a rivalry of its own. Those charming wooden ships of old were being replaced by steel giants. A typical wooden ship was between 60 and 85 metres long, and the largest wooden ship ever built (The schooner Wyoming, 450 ft or 140 m) suffered from flexure in heavy seas, causing planks to buckle, which allowed water to enter. This ship needed constant pumping: a hack made necessary by a deep design flaw, and it sank in heavy seas in 1924 with a loss of all hands. As a building material, steel allowed truly giant ships to be built, with Isambard Kingdom Brunel's ships, the SS *Great Britain*, launched in 1843 at 322 ft (98 m) and the SS *Great Eastern*, launched in 1858 at 692 ft (211 m) in length. The *Great Eastern* was like the great-granddaddy of all big ships, and was the first ship to employ a double hull, which was like having airbags before cars were invented. The *Great Eastern* was the world's largest for years to come. But the race to build the biggest, fastest ocean liner was not long in coming, and people started to believe that with enough ingenuity, these giant ships could defy Mother Nature herself- and could be unsinkable.

A STOVE BOAT AND DAVY JONES

There have been many urban legends, myths, and conspiracy theories about the sinking of the RMS *Titanic*. Some myths centred around ideas that misdeeds or omissions by the builders of the *Titanic* generated a divine influence, incurring the wrath of the Almighty and thereby bringing disaster upon themselves. There has been no shortage of conspiracy theories, from the technical to the finance-based. But the real root cause of the sinking of the *Titanic* was much more mundane: marketing. The construction and launch of the *Olympic* and *Titanic* sister ships were accompanied by widespread assumptions that were very carefully cultivated in the press. The White Star Line's owners and operators were willing partners in the construction and propagation of grand delusions.

The sister ships *Olympic* and *Titanic* were said to be the pinnacle of steamship technology, combining luxury, power, and safety for worry-free transatlantic travel and were, for all intents and purposes, unsinkable. This message was pushed into the press by both interested parties and those who were simply enthusiasts and were repeating the accepted mainstream narrative. The interested parties were able to capture the Board of Trade, the regulatory body responsible for the safety of passenger ships, and public opinion as well. The marketing messages included phrases such as 'monster ships' and 'largest vessel ever built.' While these phrases were not unique to the White Star Line fleet, of which the *Olympic* and *Titanic* were members, the language used to describe these ships led to the wide acceptance of the idea that the larger and more technically advanced the ship, the safer it is.

In order to understand how the *Olympic* and the *Titanic* actually were cast as 'practically unsinkable,' one should consider the historical context. Passenger and cargo shipping was worry-inducing at best. Shipwrecks were common, and the subject of much discussion in the press; hundreds or even thousands of lives were lost to shipping disasters in any given year up to the end of the nineteenth century. In February 1899, *The Scotsman* newspaper tallied the steam and sail vessels totally lost during the quarter ending 30 September 1898. There were 192 vessels included in the statistics, of which 34 were condemned, 14 missing, and 84 wrecked. A typical year would include over 900 vessels removed from service. Of those, over half were wrecked, 10% were lost through collision, and another 10% abandoned at sea. About 8% met an unknown fate, having been lost at sea with no additional information.

By 1899, the popular press had long featured stories of violent storms, terrified passengers, powerful currents, and the difficulties of navigation with limited information about the weather and the immediate surroundings. Those who might survive as castaways could face further difficulties such as piracy, disease, and starvation on the coast of some barely known outpost. There were also stories and novels about shipwrecks and collisions between icebergs and giant steamships. "How the Mail Steamer Went Down in Mid Atlantic by a Survivor" was a short story written by an author who was, ironically, a passenger on the *Titanic*'s maiden voyage, William Thomas Stead, and was published in the *Pall Mall Gazette* on 22 March 1896. Stead commented that 'this is exactly what might take place and will take place if liners are sent to sea short of boats.' Another book, *Futility*, published in 1898, tells of an unsinkable ship, the *Titan*, also the longest and fastest in the world, which, after a collision with another ship, leaves only a handful of survivors. While the *Titan* does not have enough lifeboats for everyone on board, the ship sinks so quickly that there is no time to lower the boats anyway. After many years of public discourse, the idea of unsinkable ships was gladly accepted and embraced by an enthusiastic but disaster-weary public.

With so much fear circulating within the public discourse, the marketing of passenger ships had nowhere to go but up – up in size, that is. In the days before modern navigation, the techniques and equipment we have now were unknown, and the travelling public was well-aware that climbing aboard was akin to taking your chances. If you were in the steamship business, it was in your interest to build your ships into the stuff of legend; as we know, myths, monuments, and legends are constructed of stories. Like Uluru, the *Titanic*-class ships had wide cultural acceptance within the culture that gave birth to the monument, but unlike Uluru, that acceptance was not unanimous. As a new monument, the gravitational force of the *Olympic*-Class Ships had to be constructed and carefully cultivated in the public discourse, since the monument had neither roots in antiquity nor any religious significance to lend authenticity. What it did have was a pedigree in ever-larger ocean-going steamships, beginning with the 106-foot (32-metre) *Aaron Manby*, launched in 1821, the first steamship with a hull completely constructed of iron. By the end of the nineteenth century, steamships had become truly enormous, with the White Star Line's 704-foot (215-metre) RMS *Oceanic*. Passenger steamships would get even larger very soon.

— — — —

Few disasters in history have been more extensively documented than the sinking of the *Titanic* in the early morning hours of 15 April 1912. The luxury ocean liner was on its maiden voyage from Southampton, England to New York City when it struck an iceberg in the icy waters of the North Atlantic. The vessel's leadership had multiple opportunities to avoid disaster, but once the cascade of events was initiated out in the open water, the design and speed of the ship presented a set of circumstances that could not be altered by human decision making, and the vessel's stewardship presented its own set of obstacles to the survival of the passengers on board. As with most new designs throughout history, *Titanic* and her sister ships had an experimental nature about them. Never before had such large ships been built to carry passengers. However, maritime disasters were mentioned in newspapers almost daily; the *Titanic* disaster was preceded by many others that could have been mitigated with updated safety regulations and basic precautions. But major lessons tend to recur time and time again with similar circumstances, yet we fail to systematically identify the basic components of disasters that recur throughout history and learn from them.

Like a sibling rivalry, there was competition between British, American, and German steamship companies. The grounds of competition were not only profit, but also the speed at which the lines could cross the Atlantic and the comfort and safety passengers could expect during their voyage. Safety was regularly tied to the size of the ship; the largest and strongest ships, it was suggested, were bound to be the safest. The race to build the largest ships was dominated by the British carriers in the 1860s. The *Great Eastern*, a British ship launched in 1859 and operated by the Eastern Steam Navigation Co. to serve the England to Australia route, was the largest ship afloat for nearly forty years. The White Star Line, founded in 1845 in Liverpool, displayed an appetite for ever larger ships, ostensibly to keep the public's attention, but the finances necessary for building them put the company in heavy debt which eventually became unsustainable, and it folded in 1867. The next year, Thomas Ismay, the grandson of a shipyard owner, bought the White Star Flag and trade name for £1,000. By the final decades of the nineteenth century, three British passenger lines dominated transatlantic travel: the Inman Line, Cunard Line, and White Star Line. Each had distinctive characteristics and corporate culture. The Inman Line was known for speed and the Cunard Line for safety. The Cunard Line was operated by Charles MacIver, a nephew of one of the original investors in the company. He was famous for his constant surprise safety inspections and was acknowledged for maintaining the reliability and safety discipline that had been demanded of the line's captains from the first by Samuel Cunard: 'Your ship is loaded, take her; speed is nothing, follow your own road, deliver her safe, bring her back – safety is all that is required.' That laudable emphasis upon safety, however, led to a marked unwillingness to try to match or beat the competition's increasing speeds across the Atlantic, with Cunard's reputation for safety tied to their slower passages. White Star was placed in direct competition with the Cunard Line, emphasising comfort and safety, and perhaps with a little speed on the side. Within the speed and safety market, the White Star and Inman Lines competed on ever faster, larger, and more luxurious ships.

THE AGE OF THE SUPERLINER

In 1897, the German-built SS *Kaiser Wilhelm der Grosse* became the largest ship in the world. At 655 feet, with a capacity for 1,506 passengers, she was the first steamer known as a 'superliner,' and the first to boast the four funnels we have come to associate with *Titanic*. The first of five '*Kaiser* Class' ships that set new standards for both speed and luxury, she and her sister ships helped the Germans wrest dominance in the North Atlantic from the British. Not to be outdone in the race for upscale customers, Thomas Ismay realised his company was beginning to lag behind the competition. He ordered a new, truly giant liner, the *Oceanic*, which was completed and launched just before his death in 1899. Before the *Oceanic* was launched, Ismay began plans for an even larger ship, the *Celtic*, which would exceed the length of even the legendary *Great Eastern*, although he would not live to see the completion of his dream. His eldest son, Bruce, was handed control of the company and the construction of ever-larger ships continued. White Star began the planning process of what would become known as their '*Olympic* Class' vessels, which would place size, comfort, and luxury over speed. The first of the three giants, *Olympic*, was ordered in 1907. Launched in June 1911, her size alone would set her apart from all other vessels in service – save her two sister ships, RMS *Titanic* (to launch the following year) and HMHS *Britannic* (not launched until 1915 and, after the fate of *Titanic*, used only as a hospital ship). At 883 feet long and with a passenger and crew capacity of over 3,300, these three ships would be the largest man-made movable objects in the history of the world.

SELLING SUPERLINERS

It is predictable that newsprint coverage of the passenger shipping services of that era would aim to cast the industry in a favourable light. Intimations of technical achievements and engineering genius, emphasising the massive size and strength of the maritime architecture as well as comfort and opulence constitute what I regard as Blue-Sky Monument Building. We are conditioned to associate propaganda with war, but propaganda is much, much more ubiquitous in our everyday lives, and has been for thousands of years. Propaganda manipulates our agency, our sense of conscious control over our beliefs, actions, and our ability to exert a degree of control over our environment. Propaganda can arise from the need to promote a business, product, or service, or to explain a war or a defence against an attack. Propaganda can define who is part of the outgroup and who is a member of one's own tribe. It can be directed internally toward a culture or outward towards the wider world. Propaganda is ultimately a narrative used to define an action, a belief, a people, a land, an enemy, a friend, a technology, or a Cultural Monument. Propaganda is entwined with the concept of monuments, those exceptional cultural entities that can be almost anything, even a huge, sun-baked rock in central Australia. Blue-Sky Monument Building is a type of propaganda designers and builders employ to focus attention on their monument-building project. Whether Blue-Sky or Dark-Sky, the monument will need definition and a sense of cause and worthiness. It will be obvious to most citizens that giant ships carrying thousands of passengers have the potential to end up in a huge, appalling disaster if things don't go well. The builders of these giant ships thus needed a story they could tell to the travelling public, some of whom certainly could imagine the terror of being lowered in a wooden lifeboat from the upper deck of a giant ship into churning waters a hundred feet below. The answer was emerging from shipbuilding technology: make the ship unsinkable.

BULKHEADS, LIFEBOATS, AND GIANT SHIPS: PROTOTYPING DESIGNS ON ACTUAL PASSENGER VESSELS

Used for centuries by Chinese wooden ship builders, compartments, also known as bulkheads, were increasingly found in ever-larger transoceanic ships, especially those which could be appropriated for State use in wartime. This concept was quite simple: the watertight compartment acted like a balloon or air bubble, slowing the sinking of a ship. If the outer compartment wall was involved in a hull breach, in theory the water could not go past the compartment to the interior of the ship.

The idea of compartments or bulkheads that made ships unsinkable was linked with the introduction of these large ships. It was a simple mathematical equation: giant ships plus bulkhead compartments equals unsinkability. White Star typically announced their newest passenger liners well prior to their launches – whilst under construction or even still in the planning stages. The language used to announce the first two *Olympic* Class liners, *Olympic* and *Titanic*, was similar to that used in the newspapers during the announcements of the launches of the *Celtic* in 1901 and the *Cedric* around 1902. Both the latter ships were claimed to be the largest ever built, and the first two of what would be known as the 'Big Four,' along with their sister ships *Baltic* and *Adriatic*. The *Illustrated London News* had a big splash about the *Celtic* on 6 April 1901, entitled: 'THE NEW WHITE STAR LINE, "CELTIC" ON THE STOCKS.' The article introduced the ship as 'currently under construction,' with a photo of the vessel in progress on the stocks in Belfast. The ship is referred to as 'the new mammoth White Star Liner ... This monster liner will, when completed, be the biggest vessel afloat.' This grandiloquence was continually used in the description of the new ocean liners with the intended purpose of convincing the public that the perils of the sea had now been reduced to an absolute minimum.

The subject of lifeboats and bulkheads was discussed in the public sphere continually throughout the nineteenth and early twentieth centuries in the context of British merchant shipping. Loss of life in those ships and the subject of what to do about it were recurring themes. The Board of Trade, tasked with shipping regulation, produced the Merchant Shipping Act of 1888, also known as the 'Life-saving Appliances Act,' and formed an Advisory Committee chaired by Mr. Thomas Ismay, founder of the new White Star Line. This committee submitted its report in April 1889 and proposed large additions of boats and equipment to the existing rules, evoking considerable pushback from shipowners. One engineer remarked that the Advisory Committee was 'driven by the conviction that life-saving appliances were best carried by a ship difficult to sink,' and that the obvious answer to making the vessels difficult to sink was the bulk-head partitioning. However, the idea of 'Unsinkable and Incombustible Ships' had been introduced to the public decades prior to the *Titanic* era:

UNSINKABLE SHIPS – THE BRITON

> This fine screw steamer, intended for the Cape mails, and built upon the invented and patented principle of Mr. Langley, of Deptford, for the construction of unsinkable and incombustible ships ... During the process of construction the vessel has been inspected by numerous shipbuilders ...

The Leeds Mercury, *15 October 1861*

The article went on to describe how the compartments worked, with each deck being watertight and able to contain the water in the event of a hull breach. This same article made its way around the newspapers of the United Kingdom from July through November 1861. This period marks the emergence and the popularisation of the idea that a steel ship could be made unsinkable by incorporating compartments within the hull.

BULKHEADS OR LIFEBOATS? THE BOARD OF TRADE'S COZY RELATIONSHIP WITH SHIPOWNERS

The Board of Trade adopted a laissez-faire policy towards the emerging bulkhead technology from this early period. However, after this introduction of the idea of watertight compartments, there were several pivotal shipwrecks that shaped the understanding of compartments within the public and regulatory sphere. The first of these shipwrecks occurred when the HMS *Vanguard* was struck by the HMS *Iron Duke* in 1875, since the *Vanguard*, a compartmentalised ship, stayed afloat for more than an hour, long enough for everyone aboard to be rescued. Newspaper editors called for a rethinking of the prior laissez-faire approach. Still, the Board of Trade and Parliament chose from the ranks of shipowners to steer the inquiry. In 1887, a committee was appointed by the House of Commons to inquire into 'the existing laws and regulations regarding boats, life-buoys, and other life-saving gear required to be carried by British merchant ships.' This committee, chaired by Lord Charles Beresford, contained many shipowners. Amongst their recommendations was 'that the proper placing of bulkheads, so as to enable a ship to keep afloat for some length of time after an accident has occurred, is most important for saving life at sea and a thing upon which the full efficiency of life-saving appliances largely depends.' The committee also recommended that the Board of Trade appoint an Advisory Committee of experts – representatives from technical societies and shipowners, ship builders, officers, and seamen – and this committee should provide a framework of rules for life-saving appliances and equipment for the various classes of ships. Thomas Ismay, founder of the White Star Line, became chairman of the Board of Trade's Lifesaving Appliances Committee.

Both committees seemed to be reflecting the general sentiment present in the newspapers – that compartmentalisation was more important than lifesaving appliances. The first report of the Bulkhead Committee arrived around 1891, but the report made only recommendations, stipulating no legal requirement to build ships to their specifications. Beresford's (Bulkhead) committee felt that all vessels, no matter the length, could be subdivided so as to be able to float in moderate weather with any two adjoining compartments in free communication with the ocean. Ismay's committee also reconsidered the additional safety equipment, and concluded that luxurious passenger ships should be able to open two compartments freely to the sea and not worry about sinking. Thus, the general opinion of both committees on how to move forward was to focus more on bulkhead design, placement, and construction, and less on life-saving appliances such as vests, rafts, and boats. In 1899, Ismay died, and his son, Bruce, already by this time a respected partner in his father's firm, became director of the family business.

THE CALL FOR COMPULSORY BULKHEADING

Possibly more than any other single disaster, the *Drummond Castle* disaster led to the call for compulsory bulkheading of ships. The *Drummond Castle*, built in 1881 by John Elder & Co. in Glasgow and essentially clad with a single iron hull, served the Cape Mail Service between South Africa and the British Isles. On her final fateful voyage, the ship approached the treacherous waters around the French island of Ushant in poor visibility, struck a reef, and sank in about four minutes. There were just three survivors, two crew and one passenger. The inquiry revealed that whilst the *Drummond Castle* incorporated bulkheads, they were inadequately constructed to prevent a disaster, and that larger ships with many passengers must stay afloat for longer periods to allow for evacuation. After the *Drummond Castle* went down, opinion had shifted from voluntary bulkheading prior to 1875 to compulsory bulkheading of future ships. This opinion was reflected in the press at the time:

COMPULSORY BULKHEADING

> The awful disaster to the *Drummond Castle* with all the pathetic and heartrending incidents connected with it, again raises the question as to whether passenger vessels, and especially ocean-going liners, should not be efficiently bulkheaded by legal enactment.

The Bristol Mercury, *23 June 1896*

The public was in need of real safeguards. Fear is a potent motivator to look for a solution, and marketers will use fear as often as they can. The travelling public was looking for a clear path to comfort and peace of mind while underway. When a ship is heavily partitioned, the utility of the closed-off areas is decreased, and thereby the space for passengers, cargo, and fuel will be reduced. Manually-operated bulkhead doors opened to obtain access also compromise the ship in the event of a hull breach. This presented a design dilemma: close off the space completely for safety, or include a bulkhead door for passage of crew members accessing the contents of the partition. The interests of business and economic viability of the ship require cargo and passenger space, directly opposing the interests of safety, which require completely watertight compartments. The solution: automatic bulkhead doors that could be closed from the bridge in the event of emergency.

RENDERING A SHIP UNSINKABLE: THE STONE–LLOYD AUTOMATIC BULKHEAD DOORS

Not long after the *Drummond Castle* disaster, a system of hydraulically-operated doorways between bulkheads, centrally controlled from the bridge, had been patented in partnership between the English firm J. Stone & Company and Norddeutscher–Lloyd of Bremen, Germany. Bulkheads are more than simple vertical walls that separate compartments of a ship; they offer structural support and stability as well as physical barriers to the ingress of water in the instance of a breach of the hull. The most forward part of the ship has the collision bulkhead, which is reinforced to withstand impact with a ship or another obstacle such as an iceberg or an oncoming wave. The collision bulkheads in a modern ship are watertight up to the bulkhead deck, and the other bulkheads are designed to limit the amount of water which can enter the ship. In a modern ship the collision bulkhead may not contain any oils, fuels, or cargo. Other bulkheads will contain doors to allow for the passage of personnel and cargo, although engineers maintain that the ideal bulkhead has no door. These passage doors were historically operated by hand, a laborious task that had to be accomplished very quickly in the event of a hull breach. If the doors were closed too slowly or there was an obstacle preventing their closure, the water would be free to enter more compartments, thus endangering the vessel.

The Stone–Lloyd innovation allowed the doors to be closed hydraulically from the bridge of the ship or automatically. Much of the 'practically unsinkable' verbiage used at the time was related to the presence of compartments, but with the additional perceived safety of these automated doorways. The kernel of intelligent design was that the mechanically-operated doors between the compartments would make the ship practically unsinkable by closing off any damaged compartment from the others automatically via the activation of a float, or all of them at once via a manual control at the captain's bridge. The newspaper articles, which read far more like client journalism, assure not only the insurance companies but also the travelling public that closing off bulkheads with automatic doors is not only the correct action in the case of a hull breach, but one guaranteeing safety in the face of a disastrous turn at sea. Further, the article asserts that the system has no real cost, as installation of the system makes ships practically unsinkable; therefore, installation costs are offset by far cheaper insurance costs. Bulkheads had a long history of use in merchant shipping in the decades prior to the *Titanic* disaster with mixed success. Unfortunately, the naval architects and engineering firms prototyped many of their ideas on actual passenger ships, something akin to the fatefully-named *Titan* submersible, an unproven design which was also tested with actual passengers aboard.

Limited information from foundering ships slowed the feedback and improvement process, since many of the witnesses either perished in the water or were unable to provide information that could enable meaningful design changes. According to the official description of the Stone–Lloyd system:

> The STONE–LLOYD hydraulically controlled marine safety bulkhead doors rendering vessels unsinkable. (J. Stone & Co. and Norddeutscher–Lloyd's combined patents.) As fitted in the largest and swiftest mail steamers in the world and highly approved. Patented throughout the world. J. Stone & Co., Deptford, London.

Many articles in various newspapers celebrated the benefits of the Stone–Lloyd system of water-tight bulkhead doors. An example is included here, along with an advertisement from a ticketing agent and an example from a newspaper serving the shipping industry. *Lloyd's List*, which provided weekly shipping news from 1734 to 2013, had a lengthy article on the subject dated 3 November 1903:

UNSINKABLE SHIPS. THE STONE–LLOYD BULKHEAD DOORS ... It is claimed for this system that its adoption will render vessels practically unsinkable, and that it is equally applicable to the largest ocean-going mail steamers and battleships, to passenger vessels of all sizes and descriptions, as well as to ocean tramps ... Besides – as a matter of fact – although the extra first cost of rendering a vessel unsinkable was somewhere about 1 per cent on its total value, the annual saving in insurance alone should more than cover the interest on this extra outlay, so that, when rightly understood, shipowners adopting the Stone–Lloyd system would not in the long run be a penny out of pocket.

Now we have a new mathematical equation being presented: giant, luxurious ship plus Stone–Lloyd automatic bulkhead doors equals unsinkability plus economic viability. Further, a financial aspect of the marketing was now apparent: the Stone–Lloyd automatic bulkhead doors actually did not cost the shipbuilder any extra interest payments; the savings on insurance premiums would make up for the extra cost of the automated bulkhead door system. The manufacturers of the Stone–Lloyd systems got an unexpected windfall in March 1907 with the shipwreck of the SS *Suevic*, a ship that had run aground. The salvage of the *Suevic* and subsequent publicity, more than any other event, convinced the public as well as those in the shipping industry that the compartmentalisation of large ships made them unsinkable. These automatic bulkhead doors – a compromise between truly sealed-off compartments, which maritime engineers favoured, and accessible spaces where freight could be stored for transport, favoured by shipowners, were set up and promoted by marketing to be the real deal, the pinnacle of nautical engineering: imparting unsinkability to ships. It became obvious, by design, to just about everyone in the shipping industry that incorporating the system of automatic bulkhead doors into any ship would bring peace of mind to the passengers. The Stone–Lloyd automatic bulkhead door system thus became the anchor of the chain of authenticity imparting this myth of 'unsinkability.'

THE SS SUEVIC: PROOF OF UNSINKABILITY

The SS *Suevic* was owned by White Star and was fitted with the automatic bulkhead doors which could be closed from the bridge in an emergency. When the *Suevic* struck the rocks off the coast of Cornwall in 1907, its captain shut the automatic bulkhead doors while the pumps kept the ship mostly free from water, allowing enough time for everyone on board to be taken to safety. The bow portion of the ship was stuck on the rocks and could not be refloated, so salvage crews cut the ship in two and brought the aft section back to harbour at Southampton for the refitting of a new bow. Photos of the severed aft section were shown in newspapers across the United Kingdom, providing visual proof that the compartmentalisation of ships did indeed make them unsinkable. There were jokes that the 12,500-ton SS *Suevic* was actually the world's largest ship since there were more than 500 miles between the bow and aft sections. The excerpt below is taken from an editorial in the *Gloucester Citizen*, 19 March 1907, and is a superb example of Blue-Sky Monument Building:

A SHIPBUILDING RECORD TRIUMPH FOR BELFAST SKILL

> In the science of shipbuilding, just as in that of surgery, there seems no limitation to its possibilities. Surgery has not yet progressed so far as to be able to add a new limb (except of the artificial character) to the human frame. Shipbuilding science on Saturday demonstrated that in its peculiar sphere, it can do much more, for it was not a mere limb but half a ship's torso, that was sent on its initial journey for active, and, one might almost say, living, union with its counterpart. The achievement is the most recent as well as the most remarkable achievement that the Queen's Island shipbuilders have secured. No similar event has taken place since the first authentic instance of shipbuilding- the launch of Noah's ark ... the vessel was successfully severed by dynamite and gelignite, and the after portion drawn clear

of the rocks on the 2nd April, the vessel's engines assisting the tugs by working full speed astern. This after portion, containing engines, boilers, etc. complete, was towed to Southampton, the engines assisting in the steering by means of the twin screws, and is now in the Trafalgar graving dock at that port. The old bow portion was hopelessly left on the rocks and is now entirely out of sight.

Editors across the United Kingdom opined that 'half a loaf is better than none,' and wrote about launching 'half a ship.' Acknowledging that it's not only the public that must believe in the safety of large ships, insurance underwriters must also be convinced, editors remarked that insurers had started to conclude that big ships equal big risks due to the difficulty in refloating a large, heavily loaded ship, but the salvage operation of the SS *Suevic* was an example which did not involve a total loss.

THE BLUE-SKY MONUMENT BUILDING OF THE TITANIC ERA

The public perception of the White Star Line's next group of luxury transatlantic ships, the *Olympic*-class ocean liners, was informed by syndicated newspaper editorials. Hyperbole builds monuments indeed. Short news articles touted the planned giants as early as April 1908:

NEW WHITE STAR LINER
A THOUSAND-FEET STEAMER

> It is announced that the White Star Line are about to construct two vessels, each 1,000 feet long. This will, of course, easily be a record dimension, for the Cunarders *Lusitania* and *Mauritania* are but 790 feet and 785 feet respectively ... The policy of the White Star Line in not seeking extreme speed will be adhered to and it is probable that twenty knots will be the limit which the new vessels will be expected to attain.

From **"NEW WHITE STAR LINER – A THOUSAND-FEET STEAMER,"**
The Londonderry Sentinel, April 18, 1908.

Later articles touted 'the two new White Star ocean monsters' and reassured readers that though the ships would not be fast, they would be very safe, 'to give comfortable passage to those who look on sea voyages with misgivings.' Terms like 'monster' and 'gigantic liners' were common, as were repeated assertions that 'everything that ingenuity can devise has been called into requisition in the construction of the steamers ... the strength of the structures will greatly exceed anything at present afloat.' Such was the case with some of the major Irish media in 1910:

WHITE STAR MONSTERS
Facts About the Wonderful Vessels Now Building in Belfast.

The White Star Steamers Olympic and Titanic, now in the course of construction at Belfast for the Company's mail and passenger service between Southampton, Cherbourg, Queenstown and New York, will each be approximately 45,000 tons and thus immeasurably the largest vessels in the world ...The Olympic and Titanic are to steam at not less than 21 knots, but they are not constructed primarily for speed, the owners' chief intention being to provide...

STEAMERS CONTAINING EVERY CONCEIVABLE COMFORT

And convenience for transatlantic passengers. It would be difficult to completely enumerate the many attractive features which may be found on these Ocean Palaces, but notable among them will be the dining saloons, lounges, drawing and smoking rooms, restaurants ...These particulars also apply to Titanic, and this steamer should take to the water a few months after the launch of her sister ship Olympic. It is anticipated that the latter will make her maiden voyage to New York about July, 1911: and as far as it is possible to do so, these two wonderful vessels are designed to be unsinkable."

From the *Irish News* and *Belfast Morning News,* 3 October 1910

This excerpt from *The Scotsman* on 20 October 1910 reflects similar sentiments:

STRENGTH OF DESIGN

Besides being the largest and heaviest vessel ever launched, the *Olympic* is undoubtedly also the strongest. Both in design and workmanship this has been kept in view, and the most approved structural arrangements suggested by the ripest experience have been adopted and every mechanical device requisitioned to secure this end. Never before in the history of shipbuilding have such elaborate means been employed, or such a combination of science, invention, and skill in the production of a ship; nothing has been left to chance; everything has been carefully thought out and skilfully planned, down to the most minute details, and from keel to truck the *Olympic* will be as perfect as human ingenuity and skill and most powerful appliances can make a vessel.

A double-page spread on *Olympic* from the *Weekly Telegraph*, appeared on 22 October 1910:

> The fact that White Star Line administration has ordered the new type of Welin davit [a small crane, on a ship or on the shore, to lower a boat into the water] to be installed throughout their new steamers, which are designed to mark an entirely new era in ocean travel, undoubtedly constitutes a magnificent certificate of the excellence and efficiency of the Welin systems. ... [A]s Mr. Welin has pointed out the launching of lifeboats is not generally required to be done under what may be termed "ordinary circumstances," nor can a shipowner be expected to sacrifice valuable deck space for machinery he trusts will never be required for actual use, or to employ hands in keeping it in a state of efficiency.

From the *Cork Examiner*, 21 January 1911:

THE WHITE STAR SS. OLYMPIC: A WONDERFUL VESSEL

> The new White Star SS *Olympic*, now fast approaching completion, has been described the "wonder ship," and the title is quite appropriate, as this noble specimen of all that is best in the world of inventive genius will, when she takes her place on the Atlantic route, be found to be unparalleled in her accommodation ... This beautiful ship, which is mighty in all that appertains to shipbuilding, is surely destined to be the realisation of all that the sea voyager had hoped for ... To make the passengers and all who travel by the Olympic as safe on

board as on the Earth's surface was the best aim of all concerned in the building of the two ships, and so thoroughly were the details worked out and with such skill that the greatest living authorities on ship construction declare that the Olympic will stand as a great monument to the mastery of science. Strength, speed, durability and absolute safety are all commanding features of this world wonder ... and before many months Titanic and Olympic will be meeting each other on the ocean journey.

From *The Sunday Citizen* (Asheville, NC), 25 June 1911:

SCIENCE AND SKILL OF CENTURY FIGURE IN NEW STEAMERS "OLYMPIC" AND "TITANIC" MASTERPIECES OF WORKMANSHIP SHOW SUPREMACY

In the White Star Line's new triple screw steamers "Olympic" and "Titanic" are epitomised all the science and skill of a century of steam navigation. The same spirit of progress which actuated the White Star Line in introducing Atlantic passenger trade the widely-known, mammoth steamers "Oceanic" the first steamer to surpass the length of the "Great Eastern" – "Celtic" "Cedric" "Baltic" and, latterly, the giant "Adriatic" – has produced these new surpassing ships.

... these latest and greatest conquerors of Neptune.

The Strongest Ships.
[Made of] solid pieces of steel ...

As already intimated, nothing has been left to chance in the construction of these superb ships, and besides being the largest and heaviest vessels ever built, they are undoubtedly the strongest. Their towering hills are moulded to battle against the seven seas ...

Safety Assured.
The double bottom, referred to above, extends the full length of each vessel, varying from 5 feet 3 inches to 6 feet 3 inches in depth and

lends added strength to the hull. The subdivision of the hulls of the "Olympic" and "Titanic" into fifteen compartments separated by watertight bulkheads of steel, further assures the safety of the vessels.

Mal de Mer Conquered
... among a hundred other fine qualities, the "Olympic" and "Titanic" will possess that most important of all, absolute steadiness at sea.

Great agent of peace.
The "Olympic" and "Titanic" represent the highest marine achievement of these progressive times, coupled with the best results of the White Star Line's long and successful experience in the fine art of passenger transportation. The addition of these, the greatest vessels in all the world, to the merchant fleet of the Atlantic, will bind men and nations closer with the immutable ties of friendship, enhance commercial relations, and, to no small degree, make the great sea less of a barrier between the Eastern and the Western Hemisphere.

A typical classified advert at the time read:

WHITE STAR LINE
ROYAL MAIL TRIPLE SCREW STEAMERS,
OLYMPIC and TITANIC, EACH 45,000 Tons.
LARGEST STEAMERS IN THE WORLD BUILDING.
From *The Scotsman*, 15 March 1911.

A PUSHED NARRATIVE BECOMES THE BANDWAGON

Ultimately, the purpose of these articles was to assure the readers that in the majority of opinion holders at the time, the universally accepted assumption was that life aboard these giant ships was worry-free. This type of client journalism constructed social proof for the consumption of the masses: it was clearly propaganda. Additionally, these news items asserted that since these ships were correctly compartmentalised, ordinary lifeboats, lifebelts, and other such implements were now unnecessary. Passengers who dreaded climbing into lifeboats no longer needed to travel in fear. This is Blue-Sky Monument Building par excellence. Those who needed to sell these ideas also needed to sell newspapers, and they needed advertising revenue to make their profits. Could these editors have pointed out flaws in thinking and assumptions without paying a dear price for expressing their contrarian views? Early on, the Board of Trade seemed to be taking a wait and see approach with the question of bulkheads. At first, partitioning was a design decision amongst shipbuilders, and the Board of Trade adopted a laissez-faire approach, allowing shipbuilders to decide whether to include them or not. As time went on, compartmentalised ships were prototyped and tested with real passengers on board. The results of this prototyping and testing were posted in newspapers throughout the English-speaking world for interpretation. Hesitant but undeterred, the public engaged in heaps of wishful thinking, and they were encouraged to do so by those who had something to sell. Were they wrong for jumping on the bandwagon?

In their endless effort to define and categorise, human beings have described themselves as *Homo sapiens*. The term was coined by Carl Linnaeus, a Swedish biologist and physician. Linnaeus is best known for the invention of Latin binomial nomenclature, the scientific system of attaching categorising labels to life forms consisting of a genus, or broader category of likeness, and species, which consists of individuals capable of interbreeding and producing fertile offspring. While these precise labels may not coincide with hard genetic barriers, they are very useful scientifically. *Homo sapiens* have also been referred to as *Homo significans*, or 'meaning makers.'

One need only look at a stadium full of cheering sports fans to understand that humans do not need any actual physical, monetary, or figurative 'skin in the game' to attach meaning to a win or a loss. And just as national pride need not be an absolute signifier of a good citizen, one does not need a ticket to support their favourite team.

In this sense, those who admired the *Olympic* and *Titanic* did not need to buy a ticket to actually admire such technically advanced, unsinkable monster ships. Further, they were free to write in to the editor of their favourite newspaper and provide their own opinion, just as the editors were free to heap additional meaning and opinion onto the subject in the same way a sports journalist writes news and opinion of the local sports teams. As we can see, if an editor felt that the *Olympic* and *Titanic* would be 'Great Agents of Peace ... representing the highest marine achievement of these progressive times ... sporting automatic-bulkhead door technology that "automatically meets every difficulty which could possibly arise,"' they were free to do so, as were their readers free to become fans and admirers. But there were likely very few fans or admirers who would welcome any predictions of disaster from a Cassandra.

CASSANDRA WEIGHS IN: THE JOHN BULL NEWSWEEKLY AND HORATIO BOTTOMLEY

The person who pointed out just how wrong the 'bandwagon' really was printed his critique regularly in a London newsmagazine called *John Bull*.

The original *John Bull* was launched in 1820 by Theodore Hook, a brilliant civil servant of a conservative bent – with the eponymous figure of John Bull meant to convey the character of the everyday Englishman. A newsmagazine of that name appeared every Sunday until 1892. It was revived fourteen years later by a Member of Parliament from the Liberal Party, Horatio Bottomley, though now running as a largely satirical and highly popular version, with an estimated weekly circulation nearing a million by 1912. There are other estimates that as early as 1907, the circulation of *John Bull* had reached half a million and that by the autumn of 1912, it had grown to 1.5 million. Bottomley had a longstanding adversarial relationship with the Board of Trade, which evolved into a considerable force charged with the implementation and interpretation of the Acts of Trade and Navigation, including standards for passenger-ship construction and their enforcement through inspections and licensing of ships carrying passengers and freight. Along with the advent of the new passenger superliners in the latter half of the nineteenth century, Bottomley had increasing concern that standards for design, including lifesaving appliances, were not keeping up with the times.

HOPELESSLY OBSOLETE REGULATIONS

A *John Bull* editorial, dated 17 June 1911, was written in response to a mishap involving the SS *Ivernia*, a 13,799-ton, 180-metre ocean-going ship of the Cunard Line with a 1,964-passenger capacity, servicing largely immigrants of limited means. The editorial was titled 'Those Boats Again.' *Ivernia*, one of the so-called 'unsinkable ones,' had grazed Daunt's Rock at Ireland's Queenstown Harbour, taking on water and quickly finding itself in the throes of a pronounced forward list. While the 775 passengers were safely taken off, the *John Bull* editorial pointed out that *Ivernia* had insufficient lifeboats for all the passengers and crew, who would be in serious trouble had an accident happened in the mid-Atlantic.

The *John Bull* editor recalled a request for a response from the Board of Trade to a prior article concerning the lifeboat accommodation on *Olympic*, which revealed that this 45,000-ton steamer carried only sixteen lifeboats. This small number was, of course, inadequate to take off a 'full complement of passengers and crew should a sudden emergency require it. Two answers were made to our statement ... that the ship had complied with the regulations of the Board of Trade and the other that she was practically unsinkable.' The editorial pointed out that the Board of Trade regulations were hopelessly obsolete and that there was an urgent need to reform the regulations. The second point is that the editor of *John Bull* maintains that 'no boat that has ever yet been put upon the waters is unsinkable.'

A *John Bull* editorial dated 26 August 1911 appeared in response to the stranding of the *Roebuck*, a steamer belonging to the Great Western Railway Company, servicing the Channel Islands. Launched on 6 March 1897, the ship survived a stranding off the coast of Jersey in July 1911, and reports from passengers stated that no lives were at risk and the evacuation of the ship calm and orderly. However, two letters written to the editor of *John Bull* were reprinted in the August issue. One letter, said to have come from a 'well-known citizen of Dover' who describes himself as a 'Continental Passenger,' discusses the claims from a witness to the incident, a Mr. Davies, whose account was published in the prior issue of *John Bull*. Mr. Davies said that the lifeboats were 'stuck so fast that crowbars had to be used' to work them free. In addition, he claimed that the davits were 'almost unworkable,' and the combined problems required nearly twenty minutes to launch the boats. The letter pointed out that had this accident occurred in deep water, the outcome could have been much worse.

White Star had a model made of its *Olympic* Class ships in 1910, complete with internal electric lighting, detail work, and an ornate display case. The model was shown at the Japanese–British Exhibition that opened in White City, London in May 1910. The *Belfast Telegraph* ran a story about the 'Remarkable Model of World's Greatest Ship.' It is no surprise that the newspaper from the city which built the *Olympic* would jump on the grandiloquence bandwagon. The *London Evening Standard* announced in November 1910 that a 21-foot model of the new *Olympic* would be on display at the Piccadilly Hotel in London. The model was also displayed in Bristol in 1911. A blurb in the *Bristol Times and Mirror* dated 25 November 1911 described the 'magnificent illuminated model, upwards of 30 feet long, of the White Star triple-screw steamer' displayed at the West India House. The article added that:

> The *Olympic* and her sister ship, *Titanic*, are the largest in the world at present, being 45,000 tons register, and embody the luxuries of a rich man's home ... The Bristol model of this marvellous steamer is an exact replica of the real thing, finely constructed, and exhibiting every outward detail of the *Olympic* when she is at sail.

The article also mentioned that the model was illuminated by 'over two hundred electric lights.'

Mr. Bottomley often criticised the White Star Line prior to the *Titanic* disaster, having observed the *Olympic/Titanic* model in 1910 in London, not far from the offices of *John Bull*:

The White Star's "Olympic"
A SERIOUS INSUFFICIENCY OF LIFEBOATS

> Our attention has been directed to the model of the OLYMPIC, the monster steamship of 45,000 tons now building for the White Star Line. This model may be seen under the Piccadilly Hotel. An examination will show that the new ship is to have only 16 boats. The Mauretania and Lusitania, very much smaller ships, have 40 boats and rafts. The Europa, which is about to be built for the

Hamburg-American Line, and will be 5,000 tons larger than the Olympic, will have no fewer than 80 boats. How, then, can 16 boats be sufficient for the Olympic? The explanation given by the company is that the ship is practically unsinkable, and that for life-saving purposes boats will not be required. That is a most unsatisfactory explanation. No vessel can be considered unsinkable if it meets with certain concussions. And presumably the Europa will be as unsinkable as the Olympic, but the builders of the German vessel do not suggest that life-saving apparatus will be unnecessary. What does the Board of Trade say?

John Bull, *19 November 1910.*

THE WHITE STAR'S "OLYMPIC"
OUR REJOINDER TO AN "OFFICIAL REPLY."

In our issue of November 19th, we directed attention to the model of the Olympic, the monster steamship now being built for the White Star Line. This model is to be seen under the Piccadilly Hotel, and anyone who cares to go there will find that the steamer has only 16 boats – 14 lifeboats and 2 dinghies. We expressed surprise at the small number of boats, and directed the attention of the Board of Trade, and here is the President's answer: "I understand that the Olympic will be provided with 14 lifeboats and two ordinary boats, of an aggregate capacity of 9,752 cubic feet, which is in excess of the requirements of the statutory rules. I have no information as to any vessel carrying four times this number of boats. The Lusitania and Mauretania each carry 16 boats."

We are quite unable to understand how Mr. Buxton could have given this answer. By his own admission, the Mauretania and Lusitania, vessels that carry considerably fewer passengers, have more boats. Mr. Buxton said that the requirements of the Board of Trade will be more than fully met by the 14 lifeboats and 2 dinghies with which the Olympic is to be provided. How can that be? The full complement of the Olympic, passengers and crew, will be 3,400. That works out at 240 passengers in each boat. Does Mr. Buxton seriously say that any lifeboat afloat can carry 240 persons? He must know that apart from men-of-war no such boat carries more than 60 or 70. And what is the boat accommodation thought sufficient by other companies?"

[The editor lays out other large steamer specs, some roughly one-half the size of the *Olympic* and *Titanic* but with nearly double the number of lifeboats]

> We invite Mr Buxton to explain how in the face of these facts and figures the Board of Trade is satisfied with the 14 lifeboats and 2 dinghies of the Olympic. We know what the explanation of the company is, namely, that the ship will be practically unsinkable. This is, as we said a fortnight ago, a very unsatisfactory explanation. The builders of the ship have cut away every possible inch to give more room for promenading on the boat deck. But that again is a very insufficient reason for sending the ship to sea with insufficient boats. We tell Mr. Buxton, without fear of contradiction from any competent authority, that if he allows the Olympic to go to sea with only her present number of boats he will have a weighty responsibility to reckon with, should disaster befall the ship, and the responsibility will not be met by saying that the Olympic has a certain number of collapsible boats and rafts not shown on the mods. Where is the sailor who will say that these are equivalent to lifeboats?

John Bull, *3 December 1910.*

A few weeks later, Bottomley claimed that the antiquated Board of Trade regulations hazard thousands of lives, and printed a letter from a naval architect agreeing that it is problematic that the same lifeboat rules applied to both a 10,000-tonne ship and one of 55,000 tonnes, with the conclusion that 'it is therefore perfectly plain that the regulations in connection with boats have not kept pace with the rapidly-increasing tonnages of the Merchant Service' (*John Bull*, 24 December 1910).

PART II: HISTORY'S MOST FAMOUS 'UNSINKABLE VESSEL' VS. ICEBERG

Ironically, the directors of the White Star Line had safety in mind when they assigned Captain Edward John Smith to take first command of the *Olympic* Class liners. Smith joined the White Star Line in 1880 as Fourth Mate, a rank just below the vessel's captain. The Board of Trade granted certificates documenting a sailor's fitness for service in a foreign-going ship. Rising through the ranks of competency, a qualified sailor could sit for the Ordinary Master's examination at the age of twenty-one years and must have spent at least six years at sea serving time in the inferior grades. For those wishing to prove superior qualifications necessary for making long voyages, there was the Extra Master's Examination. Having failed his first attempt, Captain Smith passed at the next attempt in February 1888 and earned his Extra Master's Certificate, the highest rank offered by the Board of Trade. Smith's first White Star command was received in 1887 for the steamer *Republic*, and by the time of the *Titanic* disaster, Smith was one of the most experienced and decorated sea captains in the world and had piloted the world's largest ships.

THE TIMELINE OF THE SINKING OF THE TITANIC

Having established the troubling context of the most famous 'unsinkable' vessel in history, we can move on to the disaster itself. The *Titanic* sinking has been the subject of endless rumour and speculation, but there are a number of well-accepted facts about the course of events, enumerated here for illustration and convenience.

14 APRIL 1912

9:00 AM
The RMS *Caronia*, the largest Cunard Line steamer until the *Mauretania* and *Lusitania*, radios *Titanic*, warning of icebergs and growlers (small icebergs that rise only about 1m (3ft) from the water) about a day's sailing away. *Caronia*, a 650-foot ship of roughly 20,000 tons, was roughly 400 miles ahead of *Titanic*. She was relaying information from a steamer ahead of her, the Holland–American Line's *Noordam*, concerning ice at 42° N and 49° W, almost exactly the points at which *Titanic* would founder seventeen hours later.

10:15 AM
Wireless Operator Phillips passes on the telegrams of ice fields and icebergs to Capt. Edward J. Smith. The ship would receive several reports of dangerous ice throughout the day.

10:30 AM
Captain Smith cancels the first scheduled lifeboat drill at 11 AM and leaves the Bridge to conduct a Sunday service for first-class passengers. The crew have not had a chance to practise coordinated launching of the boats.

11:40 AM
The Holland–American Line's *Noordam* radios an ice report to *Caronia*, which conveys the message to *Titanic* at 12:30 PM.

12:00 PM
As always, the ship's officers gathered on the wing of the navigating bridge with sextants to calculate their daily position and progress from the previous noon: 'Since noon Saturday, 546 miles.' That meant the ship had travelled at an average speed of 22.5 knots in the past twenty-four hours. The fast rate means docking earlier than scheduled is possible. Word spreads among the passengers, and they begin sending messages home. In the hours to come, several passengers would notice small chunks of ice adrift on the starboard side.

1:42 PM
Wireless Operator Phillips receives the second ice warning of the day, from the steamship *Baltic*: 'Greek steamer *Athenia* reports passing icebergs and large quantities of field ice today in latitude 41° 51' N, longitude 49° 52' W. [the same coordinates given earlier by *Caronia*] Wish you and *Titanic* all success". – the final part of the message likely for Captain Smith, having presided over *Baltic*'s launch eleven years earlier.

1:45 PM
Titanic transmits signals to land stations that it had picked up an 11:20 AM report of ice that the Hamburg–America Line's *Amerika* had transmitted to the Hydrographic Office in Washington, DC. Its coordinates were 12 miles from where *Titanic* would founder.

2:00 PM
White Star Chairman J. Bruce Ismay is informed of the *Baltic*'s ice report by Captain Smith. Ismay puts the message in his pocket.

5:50 PM
The course of *Titanic* is changed after a delay of twenty minutes to allow the ship to travel further south, possibly to avoid ice, and the top speed is maintained. In other years, this would have put the ship into the warmer

Gulf Stream waters free of ice, but in 1912, the Gulf Stream was much further south. The change of course put the ship directly into the colder Labrador Stream and the iceberg's path. Between 5:30 PM and 7:30 PM the temperature dropped ten degrees to 33°F (0.5°C).

6:00 PM
Captain Smith goes to dine with the first-class passengers. The shift on the Bridge is changed and Chief Officer Wilde replaces Second Officer Lightoller.

6:50 PM
The sun goes down.

7:00 PM
The radio room receives three warnings from the SS *Californian* of large icebergs in the path of *Titanic*. They advise a change of course to the south. The messages are delivered to the Bridge. The ship however maintains its course and speed and the Bridge warns the two lookouts in the crow's nest, George Symons and Archie Jewell, to keep watch for ice. As the lookouts do not have binoculars, they have to rely on their own eyesight, despite repeated requests for binoculars throughout the voyage.

7:30 PM
The *Californian* sends another report about three large icebergs two hours ahead in the path of the *Titanic*. Junior wireless officer Harold Bride takes the message to the Bridge, but Captain Smith never sees it as he is at dinner. The cold conditions increase dramatically. The iceberg is only 80 kms (50 miles) ahead.

9:00 PM
Captain Smith leaves dinner and returns to the Bridge.
The temperature is continuing to drop ...

9:20 PM
Captain Smith returns to the Bridge to check conditions before retiring. He tells Second Officer Lightoller to wake him if conditions deteriorate. He does not reduce the speed of the ship or alter its course.

9:40 PM
SS *Mesaba*, an English steamer that had spent several hours negotiating heavy ice 55 miles ahead of *Titanic*, reports an ice field of 'heavy pack ice and [a] great number [of] large icebergs.'

The warning never reaches the Bridge as Senior Wireless Operator Jack Phillips does not respond to repeated messages from *Mesaba*, asking if the warning had been received. It is later established that he was too busy with passenger telegrams and the message was not prefixed MSG (Master Service Gram), signifying that it was a message that needed to be relayed to the Bridge.

The Wireless operators work for the Marconi Company, not the ship, and passengers' messages have priority over all other radio communication unless prefixed as urgent or important. The operators have only two hours to deal with passenger messages. Both operators were weary, having been up late the previous night fixing the machinery. Junior officer Bride had retired to bed shortly before the *Mesaba* transmissions, intending to take charge from Phillips at midnight.

10:00 PM
Second Officer Lightoller's shift on the Bridge ends, and he is replaced with First Officer William Murdoch. Fredrick Fleet and Reginald Lee come on duty when the watch in the crow's nest changes. They still do not have binoculars.

Murdoch orders all lights forward of the Bridge extinguished for better visibility. The night is clear and moonless and the ocean still, making icebergs harder to see due to the lack of reflected moonlight and no waves breaking on the side of the berg.

10:30 PM
The outside temperature has dropped to 30°F (-1.1°C).

10:55 PM
Senior Wireless Operator Jack Phillips receives the final ice warning of the night from the *Californian*, about 20 miles away: 'Say, old man, we are stopped and surrounded by ice.' 'Shut up! Shut up!' Phillips retorts. 'I am busy I am working Cape Race' – i.e., he was busy catching up on a backlog of passenger's personal messages being sent to Cape Race, Newfoundland, rushing because there was only a two-hour window available for the messages to arrive.

11:00 PM
The majority of the passengers are already in their cabins for the night.

11:30 PM
The *Californian* turns off its radio (standard practice). There is no ship with communication close enough to *Titanic* to reach it in time. The iceberg is 6.5 km (4 miles) directly ahead.

11:39 PM
Lookout crewman Fredrick Fleet spots the iceberg and rings the bell three times to warn the ship. In the Bridge, Officer Murdoch reverses the engines and turns the ship 'hard-a-starboard' (right). The watertight compartments are closed.

11:40 PM
Titanic avoids a head-on collision as the iceberg scrapes along the starboard bow.

11:45 PM
The captain has arrived on the bridge, and reports of damage begin to arrive. The mailroom is filling with water, and at least five of the ship's starboard compartments have been breached. Ship designer Thomas Andrews returns from surveying the damage and advises the Captain that *Titanic* will sink in about two hours.

In the run-up to the moment of impact the ship is thought to have stayed on the same course that was begun in the early evening in the attempt to avoid the area of the iceberg. That course was slightly to the south of the originally plotted course. Pivotally, the crucial iceberg information relayed from the *Californian* was unheeded by *Titanic* leadership. This information was so crucial that ignoring it was a fatal mistake. The design and power of *Titanic* was not paralleled by the technology to survey the environment – simple binoculars – and even those were not available due to a clerical error. Essentially, *Titanic* leadership was (quite literally) blind to its environment and therefore could not account for its death-dealing icebergs.

15 APRIL 1912

12:05 AM
Orders are given to prepare the lifeboats for, famously, 'women and children first,' with crew members to handle the boats. There are only twenty lifeboats – not enough for the 2,208 people on board.

12:15 AM
At Capt. Smith's orders, distress signals are sent out using both the new SOS code and the older CQD (CQ = General Call, plus D, for Distress). The coordinates, however, are some 13.5 nautical miles off. The discrepancy between the actual position and the reported position is attributed to errors in navigation calculations, although there is some controversy as to exactly which error(s).

The three ships that first respond are all too far away to reach *Titanic*, though an English ship, the SS *Mount Temple*, en route from Antwerp to Saint John, New Brunswick and a good four hours away, reverses course to come to *Titanic*'s aid. Unfortunately, it becomes trapped in the ice fields and reaches the area some two hours after the *Carpathia* (see below) arrives. The *Californian*, thought to be roughly 20 miles away, does not hear the calls.

Titanic begins to list to starboard as the bow sections overflow, and the bow starts to sink. The stewards begin to tell passengers to put on their lifebelts.

12:20 AM
Titanic's distress signal reaches the Cunard Line's RMS *Carpathia*, en route from New York to Trieste: 'Come at once. We have struck a berg. It is a CQD, old man.' Again, incorrect coordinates of the disaster are provided, though revised shortly hereafter to the correct 41°46' N 50°14' W. After some initial understandable disbelief, the *Carpathia* turns to head full-steam to aid *Titanic*. Though normally capable of top speeds of 16–17mph, and with *Titanic* 58 nautical miles (107 km) away, the captain orders another full watch of stokers to maximise speed.

Titanic's eight musicians assemble to play together for the first and only time during the voyage in the first-class lounge to help calm passengers waiting for lifeboats. As the ship begins to list increasingly forward, four move out onto the boat deck and continue playing as the chaos of the sinking surrounds them. According to some survivors, the band continued to play until it was no longer possible. Their last song was either *Autumn* or *Nearer My God to Thee*. None of the band survived, but the body of the band's director, William Hartley, was found two weeks later, with his violin case strapped to his chest.

At the urging of officers Lightoller and Murdoch, Capt. Smith orders lifeboats to be filled, 'women and children first.'

12:45 AM
The first lifeboat lowered, No. 7 Starboard, has an estimated 28 passengers on board but a capacity of 65. The next boat is lowered ten minutes later, again with only 28 aboard. As we will see below, of the next four boats lowered, the first had 41 aboard, the next had 32, then 39, and the fourth, with a capacity of only 40, had but 12 aboard. The reasons given for the empty seats are, variously, that Lightoller and Murdoch each had their own understanding of what 'women and children first' meant, that the crew was both poorly trained and overly concerned that the weight of a full boat would be too much strain on the davits used to lower the boats,

and that many passengers were initially dubious the ship would sink: the millionaire John Jacob Astor declared, 'we are safer here than in that little boat.' A ship is sighted on the horizon fewer than 10 nautical miles away, but it cannot be contacted with radio or Morse lamp communications. The crew begin firing distress rockets, but the ship disappears. It is later found to be an illegal seal-hunting ship.

The crew on the *Californian* see the distress rockets but cannot locate the source. It is only 20 nautical miles away, but does not know *Titanic* is in trouble.

12:55 AM
The second lifeboat (far from its passenger capacity, as mentioned above) launched is No. 5, and as it is lowered, a woman is injured when two men jump into the boat.

Next is No. 6, commanded by Quartermaster Robert Hichens, the man at the wheel when the ship struck the iceberg. Aboard are Lookout Crewman Fleet and the American socialite and philanthropist Molly Brown. Hichens' refusal, some two hours later, to look for survivors after *Titanic*'s sinking angered the other passengers, and Mrs. Brown threatened to throw him into the ocean.

1:00 AM
The fourth lifeboat, No. 3, is launched with only 39 people aboard, including 12 *Titanic* crew.

1:05 AM
The emergency cutter, No. 1, with a capacity of 40, is lowered, holding only 12 people. Sir Cosmo Edmund Duff-Gordon, his wife, her secretary, two men also in First Class, plus seven crew are aboard. Duff-Gordon is later accused of offering the ship's crew £5 each to prevent anyone else from getting on the boat. He later variously denied the offer, or claimed the money was to replace the crew's lost clothing and gear. Aboard the *Carpathia* the next day, however, he wrote out a £5 cheque for each of the seven crew members.

1:10 AM
On the port side, No. 8 is lowered with only 28 people, including the Countess of Rothes, Lucy Noël Martha Leslie, who will take the tiller during the night. Macy's department store owner Isidor Straus refuses to get in the boat while the 'women and children first' order is still in force. His wife, Ida, also refuses, and says, 'where you go, I go.' Both are lost.

1:20 AM
Lifeboat No. 10 is lowered with baby Millvina Dean aboard. She will be the last disaster survivor, living until 2009 when she passed away aged 97. No. 9 at the starboard stern is launched almost full with 56 people. Millionaire Benjamin Guggenheim's alleged mistress is aboard, but he stays on *Titanic*, dressed in formal attire along with his valet. It is reported that he said, 'we have dressed up in our best and are prepared to go down like gentlemen.' Guggenheim's remains are never recovered.

1:25 AM
The *Olympic* radios *Titanic*, asking: 'Are you steering southerly to meet us?' They receive the reply, 'we are putting the women off in the boats.' The *Carpathia* informs the *Olympic* of the disaster, but both ships are still hours away. The half-full No. 12 lifeboat is launched, and this boat will later rescue so many people it will become overloaded with 70 people. Panic starts to take hold of the passengers as they realise the inevitable.

1:30 AM
As boat No. 14 is being readied, several male passengers try to board, forcing Fifth Officer Harold Lowe to fire his pistol three times. He is in command of the boat and will later move people into other lifeboats and collapsible boats, rescuing four survivors from the water and those in a flooded collapsible boat (the collapsible boats are foldable and made of canvas with a capacity of 47 people). Wireless Operator Phillips desperately continues to send out distress calls: 'Women and children in boats. Cannot last much longer.' Lifeboat No. 13 reaches the water, and as No. 15 is lowered, 13 drifts below 15; the crew manage to cut the launch ropes and get the boat out of the way.

1:35 AM
No. 16 lifeboat is lowered.

1:40 AM
Collapsible C is launched with White Star chairman J. Bruce Ismay aboard. He will later be vilified as a coward for not going down with the ship and taking up space on a lifeboat. He claimed no women or children were around when the boat was launched, but other survivors contradict his story.

1:45 AM
Emergency cutter No. 2 is launched, under the command of Fourth Officer Boxhall. Now two hours into the disaster, it is less than half full, with just 18 aboard. It will be the first to reach safety aboard the *Carpathia*.

50 people are aboard No. 11 as it is launched.

Heavily pregnant Madeleine Astor is helped onto lifeboat No. 4 by her husband, John Jacob Astor. Second Officer Lightoller, who is still following the 'women and children first' order, refuses his request to join her. Astor's body is later recovered.

2:00 AM
The ship's bow, full of water, has completely sunk, and her stern is lifted high enough from the water that the propellers are visible. Only collapsible boats A, B, and D are left on *Titanic*. More than 20 are aboard D as it is lowered from the roof of the Officers' Quarters. A is washed from the deck when the ship's bow goes under, but 20 people manage to get onto the partially flooded boat. When Fifth Officer Lowe in Lifeboat 14 finds them, only 12 are still alive to be rescued. The bodies are left in the boat, which will be found three months later. Collapsible B falls as the crew lowers it, and it is swept off *Titanic* upside down. 30 men, including Wireless Operator Bride and Second Officer Lightoller, survive, clinging to the upturned boat. Lowe will rescue them and put them on boats 4 and 12. Captain Smith tells the crew members, 'now it is every man for himself,' and is last seen on the Bridge. His body is never found.

2:17 AM
Wireless Operator Phillips sends his last distress signal and abandons the ship. He makes it to the upturned boat, but is overcome by exposure. His remains are never located.

Funnels No. 1 and 2 have broken off as the bow begins sinking quickly into the ocean.

2:18 AM
The power finally fails, and the ship is plunged into darkness as the lights go out.

The sinking bow lifts the stern higher out of the water until the strain breaks *Titanic* in half between the third and fourth funnels. Hundreds of people are now in the freezing water.

The stern slaps back down onto the ocean surface, killing survivors in the water and on the ship. It settles momentarily before it, too, begins to take on water. The stern lifts vertically where it briefly remains, then plunges into the ocean. Scientists later speculate that it took six minutes for the bow travelling at 48 km (30 miles) per hour to reach the ocean floor.

2:20 AM
Titanic has sunk. The ship will not be seen again until 1985, when a submersible takes photos of the wreck on the ocean floor. A combination of air trapped in the back section of the ship and the intense water pressure from outside the hull cause it to implode as it sinks, and the shape makes it spiral 180 degrees, so the stern rests on the ocean floor first. It is found 610m (2,000 ft.) away from the bow.

There is room in the lifeboats, but crewmen are reluctant to rescue those in the water for fear of the boats being swamped. Some people are pulled to safety, and boats return for survivors, but it is too late for most. The majority die quickly from exposure in the freezing water. Numerous ships continue to try to contact *Titanic*, and the wireless operator of the *Birma* thinks he hears *Titanic* send the message: 'Steaming full speed to you; shall arrive to you 6 in morning. Hope you are safe.'

3:30 AM
Rockets are seen as the *Carpathia* arrives in the vicinity.

4:10 AM
The first boat, the emergency cutter No. 2, gets to the *Carpathia*. The rescue of the remaining survivors takes several hours. When Ismay reaches the ship, he telegraphs the White Star Line offices: 'Deeply regret to advise you *Titanic* sank this morning fifteenth after collision iceberg, resulting serious loss life; further particulars later.'

8:30 AM
After turning the radios on and learning of the disaster at 5:30 AM, *Californian* arrives and searches for survivors for hours without luck.

8:50 AM
705 survivors of *Titanic* are aboard the *Carpathia* as she begins the sad voyage to New York City. The ship is greeted by massive crowds when she docks on 18 April.

HOW THE MIGHTY FELL

The *Titanic* disaster occurred due to a symphony of errors, biases, and environmental conditions. While a repeat of these exact conditions was unlikely to occur in this exact sequence, key elements of the loss of *Titanic* can be found in disasters prior and since.

The *Olympic* Class liners were truly technological masterpieces for their time. They were fully capable of traversing the Atlantic safely, as demonstrated by the *Olympic*, which despite also suffering collisions that led to flooding of watertight compartments, including one 1911 incident with Captain Smith at the helm, never went down. The *Olympic* was retrofitted with a double hull and augmented with lifeboat accommodation after the *Titanic* disaster and went on to have a career that included 514 Atlantic crossings, carrying more than 400,000 passengers over its 24-year commercial lifespan. The durability and reliability of the *Olympic* is a testament to the design of the *Olympic* Class liners – albeit with the addition of the double hull. They were equipped with the best technology of the day, including wireless radio, but the famed and much-lauded Stone–Lloyd automatic bulkhead doors were unable to account for catastrophic flooding, as was predicted in letters to newspaper editors written prior to the disaster.

Further, the ballast pumps were not intended for catastrophic flooding; they were intended mainly to pump water from one compartment to another to correct listing and restore trim. The bilge pumps were able to pump about 2 tons of water per minute. The pumps in *Titanic* were located in the centre of the ship and were incapable of drawing water from the more forward parts of the ship. The engineers aboard the ship were attempting to run temporary pipes from the stationary pumps up to the forward compartments, in an attempt to pump out the water from those compartments and keep the ship afloat long enough for an orderly evacuation, but were simply unable to do so. First, the stationary pumps were too small for the amount of incoming water, and second, they were located in the wrong compartments with respect to the location of the iceberg damage. Edward Wilding, Harland and Wolff's senior naval architect, calculated that approximately 16,000 tons of water would be required to bring *Titanic*'s bow down 40 feet, the point at which the bow was at approximately 2 AM. If all of the bilge pumps and transfer pumps were plumbed to pump water out of the forward compartments, they could have removed only about 1,560 tons of water per hour, versus 8,000 tons of seawater influx. The pumps would not have been able to delay *Titanic*'s sinking long enough for the arrival of the *Carpathia*, even if they were connected correctly and operational. The quality of the steel, which was normal and typical for shipbuilding of its time, was furthermore brittle at the temperatures that were encountered when the ship struck the iceberg. This was unknown until pieces of the hull were brought up for examination after the discovery of the wreckage.

Finally, the complement of lifeboats, as discussed earlier, was totally inadequate for the number of passengers and crew on board *Titanic* that fateful night. But the question remains, what is the root cause of the sinking of *Titanic*? The long career of the virtually identical *Olympic* suggests human factors were largely responsible. To understand the disaster more completely, one must first distinguish between the ship's design and construction, and its operation and the environment in which it sailed. *Titanic*'s design, as discussed above, was state-of-the-art for its time, and in other instances proved perfectly seaworthy. Yet the operation and environment were affected by human factors, which take more time to separate out and examine.

Newspaper coverage after the disaster reflected the realisation that the assumptions formed over many years and widely held were wrong. Assumptions included the ideas that the ships built with compartments were 'practically unsinkable,' and the safety factor imparted by the automatic bulkhead door system was also called into doubt.

The human factor of this disaster opens with the broadly-held assumptions, starting with the dreaded lifesaving appliances. Life vests were bulky, heavy, and uncomfortable to wear, and just the sight of them was an admission of ship vulnerability. Lifeboats were likewise unpopular with passengers and crew, often requiring a leap of faith to step off the giant ship and onto the small wooden boat in the middle of the ocean. Those assumptions, carried by popular opinion, went up to the regulatory level. The Board of Trade's primary perception of the nature of *Titanic*, by design, was that 'life-saving appliances were best carried by a ship difficult to sink.' It was very useful fiction, and the Board of Trade was in a kind of collusion with this perception. The stories needed to be compatible with the experiences of actual travellers, but the underlying narrative was clear: yes, there are life vests, and yes, there are lifeboats, but we probably won't be needing them, except to ferry passengers to the rescue ship. Those same assumptions were probably held by the captain, crew, and many of the passengers via social proof as described by the psychologist Robert Cialdini. It was simple mathematics: the editorials of grandiloquence describing so many unsinkable 'gigantic liners', together with the obvious physical proof of 'launching half a ship," as photos of the SS *Suevic* showed the world, combined to make unsinkability a matter of course. The active 'Blue-Sky Monument' building around those gargantuan liners took effect; the mere fact that so many members of society already held the same beliefs encouraged others to adopt the cultural 'box set.' Society's widely-held opinions of the ship were reflected in the mentality of those aboard the ship, and those opinions had been carefully groomed by years of not only client journalism, but years of active Blue-Sky Monument Building in the press. After the accident it became apparent that there was a degree of regulatory capture, but not in the traditional sense. The regulatory apparatus, the state charter designed and purposed to intervene in maritime commerce, was captured by the Blue-Sky Monument, those giant ships whose 'towering hills are moulded to battle against the seven seas.'

On 13 March 1913, addressing the hubris of the 'unsinkable ship' approach, *The Daily Citizen* (Manchester, UK) wrote:

> The *Titanic* disaster destroyed the legend of the "practically unsinkable" ship. For years the Advisory Committee of the Board of Trade on Shipping – a committee to all intents dominated by shipowners – persuaded the official mind that the "practically unsinkable" problem had been solved. In spite of the mercantile marine

service, the regulations on life-saving appliances were neglected. But the *Titanic* calamity proved that the shipowning interest had led the Board of Trade into a fool's paradise. The shipowners and naval architects have nevertheless not given up on their search for safety. At vast expense the *Olympic*, the sister ship of the *Titanic*, has been fitted at Belfast with an inner steel shell, extending to nearly two-thirds of her length from the bows aft. At the same time the scheme of watertight bulkheads has been replanned. After this [in order to sink] the *Olympic* would have to be so damaged by collision as to be "holed" through both skins."

THE REGULATORY ENVIRONMENT OF THE TITANIC DISASTER REFLECTED IN THE PRESS

I include here the proceedings and statements by the actual members of the House of Commons as they questioned Mr. Buxton. These individuals lived and worked in that time, and they bear witness to the events that surrounded the *Titanic* disaster, and I feel there is no better way to convey the essence of that time than the opinions and statements of those who were there. I have selected the most revealing statements, and omitted many others. The following news piece provides an excellent overview of the inquiry:

> At the post-disaster inquiry in the House of Commons which occurred on 18 April, 1912, Mr. Sydney Buxton, President of the Board of Trade, addressed the members present in a statement: "I think it will be convenient if I deal in a single statement with all the questions relating to the boat accommodation of the *Titanic* and the Board of Trade regulations relating to boat and other life-saving appliances. The Board of Trade are empowered by section 427 of the Merchant Shipping Act of 1894, to make life-saving appliances on British ships, and section 428 requires their owner and master to give effect to the rules. The rules now in force were originally drawn up in 1890, and were revised in 1894 and subsequently, and prescribe a scale indicating a minimum number of boats to be provided in accordance with the gross tonnage of the ship. The highest provision made in this scale is for vessels of 10,000 tons and upwards. In view of the increased size of modern passenger steamers, the Board of Trade early last year referred to the Advisory Committee on Merchant Shipping the question of the revision of the rules, and in particular of the provision to be made in the case of steamers of very large size.

Mr. Buxton was questioned by other members present.

Mr. William O'Brien – Will not the Board of Trade do something to discourage the racing for time records across the Atlantic, which was the cause of this disaster?

Mr. Buxton – I am afraid we have no power over that.

Mr. Fred Hall – Will careful consideration be given to the question of the penalties under which steamship companies labour at the present time in consequence of any lateness of arrival? And may I ask whether, in consequence of the explosion of the theory that a ship can be unsinkable although she may have 16 bulkheads as in the case of the *Titanic*, the right honourable gentleman will do all he can to facilitate this inquiry?

Mr. Buxton – It will be my desire, and that of my Department, to facilitate this inquiry as far as possible, but there must necessarily be an inquiry into the loss of the *Titanic*, and it is quite clear that, until we have such information as is available with regard to the disaster, we shall not be in such a strong position to know what to do. I will assure the House there will be no delay. We fully feel the great responsibility the Board of Trade has in the matter; but it is far better that we should give a little more time and come to a really satisfactory conclusion than act rapidly which might possibly lead us into other evils.

Mr. Lough – Having regard to the rapid growth in the size of vessels in recent years, does not the right honourable gentleman consider that it was a long time to wait from 1894 to 1911 without making any regulations for vessels over 10,000 tons?

Note: this question was not answered by Mr. Buxton.

Mr. Cooper – May I ask the right honourable gentleman if it is not a fact that Atlantic liners of Germany and United States nationality do not to-day actually carry close or double the lifeboat accommodation required by the Board of Trade regulations for ships of this country?

Mr. Buxton – I do not think that is so as a matter of fact, but perhaps the honourable gentleman will give me notice.

The article continues:

> Mr. Bottomley [the editor of *John Bull*, the Cassandra we met earlier] called attention to what he regarded as the lack of provision made by the Board of Trade for the safety of the passengers upon British Liners. The sole responsibility for their safety rested upon the Board of Trade. According to the answer given by the President, the utmost requirement of the present rules of the Board for life-saving accommodation on the Titanic amounted to 960 people only, against the fact that she was authorised to carry 3,500, and on this particular voyage she carried 2,200. He submitted that the Board of Trade was really to be seriously censured for allowing obsolete rules to remain in force which legalised such inadequate boat accommodation. [Mr. Bottomley] ... had seen that report. It indicated the same stupendous failure to comprehend the new condition of things as was shown by the rules of the Board of Trade. Either for the purpose of breaking records or for the purpose of saving fuel there was a tendency on the part of these ocean liners to take a northerly route, and ignore the recognised dangers at this season of the year of the icefield or icebergs. ... With regard to the calamity itself, he must point out that there was not a single expert throughout the country who did not think that the fact of a large ship of this sort being built in water-tight compartments was not a factor for safety, and that such a ship would require a smaller proportion of boats than the one not so constructed. Unfortunately this calamity had shown that those compartments could not be relied upon in certain circumstances ... Mr. Bonar Law said he entirely agreed with the general views expressed by Mr. Buxton. Undoubtedly a new factor had arisen in regard to watertight compartments, because undoubtedly everybody had been under the impression that these water-tight compartments rendered a ship unsinkable.

-From a report published in the Belfast News-Letter, 19 April 1912.

INTELLIGENT, SEMI-INTELLIGENT AND BLIND

/ NO VESSEL CAN BE CONSIDERED UNSINKABLE IF IT MEETS WITH CERTAIN CONCUSSIONS.

Horatio Bottomley

Albert Einstein described the measure of intelligence as the ability to change. Intelligent design must account for its environment, whilst evolutionary design links success to the ability to adapt to a constantly changing environment. This can be shown simply by an example of a railroad-building operation. A railroad can go almost anywhere, as long as obstacles are accounted for: mountains have tunnels blasted through them, rivers and gorges require bridges to span them, sandy or shifting soil needs to be accounted for, and earthquake fault lines avoided. The bulk of the intelligent design of railroad construction is done long before the first passenger train crosses that line, the train operator needing only to look directly ahead for incidental obstacles, such as vehicles, cattle, trees, and perhaps sabotage (in the Old West). The incidence of truly novel situations will be infrequent in such an embedded intelligent design. This allows the train operator to limit necessary changes largely to foreseen situations – i.e., obstacles directly on the track – in which he will have few choices: a whistle warning, to continue at speed, continue at a lower speed, to stop, and to reverse. Truly novel situations that would require a fast response are kept to a minimum.

Compare this scenario to that of an ocean liner. The first difference is that the ocean liner has freedom regarding the route. A northern route across the Atlantic in April 1912 would have been shorter, but more hazardous due to the presence of icebergs. In order to lower the risk of failure,

Captain Smith decided to take a more southerly route, the alteration made at 5:50 PM on the night of the disaster. This route of course was not completely risk-free, but more of a calculated risk, and not a large one, in normal circumstances: the new route steering into an area of the Gulf Stream typically free of icebergs in April. A lookout was still necessary, but the perceived hazards were low, and therefore any intelligent design embedded in that route would have been limited to prior knowledge – prior sightings of icebergs in the area and the knowledge that iceberg frequency is lower the further south one goes.

The year 1912 was not a normal one for ice floes, since cold water had pushed the warmth of the Gulf Stream further south. Thus the change in direction ordered by Captain Smith actually put *Titanic* on a collision course with the iceberg it struck. Note the delicacy of the timing here: the original change in course was to have been made at 5:30 PM, but was delayed for further travel south, to avoid contact with the ice that the *Baltic* had earlier alerted the ship to.

Embedded intelligent design would also be limited to the navigation maps which contain the shipping route lanes and known ice hazards. The quality of that embedded intelligent design is completely dependent upon accurate knowledge of the exact location of the ship. Updates to that knowledge would be limited to visual sightings from the crow's nest and the updates received from the Marconi wireless room, again dependent on the accuracy of the navigation information. The ocean liner would need to continuously monitor its environment due to the latency of knowledge of the local environment: i.e., the time elapsed before the information received. Unless there is a ship directly in front of the ocean liner, all information received by the 'navigational design team' would be out of date, i.e., the iceberg which was spotted yesterday by the prior ship may have drifted away from that particular location, but pack ice may have taken its place by the time the ocean liner gets to that location. The lack of embedded design in the pathway of a ship out in the open water increases the chance of a situation containing novel complexity.

Back on land, the surveyors would have told our hypothetical railroad design office that there was an obstacle to be avoided or bridged long before that route was planned and the track built. In 1912, out in the open water, there is merely the prior knowledge from another ship that was relayed to the Marconi room, or by a direct sighting of the obstacle. Whilst intelligence displays the ability to change, intelligent design is knowing what change to make. Accounting for the environment is dependent on an intimate, real-time knowledge of that environment, followed by judgement: an understanding of what change to make and when to make it in order to achieve success.

Piloting a ship in the open waters of the North Atlantic is a situation where the environment must be taken into account for both survival and success. One would expect the open water to produce novel random situations at relatively lower rates than those expected the nearer a ship gets to harbour, where an increase in collisions with other ships or docks in conditions of fog or heavy weather becomes a greater possibility. On the night the *Titanic* collided with the iceberg, the water was still, the sky clear and moonless, and the perceived hazards low. Captain Smith had already adjusted the course of the ship from southwest to due west, and in his mind the risks of collision on the new route were at a minimum. Collision with another ship on a clear night was unlikely, given that ships normally have lighting. Still, mariners knew that the environment could throw an iceberg at them with a certain random, if not rare, frequency. I propose that Captain Smith subconsciously assessed the open seas ahead of *Titanic* on that fateful night as low risk and thus he allowed the ship to continue on its course at speed. If we consider the thinking of Captain Smith on that fateful night, I argue that he may have imagined the risk of a collision in the open waters as low, not understanding the true nature of the ice field the ship was traversing. That is, the highest frequency of naval accidents occur near to shore or port, whereas the frequency of mishaps out in the open ocean is relatively low. I also propose that Captain Smith displayed a normalcy bias. Maritime mishaps were actually a relatively common occurrence throughout the seventeenth to the twentieth centuries, but the typical ship captain experienced them only rarely. This cognitive bias, developed through the combination of his own experience, acted synergistically with his culturally-induced cognitive bias, a deeply embedded bias resulting from years of exposure to active Blue-Sky Monument Building by the interests and admirers of the *Olympic* Class steamships, led the captain to underestimate the likelihood of a disaster involving the *Titanic*.

DIAGNOSING THE SINKING OF TITANIC

Let us go over the key events:

1. The Merchant Shipping Act of 1894 was designed to account, amongst literally hundreds of concerns, for ships on the water at the time the law went into effect. It had not been updated to account for the larger passenger ships of the twentieth century, and certainly not for the enormity of the *Olympic* Class liners. The Act is thus another case of intelligent design that could not account for its environment. Even so, this law did not prevent passenger lines from having enough lifeboats for everyone on board. Had the law been updated and enforced correctly, the required boats would have been added to *Titanic* to provide a place on a boat for every passenger and crew member.

   Therefore, this law deficiency component was required but not sufficient. This means that the law deficiency by itself could not have resulted in the sinking of *Titanic*. As a component of the event, one could point out that the coupling was loose. The origin of the design of the law and its participation as an input to the *Titanic* disaster were separated by decades.

2. The Stone–Lloyd automated bulkhead-door closed-compartment system. This bit of intelligent design, in tandem with its subsequent treatment by the press, ultimately led almost everyone involved to believe *Titanic* was all but unsinkable. It contributed to the disaster by leading the Board of Trade, the Advisory Board, White Star Line, Captain Smith, passengers, and the public into a fool's paradise. It is possible that the *Titanic* may have survived the disaster by simply ramming the iceberg head-on, which would have crushed the forward compartments and severely damaged the ship, but may not have completely sunk it. Without the allegedly-invulnerable compartments, the operators of the ship may have been much more careful about operation, since the

false security of the automatic closed-compartment system would not have been present. Further, with the compartments being open on the topside, the water collected towards the front of the ship, causing the bow to sink more quickly. Had the water distributed more evenly along the ship, there may have been more time before the ship actually sank, perhaps enough time for the *Carpathia* to arrive.

The watertight door component was therefore contributory, but not required and not sufficient. The presence of these doors was a loosely coupled event. They had been invented years earlier and had been installed on many other ships, including the SS Suevic (half a ship) prior to their use on the *Olympic* and *Titanic*.

3. Lack of binoculars in the crow's nest. Binoculars may have helped the lookout see the iceberg perhaps even one minute earlier than they did, allowing sufficient time to turn the ship and avoid the iceberg altogether. One could argue that had there been no lookout, the ship would have run directly into the iceberg, which may have saved the ship and averted disaster. But that collision would have been at full speed, and may have been a more severe accident. Therefore, this component was required but not sufficient. This event was loosely coupled, since there was a time gap between the event that caused the binoculars to be unavailable at the moment the binoculars were required.

4. The iceberg. The iceberg was an incidental obstacle in the path of *Titanic*. As we discussed previously, *Titanic* had many degrees of freedom to avoid both the iceberg and the iceberg-heavy region, simply by taking a more southerly route. Had the binoculars been available to the lookout watchman in the crow's nest, there could have been ample opportunity to manoeuvre around the iceberg. Because the iceberg may have been avoided or rammed, both scenarios would have likely saved lives and the ship. Therefore, the iceberg collision was required, but not sufficient for the *Titanic* disaster. I characterise this event as loosely coupled, since the paths of both the iceberg and *Titanic* were independent. Further, there could have been weeks

or months elapsed since the calving of the iceberg off the coast of Newfoundland and the appearance of the berg in the shipping lanes.

5. Communication failure. The disaster hearings discovered that there was a profound communication failure. *Titanic*'s Marconi operator had received two recent messages from a neighbouring ship, the SS *Californian*, the first two hours before and the second 45 minutes prior to the disaster. These warnings were never relayed to the Bridge. By itself, this failure could not have caused the accident; but when combined with the lack of binoculars and the speed of the ship, the events were synergistic. Therefore, this communication failure was contributory, but not required and not sufficient to cause the disaster. The communication failure was therefore a loosely-coupled event.

6. Brittle, single-layer hull steel and rivets. It was determined later by materials scientists that the steel that made up the hull and rivets of *Titanic* was brittle at freezing temperatures. While this steel would not pass quality testing in modern times, in 1912, it was not only more than adequate but considered top of the line. The steel was about 1 inch thick in the impact area. Thicker steel or a double-hull may have changed the outcome dramatically. Therefore, the brittle steel component was required but not sufficient to cause the disaster. I characterise the event as loosely coupled. The manufacture of the steel and the iceberg breach were separated by significant time. Since the steel was made brittle by the near-freezing water, it remains unclear whether the steel could have been made sufficiently ductile to produce a different outcome.

7. Lack of sufficient boats. Whilst this component did not contribute to the cause of the disaster, it did transform what was a survivable disaster for many if not all passengers into a non-survivable disaster for most people aboard *Titanic*. There have been claims that the passengers would have been unable to board the boats due to the confusion and panic, but I disagree. Once Mr. Andrews, the ship's designer, told Captain Smith the ship would be lost, Captain Smith knew there was no way to save the majority of the people aboard the ship. He knew that to avoid panic and engender an orderly evacuation,

he could not announce to the entire ship to head to the boat deck. If there had been enough boats on board, the passengers reluctant to board the boats would have ultimately made a choice to go down with the ship or chance it aboard a boat. Therefore, the lack of boats on board for all passengers converted a disaster resulting in the loss of *Titanic* into a disaster also resulting in the loss of the 1,517 lives estimated by the US hearings or the 1,503 lives lost by the British hearings. This was a loosely coupled event from the standpoint of the law dating from 1894, but once the iceberg was struck, it became a tightly-coupled event.

8. *Titanic's* speed was too high. *Titanic* was on the customary 'southern track' at the time it struck the iceberg. This was the agreed outbound track (from Southampton) formalised in 1899. *Titanic* was in Iceberg Alley when it struck the iceberg and sank. Studies and logs have shown that the year 1912 was average in the number of icebergs crossing the 48th parallel north, which marks the northern boundary of the transatlantic shipping lanes. In 1912 the locations of iceberg zones were known from three sources: Mariner's books and piloting guides, direct observation and reporting by wireless, and by direct observation from the crow's nest. There had been reports of sea ice on both *Titanic's* original track and the altered route. This sea ice was noticed by *Titanic* passengers on the afternoon of 14 April, indicating that the captain and crew were well aware they were in the midst of an ice hazard. Though Royal Statistical Society records for the year 1912 do not indicate an exceptional number of icebergs that crossed the 48th parallel into the shipping lanes – the total number spotted in 1912 was 1,038 – coast guard records show that in 1909, a total of 1,041 icebergs drifted from Arctic waters into the shipping lanes. Limited visibility on a clear, still, moonless night reduced the quality of input of local data concerning the immediate environment of *Titanic*, increasing the looseness of the coupling of the embedded design (shipping maps and navigation books) with the ship's assumed location and route design. Therefore, there was a disconnect between the assumed location and the actual location of the ship, rendering the embedded design (maps) as merely approximate. The high speed of the ship decreased

the coupling time between the sighting of the iceberg and the impact event. This is called a tightly-coupled event. The higher the speed, the more tightly-coupled the events would be. Unfortunately, this particular tightly-coupled event cascade left little room for error, and the rest is history. Further, the unfortunate lack of lifeboats turned what could have been a mostly survivable disaster into a mostly unsurvivable disaster in which 1,517 people perished.

Therefore, *Titanic*'s high speed on the night of the disaster was required but not sufficient to cause the loss of life.

THE DNA OF DISASTER RULES APPLIED TO THE SINKING OF THE TITANIC

In general, the period of time between when a design decision is made and the moment it is needed to account for the environment is the key to determining the degree of coupling of events. Embedded designs always have the potential weakness of being outdated; that is, the design decision was made well before the event in question. The majority of the design decisions embedded in the RMS *Titanic* were made decades prior to the moment they were relevant in a crisis: the approach of the ship to the iceberg.

1. Merchant Shipping Act of 1894: Intelligent design must account for its environment.

Intelligent design that cannot account for its environment can be called semi-intelligent design. The less perfect the fit of the design to the environment, the closer the design is to evolution (pure chance, thrown to the randomness of the universe). In some cases, the antiquated design is so far removed from the present reality that it can become dangerous. The Merchant Shipping Act of 1894 is one case that resulted in needless risk-taking with large ships. It is possible to conclude with reasonable certainty that those who were empowered to update the law did not see the need to do so, in light of the popular opinion that large ships fitted with the watertight compartments were obviously unsinkable. These events were loosely-coupled, given the years between the design decisions, both regulation design and ship design.

Human folly #3: Misunderstanding the true nature of an intelligent design (Trojan Horse Folly). The twentieth-century gargantuan liners were carrying passengers in numbers far beyond the design of the applicable law. Popular opinion was influenced by monument building, the awe of the monuments blinded decision makers to the need to adapt, and the law was not changed at the correct time to prevent the tragedy. Popular opinion engendered a cognitive bias which in turn produced a blindness, rendering the design unable to account for its environment completely.

2 Excessive speed of the vessel in the immediate environment: Tightly-coupled event cascades leave little room for error.

The collision could not be avoided due to excessive speed. The speed at the time of impact – 22 knots – was close to *Titanic*'s top speed. The reasoning (if any) that Captain Smith could have used would absolutely need to be based on his belief that *Titanic* was unsinkable. To this day, there is no direct evidence that Bruce Ismay cajoled Captain Smith to set any speed record.

Human folly #3. Misunderstanding the true nature of an intelligent design (Trojan Horse Folly). Not only was the ship not unsinkable, but the operation of the ship was plagued with miscommunication and assumptions that were incorrect. The communication both within the ship and between Titanic and surrounding vessels was broken, and there was no priority channel for ice warnings or SOS distress calls. The embedded design of the automated bulkhead door system was unable to account for the immediate physical environment of the *Titanic* as it approached the ice field.

3 The ship operators could not identify and account for the ice hazards at the correct time and in the correct way: Intelligent design must account for its environment.

Human Folly #4. Misunderstanding of the nature of evolutionary forces (failure to understand nature, Marie and Pierre Curie Folly). Those who were operating the ship were unable to account for their environment in Iceberg Alley. They were unaware of the large iceberg directly in the path of the ship until it was too late to make the necessary correction.

4. Unfamiliarity with the designed and built ship: The operators did not know how the ship should encounter the iceberg: avoidance or ramming.

Human Folly #3. Misunderstanding the true nature of an intelligent design (Trojan Horse Folly). The operators did not know the new ship well. Avoidance was attempted, and the ship was unable to make the necessary change of course in the time and distance that was available prior to the iceberg encounter. They clearly did not understand the design and capabilities or the fragility of the ship adequately to make a sound decision. By the time the *Titanic* disaster occurred, it was well-known that in ships involved in collisions, the ship which rams another ship with its bow portion will be less likely to sink, whereas the ship that gets flanked has a much higher chance of sinking. Whether or not this would hold true in a ramming collision with a giant mountain of ice is not known.

5. Disconnect between ship designers and ship operators: Intelligent Design must account for its environment.

The designers of the ship could not account for the ship's operators and the operators could not account for the ship's design: a two-way street regarding assumptions. The designers and builders handed over the keys to what they considered to be a perfect example of a ship made unsinkable by the automatic compartment doors, and further assumed the operators knew how to operate the ship correctly when they embarked on their maiden voyage. Likewise, the operators took the keys to what they considered an unsinkable ship, assuming the ship's designers accounted for all manner of obstacles and mishaps the ship could encounter in the embedded design of the ship. This assumption of unsinkability blinded the operators to the ship's embedded vulnerabilities. While the ship was indeed sturdy, it was incapable of surviving being flanked by a giant iceberg at full speed.

Human Folly #1. Assuming the presence of intelligent design where none is present or is mere semi-intelligent design. (the Divine Intervention

Folly). The intelligent design embedded in *Titanic* was remarkable for its time, but it could not account for the manner of mis-operation as was the case in the disaster. The designers and the operators of the Titanic assumed the presence of intelligent design that did not actually exist: it was closer to semi-intelligent design. For the manner in which they operated the ship – full speed through an ice field – the Titanic was closer to semi-intelligent design. From the point of view of the designers, the operators committed the folly – their assumptions about the capabilities of the ship were off the mark. Captain Smith and his crew were driving a luxury car in a demolition derby. From the lack of communication in the Marconi room to the failure to supply the crow's nest lookouts with binoculars, and the absence of intelligent observation of the environment to avoid obstacles, the mistakes of navigation, the lack of sufficient boats and other lifesaving appliances, the failures in the intelligent design of operation were many. In this disaster, Human Follies #1 and #3 and #4 were interdependent.

Social psychologist Jonathan Haidt uses an elephant-and-rider metaphor to explain the concept that intuitions (the elephant) are the dominant forces that control human behaviour, whilst rationalisation (the rider) primarily acts as a post-hoc support to the conclusion made long before. In this instance, the conclusion was that the *Olympic* and *Titanic*, as printed in almost every newspaper that mentioned these 'wonder ships,' elevated them to the status of a 'great monument to the mastery of science.' Yes, Captain Smith and almost everyone on board believed that *Titanic* was unsinkable, and that made all the difference. The smoking gun in the sinking was not the quality of the steel, the lack of binoculars, the successive flooding of the compartments as the bow began to sink, nor the unhelpful Marconi wireless room. It was a cognitive bias in the minds of the beholders of *Titanic*: the Board of Trade, the Advisory Committee, the White Star Line, Harland and Wolff, newspaper editors and journalists, passengers, the crew, and Captain Smith himself. They allowed themselves to be fooled that the ship was, in fact, as indirectly advertised, unsinkable. A monument, like beauty, is indeed in the eyes of the beholder.

Every Atlantic Crossing is, in a way, a maiden voyage.

THE NASA SPACE SHUTTLE CHALLENGER DISASTER

/ YOU'LL BE A WITNESS TO THAT GAME OF CHANCE IN THE SKY
YOU KNOW WE'VE GOT TO WIN.

Donald Fagen, *'I.G.Y.'*

For me, Ronald Reagan was the Space Shuttle president. He was the puppet master calling the shots for the Shuttle Programme, and the Challenger disaster happened because nobody in NASA could tell him no.

I have never actually met the Gipper, but I'm certain he was an affable fellow. I've also never met any of his staff or relatives, sycophants or yes-men, but I did know some of his voters. I was one of his voters myself, but that is another story, and I am older and wiser now. Reagan got his start in politics in California with the help of Barry Goldwater and became its governor in 1967. My parents lived in California during that period, and for eight years of my childhood, Reagan was the state's governor. During those years, I do not recall hearing much about Governor Reagan, since the Vietnam War and Watergate sucked up all the attention at the time. As the seventies progressed, my parents were especially spooked by the Vietnam War after one of the kids in our neighbourhood was drafted and sent to Da Nang in 1973, and this had the effect of keeping one's eye off California's governor at the time, at least in our house. Reagan, though, was a bit of an environmentalist back then, and as I see it, he was the real ozone man, at least for California in the seventies. But if you're an American youth, the governor of your state is something like a water heater. You know there's hot water, but you're barely aware of where it comes from. Perhaps that is what the executive branch of government should be like – an appliance happily chugging away unnoticed, until the dishes are clean: something we actually need.

But that, dear friends, is not what we get in the box set included with our American President. Nope, we Americans always have something to prove, don't we? The foundational generation got rid of a king, but now we're stuck with kings of one-upmanship, depending, of course, on who is occupying the Oval Office or who is rubbing Elon Musk up the wrong way. Sputnik beat us to the punch, and the resulting alarm became another tool for the righteous – lest the godless Soviets get the upper hand. By the 1980s we were witnessing the onset of the death rattles of the Soviet system, heralded by bread lines and shortages of just about everything but propaganda and surveillance. But back home in the States, the fear of the spread of communism could still be used to sow the seeds of yet more fear. Should Reagan get the credit for ending the Cold War, like so many right-wingers want us to believe? Perhaps he had a hand in it, but I think his influence on the waning years of the seventy-year history of the Soviet Union was more that of a circus ringleader announcing the participants of some duel of words. After all, the Soviet Union was voted out of existence by the leaders of the individual nations that made up the communist bloc, and to credit President Reagan for that is also asserting that the Soviet Union was viable to keep operating – doing business as usual. But there is ample evidence that wasn't the case, and no amount of right-wing disinformation to the contrary will erase the images I have in my mind of the Soviet breadlines on Tom Brokaw's news broadcasts. No one thanks a dumpster fire for getting rid of the rubbish, and this one was spontaneous combustion anyway. Just let it burn.

Anyhoo, I have long suspected that there was a connection between President Reagan and the Challenger disaster. I'm not saying it was all his fault, but there is a lot of damning evidence I want to bring up and a few fingerprints here and there. Reagan was able to insulate himself from the part I suspect he played in the Challenger disaster in a way the Soviets could not when confronted with the fallout of the Chernobyl disaster right inside the Soviet Union just a few months later. President Reagan had an awful lot riding on the Space Shuttle Programme, and his administration had a 'Shuttle only' policy, to the point of shutting down all other launch vehicle programmes that could compete. The Shuttle could have no challengers, nothing would be allowed to outcompete it for attention-grabbing potential. In Reagan's second term, the Shuttle had launched congressman Bill Nelson and prominent NASA backer Senator Jake Garn into space, and somewhere in cooking up Reagan's reelection campaign strategy, he and his stunt men came up with the shameless geopolitical circus act which became known as the 'Teacher In Space Project.' They hatched a plan to put the first ordinary citizen into space on the Shuttle. Further, that 'ordinary citizen' would be a schoolteacher, and to top it off, would teach classes directly from space in real time. It would be a public relations bonanza for NASA, and an absolute, ultimate coup for President Reagan, who could figuratively bury his geopolitical competition, the Soviet Union.

In the 1980s, the Soviet Union had not yet failed, and was still in the race. We could not foresee the exact moment it would cease to exist; at the time it seemed the wounded but still brutal Soviet beast could go on ad infinitum, gobbling up more territory and living rent-free in the heads of the susceptible. President Ronald Reagan had a weighty task in front of him: not only did he need to decry the inevitable failure of the home of Soviet Marxism, but he also had to demonstrate to the world that the non-Marxist West was indeed better. As an American Blue-Sky Cultural Monument, the DNA of the Space Shuttle Programme included, at its genesis, a built-in mission to outshine the Soviets. But if this American entry into the space race was intended even partly to inflate the pride of the United States, is it possible that this overarching priority interfered with other priorities, including the safety of the mission and crew?

The Space Shuttle Programme was undoubtedly the pride of the United States of America during the 1980s Cold War period. It was America's latest entry into the space race which began decades before in the run-up to the period when the Soviet Union launched Sputnik. As such, it became the focus of national pride as ordinary Americans and American Politicians alike projected their hopes and dreams upon the programme. After twenty-four successful launches, NASA and the Reagan White House assumed that the Space Shuttle was a completely known and ultra-reliable system which could be ramped up to one or two launches per month. However, the Shuttle Programme was plagued by technical problems that were not yet acknowledged by NASA management, nor Morton Thiokol, the contractor responsible for building the solid rocket boosters.

28 January 1986. After a very cold night at the Kennedy Space Center, the STS-51L Shuttle mission lifted off, carrying teacher Christa McAuliffe and six other crew members. As millions watched on live television alongside those on the ground, seventy-three seconds after lift-off, the Shuttle broke up into a billowing cloud of fire, smoke, and vapours.

THE SHOCK OF SPUTNIK AND THE BIRTH OF NASA

On the front page of the NASA.gov website, the very first sentence reads: 'The Cold War between the United States and former Soviet Union gave birth to the space race and an unprecedented program of scientific exploration.'

If anything kicked off the space race, it was the launch of the Soviet satellite Sputnik I on 4 October 1957. The International Geophysical Year (IGY) was to be a huge collaborative effort to increase knowledge about the Earth, and was set to coincide with the increased activity of the sun's eleven-year cycle. Both the Soviet Union and the United States announced plans to launch a satellite into Earth's orbit during the IGY, an eighteen-month period ending on 31 December 1958. But the Soviets leapfrogged the US plans and launched Sputnik early in the IGY time period. This created a certain alarm in the American public, often compared with the effect of the Pearl Harbor attack on the nation. President Eisenhower created NASA in response to Sputnik, and the National Aeronautics and Space Act was signed into law on 29 July 1958. By this time the seed of the Space Shuttle Programme had already been planted. The need for reusability was recognised early, and the X-15 hypersonic research programme was planned in 1954 and consisted of rocket-propelled aeroplanes launched from an airborne B-52, which, after running the test flight, landed horizontally on a landing strip or a dry lake bed. These aircraft made a total of 199 successful flights, resulting in a wealth of knowledge and technology key to the building of the successful space transport system commonly known as the Space Shuttle.

A FAINT SIGNAL EMERGES FROM THE NOISE

As the Apollo Programme matured, the need for a reusable spacecraft was recognised as the most cost-effective solution, and by 1968 this plan was made public. Where the Apollo Programme relied on single-use, disposable vehicles, the new Space Shuttle Programme featured:

> Three major components: the Orbiter which houses the crew; a large External Tank that holds fuel for the main engines; and two Solid Rocket Boosters (SRBs) which provide most of the Shuttle's lift during the first two minutes of flight. All of the components are reused except for the external fuel tank, which burns up in the atmosphere after each launch – www.NASA.gov

By the early 1970s the design for the Space Shuttle was finalised and contracts were awarded, with the solid rocket booster contract going to Morton Thiokol of Ogden, Utah due to their well-developed technology in solid rocket motors, called SRBs.

After pushing the Shuttle Stack to the edge of space, the SRBs parachute back to Earth and land in the ocean, to be recycled and refurbished for re-use on another mission. The built-in feature of this method of operations is that the orbiter and the SRBs can be thoroughly examined after each use for clues pertaining to their operational soundness.

Morton Thiokol technology used solid rocket motor sections that were stacked up to make the final rocket booster. The design of the booster sections was completed in the 1970s, and was not that different to rocket systems in use at the time. Since these conjoined sections were assembled not at the Morton Thiokol factory in Utah, but at the Vehicle Assembly Building (VAB) at Cape Canaveral, they were called 'field-joints.' When stacked up, the sections all had tiny gaps between them due to irregularities in manufacturing large objects, and these gaps were filled in by O-rings, special heat-resistant rubber rings: a primary and a secondary backup O-ring to contain the high-pressure, extremely hot gases inside the interior of the SRBs. The seal of these O-rings was checked after every launch for evidence that the hot burning gas from the interior of the rocket booster got past the O-ring seal. Soot that reached the outside of the O-rings was called 'blowby,' and this soot indicated that hot gases had escaped past the O-ring seal, possibly even damaging it.

After finding soot between two O-rings after a very cold launch in January 1985, blowby became a known problem to the Thiokol SRB engineering team, and was correlated with lower temperature launches below 53°F (11.6°C). A lead expert Thiokol engineer named Roger Boisjoly suspected the correlation between O-ring resiliency and temperature. Boisjoly was considered the US's leading expert on O-rings used in rocket joint seals, and by 1985 had twenty-five years' experience as an aerospace engineer. In March 1985, Boisjoly had recognised the need for further studies to link the low-temperature operating environment with the observed hot gas blowby, and worked with Ernie Thompson, supervisor of Rocket Motor Cases at Thiokol, on laboratory bench-testing of the cold weather effects on O-ring resiliency.

The tests revealed that low temperatures indeed affected the ability of the O-rings to pressurise and move into place quickly enough to prevent the escape of hot gases. Another Thiokol engineer, Allan McDonald, along with Boisjoly, concluded that lower temperatures caused stiffness in the O-rings, and this cold-induced stiffness also delayed the movement of the O-rings into the maximum sealing position within the field joint. Within the small group of engineers involved in the project, it was suspected that escaping hot gases could cause an explosion of the Shuttle on the launch-pad or shortly after lift-off.

RED FLAGS IN THE FAMILY

As we have now established, noise in a designed system is the presence of chance or randomness creeping into or affecting that designed system. The noise is manifested by the occurrence of repeated incidences of unexpected or unintended outcomes. The history of maritime disasters such as the *Titanic* reflects that the operator(s) in control of the designed system do not fully understand and control all the components of the system, or that the system has one or more embedded flaws. An earthquake, tornado, or simply a very cold or windy day constitute the natural environment a designed system must operate within. A misunderstanding in the way a designed system will operate within its environment could constitute both a Trojan Horse Folly, combined with a misunderstanding of the natural phenomena and how it will affect any system, natural or designed. (Marie and Pierre Curie Folly).

The Space Shuttle booster rockets were known for their blowby problem in the O-rings, knowledge which may have been completely unknown had the SRBs been designed as expendable and not recovered. But despite the physical evidence and observations made by Boisjoly and Thompson, the blowby was not taken seriously by NASA or Thiokol management. Nonetheless, it was clearly the result of a designed system producing noise consistently. The SRBs were not the only Shuttle system displaying a noise problem: the Space Shuttle Columbia disaster in 2003 occurred due to a foam-insulation impact problem of which NASA managers had been aware.

The foam shedding problem was acknowledged by NASA, but there was no concerted effort to understand how it could affect the designed system until after the disaster. When a piece of foam breaks away from the External Tank during a launch, it's essentially now in the environment, and becomes the manmade equivalent of an iceberg. Therefore, the environment 'threw' a piece of foam at the Shuttle during the launch. This is a classic example of the Trojan Horse Folly. In an interview after the Columbia disaster in August 2003, Dr. Sally Ride, who was on both

/ 153

the Challenger Accident Investigation Board (The Rogers Commission) and the Columbia Accident Investigation Board, answered questions from *New York Times* reporter Claudia Dreyfus:

Q. Are there parallels between the Columbia problem and the famous O-rings, where rubber rings on the Challenger rocket boosters froze, leading to the explosion?

A. Yes, and it was recognised, dealt with in some way. But they never spent the money to do the required engineering tests to understand exactly what was going on. The problem occurred a second time, but Challenger got to orbit fine. Gradually, over the course of several flights, the mindset became: "We have seen this problem before. It did not cause a catastrophe. It is probably O.K." It was seen as something that should be fixed, eventually.

With Columbia, there was a history of foam coming off the external tank during launch. Each time, it was identified as a problem. But there was never a real significant engineering effort to understand why this was happening, what the potential implications were and what needed to be done to stop it. There was no catastrophic damage the first time, the second time or even the third time. It got to be accepted as almost, "in the family."

TWO CASSANDRAS: ROGER BOISJOLY AND ALLAN MCDONALD

In his book *Truth, Lies and O-rings* (2012), Allan McDonald takes a deep dive into the history of the Space Shuttle Programme and the conditions leading up to the Challenger disaster. Up to the time of the disaster, there had been twenty-four successful launches and landings, but there were known maladies in the system producing and testing the SRBs. While working on an engine nozzle erosion 'spalling' (a type of surface erosion) problem in 1981, McDonald 'first learned about an O-ring erosion problem in the field-joints of the SRMs.' Since the Space Shuttle is a manned vehicle, redundancies are required in certain critical components which can contribute to a catastrophic failure.

It was recognised early on in the design process that superheated gases escaping from this field joint could lead to catastrophic failure. Therefore, the O-ring system was actually two O-rings, a primary and secondary O-ring consisting of highly heat-resistant fluorocarbons. McDonald wrote that he was surprised to learn about the erosion problem, and even more surprised to find out that 'this anomaly had been observed as early as the Shuttle's second flight ... in November 1981.' Later in the chapter, McDonald says something very revealing: 'The O-ring erosion problem was not something that was occurring on every flight. Nor was it considered by either NASA or Morton Thiokol to be nearly as critical as the pocketing erosion of the nozzle.' Both organisations placed the blowby problem on the back burner.

McDonald later discovered that his boss was personally going inside rocket motors prior to static burn tests, which were done in a horizontal position, to apply 'strips of zinc chromate asbestos-filled vacuum putty on the rubber insulation in the area of the field-joints and had squeezed putty into the voids that formed between the insulation surfaces during the mating operation.' McDonald confronted his boss about this interference in the validity of the tests, explaining: 'we did not fly the vehicle in that condition, so we needed to test in the exact same condition.'

Out of a total of four shuttle flights in 1984, according to McDonald's book, only the November 1984 flight of STS-51A Discovery 'showed no evidence of O-ring erosions,' but all three of the other missions 'had shown signs of O-ring thermal distress.' Furthermore, 1985 did not start well, since the Discovery flight on 24 January 1985 'revealed a very serious problem' in two of the field joints, one on each of the two SRBs, which 'not only exhibited erosion of the primary O-rings, but large quantities of dark black soot sat between the primary and secondary O-rings in both field-joints.' After searching for clues to explain their observations, nothing could be directly found in the physical state of the recovered SRBs, and the engineers finally concluded that the blowby and soot were correlated with cold temperatures, confirmed by news publications that stated the three nights prior to the launch had become so cold the SRBs were exposed to temperatures in the teens; engineers calculated an O-ring temperature at 53°F.

Roger Boisjoly wrote a report to Bob Lund, at the time Thiokol's Vice President of Engineering and Boisjoly's supervisor, explaining that the engineers were confident they had found the root of the problem – cold temperatures – and that failure of this system could result in the 'loss of the Shuttle vehicle and its crew.' As 1985 progressed, however, the pressure mounted from NASA to rapidly increase the flight rate, and yet the engineers comprising the newly formed O-ring task force were having difficulty getting the necessary resources to correctly identify the parameters under which the O-ring design was operating correctly. Consequently, the problem was not solved by January 1986, at which time NASA's flight-rate goal had increased to twenty-four shuttle flights per year.

As the fateful date approached, NASA successfully launched STS-61-C (Columbia) on 12 January 1986, a flight which had been scrubbed and rescheduled on six different occasions, two of which were associated with bad weather. It was regularly pointed out in the press at the time that if it took an entire month to launch one shuttle 'after it had been declared ready to go,' NASA had little hope of successfully launching two shuttles per month.

The forecast on 26 January 1986 predicted 'no-go' bad weather conditions during the launch window that never materialised. The launch was pushed to the 27th, which turned out to be a very cold day on the Cape. After an embarrassing stuck door handle caused a scrub, newspapers quipped: 'Frozen part puts shuttle on ice.' The door's exterior handle to the crew compartment had to be removed prior to lift-off and would not budge. Newspapers reported that after the two hours it took to remove the handle, which had to be crudely cut off manually with a hacksaw, 'strong winds whipped into the area, and lift-off was cancelled.' Launch commentator Hugh Harris explained the handle is only necessary when the Orbiter is on the ground to close the crew compartment door. 'When they tried to take it off, the screw was frozen.' That night, on the eve of the planned Challenger launch, Thiokol engineers brought their concerns to NASA management. The engineers considered 53°F to be the minimum temperature for the O-rings to move into their sealing positions when the SRBs were pressurised at ignition, but the expected temperature was only 22°F at 7 AM, and only 36°F by midday. Over the course of several late evening meetings the night before the launch, the Thiokol engineers explained to NASA management that the expected temperatures on the 28th were outside what they considered safe to launch.

Just as the Thiokol engineers were bringing their safety concerns to NASA, the presence of other priorities were beginning to raise their heads; priorities other than the safe operation of the Challenger mission. After a run of several years of successful launches, the Space Shuttle Programme had become routine and perhaps even mundane, and public interest began to wane. But the TISP was already churning, having been set in motion in an effort to recapture the interest from the Shuttle's earlier days, and the recent negative publicity over NASA's cold weather launch difficulties was unwelcome at best. NASA would push ahead with the grand plan: The presence of a female civilian teacher aboard the mission fulfilled an early promise of the Space Shuttle Programme – that it could carry cargo, astronauts, engineers, scientists, and eventually civilians, into space. What was not mentioned, though, was that NASA was prepared to toss aside its prior launch criteria and simply ignore the engineer's concerns. The Thiokol engineers were about to find that a cold weather launch was, despite all the prior talk about mission safety, non-negotiable.

THE CASSANDRAS' UNSUCCESSFUL ATTEMPT TO PREVENT THE DISASTER

Allan McDonald and Roger Boisjoly presented handwritten charts to NASA management on the evening prior to launch
(NB. these have been summarised for clarity):

Conclusions:
The Solid Rocket Motors are basically no different from one-another except for:
- Ambient temperature when tested or launched
- Whether or not putty packing had been used.

Blowby is expected in joints which operated at 50°F and had no putty packing

Test Motor joints that were 53°F performed the best –

Therefore the ambient temperature must be 53°F or greater to launch.

Tomorrow's Launch –

Expected Temperature of the O-rings:

29°F at 9 AM

38°F at 2 PM

Thiokol's Recommendation: No Go for Tomorrow's Launch

This recommendation prompted the infamous outburst from NASA Manager Larry Mulloy, who immediately retorted that he would not accept the engineer's recommendations, a response NASA director George Hardy said appalled him. Mulloy then shouted at the engineers: 'My God, Thiokol, when do you want me to launch, next April?'

McDonald revealed how he felt pressure from NASA management to allow the launch to proceed, though in the past the same NASA managers would challenge his 'rationale on why it was safe to fly.' Reflecting on this sudden perplexing change of philosophy, McDonald observed that 'this was the first time that NASA personnel ever challenged a recommendation that was made that said it was unsafe to fly.' The review process to assess flight readiness had, in the past, always stressed 'safety first' and was centred around the core philosophy that the contractors must 'prove beyond the shadow of a doubt that their hardware is safe to fly.' The NASA managers on this occasion did not accept the no-go recommendation from McDonald, Boisjoly, and the other Thiokol engineers, citing 'inconclusive' data, and recommended going ahead with the launch. McDonald refused to sign off on the launch, leading NASA managers to pressure Thiokol's management, which in turn pressured its VP of engineering, Bob Lund, into reversing his decision. McDonald later described not signing off on the launch as 'the best decision I ever made in my life.'

The next day's launch attempt was met with Arctic air and record low temperatures across Florida. Ice covered the launch pad, and the extremely cold liquid oxygen and hydrogen fuel in the tanks could further cool the area surrounding the Shuttle Stack. Overnight temperatures recorded by the Kennedy Space Center 'Ice Team' found the external surfaces of the Shuttle Stack, including the boosters, which were recorded as: Left 25°F (-3.8°C); Right 8°F (-13.3°C). Challenger lifted off from the pad at T +0, 11:38 AM on 28 January at an ambient temperature of approximately 36°F (2.2°C). The coldest prior launch, out of the previous twenty-four, had been 53°F (11.6°C).

Simplified Timeline

0 Seconds: Solid Rocket Booster ignition

.678: For almost 3 seconds, 9 puffs of grey smoke were recorded escaping from the right-side SRB near the strut connecting the Booster to the external fuel tank (ET)

37: Wind shear conditions encountered, but within design limits of the Shuttle Stack

58.7: Tracking camera captured a plume of flame emanating from the right-side SRB

72: The right SRB pulled away from the strut connecting it to the ET, causing a lateral acceleration felt by the crew

72.2: Structural breakup of the Shuttle Stack caused by excessive aerodynamic forces beyond the design basis of the vehicle. Rupture turbulence of the ET and release of the liquid oxygen and liquid hydrogen contents into the immediate area surrounding the orbiter, causing its breakup and the loss of the crew.

The two SRBs built by Morton Thiokol Corporation continued to fly until destroyed by remote control. Surface recovery operations wrapped up on 7 February, but submarine recovery operations continued for weeks. Significant portions were never recovered from the depths.

— — — —

Boisjoly and Allan began to recognise the emerging noise pattern and presented their findings to NASA management, but could not prevent the launch. The emerging pattern of noise was likely hampered and delayed by the masking of the cold weather launch effects by McDonald's boss, Joe Kilminster, who was packing the asbestos-filled putty in between the joint spaces for the horizontal rocket motor tests. In my view, the technical DNA of the Challenger disaster was related to the unscientific way the rocket motor tests were done: the putty packing of the joints masked the fundamental flaw in the design of the system, obscuring and delaying the recognition of the pattern of noise by those who had the most intimate knowledge of the intelligent design of the system – those who are often the Cassandras or whistle-blowers. This handicapped their ability to make the case for a launch delay to their superiors: a history of success is a powerful force which propels a human-designed system forward. NASA was and still is a human-designed system, and at least in the past, displayed characteristics of a layered hierarchy. Stepping out of one's level in an organisation to blow the whistle could be a career-ending act of conscience. Due to the power structures and hierarchies embedded within organisations such as NASA, it is unlikely that any human-designed hierarchical system possesses a mechanism by which disasters or even poor outcomes can be reliably prevented by default. This is at least partly due to the nature by which these hierarchical systems themselves are established: mainly due to power relationships. Power hierarchies, as systems, do not naturally possess veto mechanisms that function as a curb to that power: veto mechanisms must be designed and implemented within the system to avoid suboptimal outcomes, and we can expect those in power to be tempted to dismantle or neuter any embedded safeguards within these systems for their own purposes and interests. Commercial and Political success is the fuel that pushes these systems forward. Western capitalist systems typically display a type of bias- a bias centred around the other Golden Rule: that is – 'he who has the gold makes the rules.' This is based on an underlying assumption that the one who has the actual or metaphorical 'gold' arrived at that position of power via merit. The 'yang' of this 'yin' is that the system's subordinates did not merit that power and position, and whose opinion is, by default, less credible. We should therefore also assume that by default, the C-suite is at best neutral or even slightly hostile to bad news from the playing field, including regulatory bad news. Further, we should always assume that the C-suite is at least slightly susceptible to the bias-inducing gravity of Cultural Monuments- even if that susceptibility is indirect, passing through all the President's men.

The design of the SRB O-ring system had a designed and built-in temperature operating range: from a typical hot Florida day all the way down to 53°F. Operation of that system out of its designed temperature range was an invitation for chance or randomness to enter the system. A designed system has a dynamic range – that is, the ability of the system to account for events of novel complexity presented by the environment. When any system is presented with conditions that exceed the dynamic range of that system, either a veto node must be enabled to prevent disaster or any embedded failure compensation mechanisms must be triggered. If the failure compensation mechanisms are human-based, i.e. designed and intended to be triggered and carried out by humans, judgement automatically factors in to the equation. Any looming majoritarian geopolitical Cultural Monument wars such as the Cold War will have the potential to produce a gravitational effect upon that human judgement, and when combined with the follies, those typical misunderstandings and culturally-embedded assumptions that cloud judgement, the stakes can be very high. With a system that displays these defects but that also has not yet demonstrably failed, there is no basis for a unifying call to action. One must look for and recognise the noise patterns produced by such a system. Whether from within the system or without, the brakes may need to be applied- but they must be in workable order. In many cases the brakes will have to be applied from outside the system, but as we know that may not always be enough – Ross Perot originated from outside the American political system, but he had no access to the brakes and was unable to prevent a disaster for the working class Americans whose jobs were moved to Mexico or China. Thiokol engineers resided within the Shuttle system, recognised the catastrophic potential of the launch in cold weather, but were also unable to prevent the disaster. When there is seemingly no other hope, people naturally seek divine intervention to apply the brakes from outside the system, but that, as we know, constitutes wishful thinking, not good design.

THE OPPORTUNITY TO WRITE THE HISTORY THAT FOLLOWS

The TISP was organised by NASA and announced by President Ronald Reagan in 1984, with the goal of stimulating student interest in mathematics, science, and space exploration. The teacher-astronaut was to be chosen from among the interested applicants. After a lengthy process, Christa McAuliffe, a teacher from New Hampshire, was selected to be the first teacher in space. Described as a vivacious person and a natural leader, her mission was to teach two fifteen-minute lessons from the Space Shuttle Challenger. Her sudden loss was truly felt around the world and was an especially tragic moment for students, who lost a role model. The death of a teacher is an especially traumatic moment for kids, and even more so for those who knew her back in Concord, Massachusetts.

Reagan thus sent a letter to the faculty and students of Concord High School, where Christa McAuliffe taught social studies, somehow managing to derive a patriotic moral from a totally avoidable disaster in which he was clearly involved:

> Today all America joins with you in paying tribute to the memory of a teacher, a friend, a wife and mother, a leader.
>
> The shock and grief, the numbness we all experienced at having Christa McAuliffe so suddenly taken from our midst Tuesday morning is beyond the power of words to express. But through the silence of sorrow we can say that your burden is not only the burden of all Americans, but of people throughout the world who saw in Christa what you who knew her best saw in her – a woman of courage and caring, an educator of boundless energy and inexhaustible enthusiasm, an inspiration to young and old alike.

In 1961, when the first manned missions were flown into space, Christa McAuliffe was 12 years old, younger than virtually all of you gathered here. She said recently that at the dawn of the space age she was fascinated by the possibilities it opened to the imagination, but that she never considered becoming an astronaut because there were no role models. And when she herself became a role model for others, she characteristically looked back in American history to others who had challenged a trackless frontier. On her application for selection as the first teacher in space, she wrote that, like the pioneer travelers of the Conestoga wagon days, she intended to keep a journal of her passage.

We will never have the opportunity to read that journal, but all of us – all of you – will have the opportunity to write the history that follows. And as you move forward from this day, as its clouds and shadows give way to fresh sunlight, I know that you will ponder many times how best to honor the memory of your dear friend. You could hardly do better than believe as she believed, that the lives and example of every citizen alike – teacher, engineer, lawyer, policeman, mother, father – have the power to change the course of human events for the good…

THE ROGERS COMMISSION INVESTIGATES

President Reagan appointed a commission to investigate the disaster. Chaired by William P. Rogers, notable members of the Rogers Commission included Neil Armstrong, Sally K. Ride, Charles E. Yeager, and physicist Richard P. Feynman.

Summary of Commission Findings: technical causes

The Commission findings were damning. The technical causes began with the faulty O-ring design and increased as both NASA and contractor management first failed to recognise it as a problem, then failed to fix it, and finally treated it as an acceptable flight risk since it was a repeating occurrence that could not be controlled. Due to the size and cost of the SRBs, a redesign would need to have been budgeted for, and the issue was not seen as a significant enough risk at the time to allocate resources. The Commission found that neither Thiokol nor NASA expected the hot gases from rocket motor ignition to even reach the rubber O-rings sealing the joints, much less to be partially burned. Regardless, as tests and then flights confirmed damage to the sealing rings, the reaction by both NASA and Thiokol was to increase the amount of damage considered 'acceptable.' At no time did management either recommend a redesign of the joint or call for the Shuttle's grounding until the problem was solved.

The inclusion of typical operating conditions could have been more convincing to NASA managers. The team of engineers should have included all temperature data when presenting their case to NASA managers the night before the launch; the cold weather data was not presented in contrast to that from normal weather launches. The pattern present in the data may have been more convincing had all of the data been presented to NASA, including the temperatures at which there was no O-ring damage. The data contained a single outlier, where soot between the O-rings was found after a 75°F (23.8°C) launch. This one outlier was enough to throw off the interpretation of the system as a temperature-dependent malfunction. Another point is that as early as 1985 the Thiokol O-ring expert engineer Roger Boisjoly wrote a memo to his boss, and urged a delay of further launches until the O-ring problem had been solved, adding that to 'fly without fear of failure' was a 'mistaken position,' which could result in catastrophic failure and loss of human life. This second point suggests, in contrast to the above, that no amount of data from the Thiokol engineers would persuade Thiokol and NASA management to take the O-ring problem seriously.

The Morton Thiokol engineers told the Rogers Commission that they had unanimously recommended against launching the Challenger in weather any colder than the low fifties because of fears that the cold might cause the synthetic rubber seals in the booster rockets to fail, causing a catastrophic explosion. One of the engineers, Brian Russell, told the Commission that he 'felt pressure' that 'we were in the position of having to prove it was unsafe instead of the other way around.' Roger Boisjoly testified that he cautioned his superiors and was frustrated that top management would not stop the launch given his warnings, telling the Commission he 'expressed deep concern about launching at low temperature' because he knew cold could make the rubber seals hard and stiff, shrink them, and increase the time it took the seals to close. Describing the pre-launch meetings between NASA management and Thiokol engineers, Boisjoly told the Commission that he felt that NASA was determined to launch the Challenger despite warnings from qualified engineers.

Key facts revealed by the Rogers Commission concerning the solid rocket booster O-ring design and applicable Human Follies

Both Thiokol and NASA failed to respond to facts which emerged during the testing phases of the O-ring design. After repeated internal warnings that there were problems with the original design, both Thiokol and NASA failed to respond appropriately by developing a new seal design. Human Folly #3, Trojan Horse.

The Solid Rocket Boosters were tested and O-rings evaluated in a horizontal position, not in the actual flight position during the static testing. This is a common testing method, and is useful if the position of the O-rings is not critical during the testing phase. Blowby was being generated, which means that a designed system was throwing off noise, and the mechanism producing the blowby was not investigated and corrected. Human Folly #3, Trojan Horse.

Prior to the accident, neither NASA nor Thiokol fully understood the mechanism by which the joint sealing action took place. Human Folly #3, Trojan Horse.

NASA and Thiokol accepted escalating risk apparently because they 'got away with it last time.' This is a once-good, always-good bias. The information contained in prior events was not investigated. They were essentially handling a loaded gun, unaware of the live bullet in the chamber. Human Folly #3, Trojan Horse.

Getting away with it last time is no basis for lowering standards for future flights. Despite persistent O-ring erosion and blowby, flights were still permitted. The omission of persistent anomalies from tracking and reporting systems allows major problems to persist without serious efforts to elucidate and solve the problems. Again, there was a significant amount of noise generated by the designed system, which was completely ignored by the designers and operators of that system. Human Folly #3, Trojan Horse.

Commissioner Feynman observed that the decision-making process was 'a kind of Russian Roulette.' The Commission also stated that they had sufficient information to assert that a careful analysis of the flight history of O-ring performance by either NASA, which failed to request such documentation, and Thiokol, which failed to produce such documentation, would have revealed the correlation of O-ring damage and low temperature. Since both NASA and Thiokol failed to carry out such analysis, they were unaware of the designed system's vulnerability: cold weather. Again, Human Folly #3, Trojan Horse, and since the cold weather is a product of nature, The Marie and Pierre Curie Folly, Human Folly #4, also applies.

The Commission concluded that the O-ring erosion history McDonald presented to NASA Headquarters in August 1985 was sufficiently detailed to require corrective action prior to the next flight. Allan McDonald and Roger Boisjoly both played the Cassandra part but were ignored by both the manufacturer, Morton Thiokol, and the client, NASA.

COMMISSIONER DR. RICHARD FEYNMAN'S FAMOUS O-RING C-CLAMP EXPERIMENT

During the hearings, when Larry Mulloy was in front of the panel claiming that, 'during the configuration that we ran ... the seal would function at that temperature,' Richard Feynman conducted his famous C-clamp experiment on the tabletop right in front of him. The physicist learned that the heat-resistant rubber used to seal the solid rocket booster joints using O-rings, became less pliable and significantly stiffer at colder temperatures. Feynman now believed that he had the solution, but to test it, he dropped a piece of the O-ring material, squeezed with a C-clamp to simulate the actual conditions of the Shuttle, into a glass of ice water. 'There is no resilience in this particular material when it is at a temperature of 32 degrees [Fahrenheit],' he explained. Feynman then took the clamp off of the rubber material for all to see. The material retained its 'clamped' shape well after it was removed from the ice water. Headlines proclaimed: 'NASA Admits Cold Affects Shuttle Seal.'

The early years of the STS programme saw NASA proposing some very ambitious schedules for shuttle missions. One early plan mentioned in the Rogers Report contemplated one mission per week, but as reality set in, these projections were revised significantly downwards. From the inception of the STS programme, the assumption had been that the reusability of the Shuttle and its components would make space operations 'routine and economical.' The rationale included the notion that the 'greater the number of flights, the greater the degree of routinisation and economy, so heavy emphasis was placed on the schedule.' The Rogers Report concluded that the 'attempt to build up to 24 missions a year brought a number of difficulties, among them the compression of training schedules and the lack of spare parts, and the focusing of resources on near term problems.'

The authors of the report concluded that 'the agency's determination to meet' the accelerated flight rate diluted the 'human and material resources that could be applied to any particular flight.'

THE DNA OF DISASTER DIAGNOSIS

Physical Environment of the Challenger

On 28 January 1986, the Challenger Orbiter stood on the launchpad during weather that was extreme for the region. Several communities experienced the coldest 28 January temperatures on record. Just two weeks earlier, the Space Shuttle Columbia went to space when ground temperatures were about 55°F, considered by Morton Thiokol engineers to be near the lowest temperature the SRBs were qualified to operate in. On the morning of the Challenger launch, however, launch pad workers found ice completely covering equipment and a layer of ice on the launch pad. The Chief of Rockwell, builder of the Orbiter, advised against the launch. Overnight temperatures had reached as low as 22°F at Kennedy Space Center as an Arctic air mass settled over the area, setting record lows over the southeastern seaboard. Armed with the knowledge that all intelligent design must account for its environment, a wary astronaut or NASA manager could simply ask: how does this extreme weather affect the operation of the vehicle? Has the Shuttle ever flown in these conditions before? Were shuttle components even tested at these temperatures? What is the lowest temperature the Shuttle and its components are qualified to fly in?

Let us now look for the iceberg. To clarify what will be considered the iceberg, we can broaden and extend our definition of the iceberg as something thrown at the environment that is being traversed by or contains the intelligent design of interest. The obstacle (iceberg) may be produced by the environment itself, or may be a chunk of debris that came from an intelligent design (an artefact) that is present in that environment or was present at one time in that environment. The *Titanic* struck an iceberg that formed perhaps thousands of years ago in a glacier in Greenland, calved into the ocean, and arrived in the path of the *Titanic* in the days preceding the collision. You can now extend this line of reasoning to understand how a city like Jakarta, Indonesia, which is built on a delta of thirteen rivers, is starting to sink. In contrast, the iceberg in this situation is manmade. Groundwater was pumped out from under the city, causing the sinking, but the city is also being inundated by rising sea levels, a result of climate change. In that case, the pumping of groundwater is inducing a vulnerability in a designed system, and the iceberg is clearly the sea-level rise due to climate change. DNA of Disaster rule of thumb: catastrophes can have as many maladies as they please.

In terms of aircraft design, a Shuttle Stack contains highly flammable cryogenic liquid fuels, solid rocket boosters, and a space plane connected to the giant foam-insulated fuel tank (ET), with the SRBs strapped onto the sides of the giant ET. SRB intelligent design: segmented solid rocket motor with cold-sensitive packing material between segments which have a history of leaking hot gas while in operation (semi-intelligent design).

We should also look at external factors, such as the operating environment. For 28 January, this was the coldest day on record. Mean January temperatures are 62.6°F (17°C) with a low of 51.8°F (11°C), but on this particular day the overnight temperature was 22°F (-5°C). Given that with large, deeper internal structures, there will be a degree of thermal latency, without active heating it would take some hours for the O-rings to warm up to ambient temperatures. One must also take into consideration that the large External Tank is filled with cryogenic fuels, which characteristically must allow extremely cold gases to escape through vents. This is a normal function, but which can further cool any local cold-sensitive parts as the shuttle stack sat on the launchpad overnight, and any sections or components blocked from the sun will be delayed in warming up to the ambient temperatures. Internal Environment of the SRBs: on 28 January 1986, it was very cold, and the O-rings were in a state of reduced resiliency, hindering their function. The Challenger Iceberg: record cold snap from an Arctic blast.

> The Shuttle had been sold as a reliable space truck ...There was just a whole party line and propaganda that the thing was a completely understood, completely reliable vehicle, and it was not.

Richard Cook, *former NASA budget analyst*

KNOWN MALADIES

Temperature sensitive field-joint seals, a design flaw. Human folly #3 Misunderstanding the true nature of an intelligent design (Trojan Horse Folly). This applies mainly to NASA, but also to Thiokol. The engineers Allan McDonald and Roger Boisjoly understood the design weaknesses far better than any management person at either NASA or Morton Thiokol, but tragically they were unable to convince the NASA management that their concerns were valid, instead being forced to prove their design was unsafe.

Solid Rocket Boosters developed and tested with putty packing in the joints. Developing the solid rocket boosters with putty packing masked the design problem (Human Folly #3). Further, the SRBs were tested in a horizontal position, but operated in a vertical position. This should have been a red flag for everyone, since the SRBs were not flown in this arrangement. As the Challenger ascended, it encountered wind shear, which can cause micro-movements between joined parts. But the most egregious violation of the scientific method in this case was the use of putty packing in the joints by Allan McDonald's boss, Joe Kilminster. The blowby would only have been noticed if it had been severe enough for the hot gases to have penetrated both the putty and the joint seals.

Lack of a feedback mechanism in the processes (Human Folly #3). With any sort of top-down control where an agenda is pushed, there must be a feedback mechanism whereby the information from the environment can make its way back to cognitive control (the C-suite, the nervous system, the autopilot, etc.) so the information can be considered for the purpose of adapting the entire system to the environmental conditions.

This information feedback must come from the people who are closest to the environmental conditions: those who are on the assembly line, i.e., the origin point of the Value Chain, those on the ground serving customer needs, or those surveying the ocean for icebergs. Sensory input is required to make corrections. It is how markets drive production: sales are a form of feedback that enables production through the Chain of Tribute. In the Challenger disaster, the engineers who knew the O-ring system the best were unable to get their concerns taken seriously. Thus, either a veto node was formed blocking the flow of this information to NASA management or their own judgement and agency was overruled by someone in the hierarchy: i.e. President Reagan. The information so critical to the success of the mission was either blocked or disregarded: NASA was blind by design. The critical information was handed directly to NASA management during the pre-launch meetings, and this was the dreaded bad news from the playing field. But it was also known even closer to the DNA of Disaster, when Roger Boisjoly and Allan McDonald first noticed a designed system producing noise in the form of an unexpected result. They first learned of the O-ring problem in 1981, and made efforts to address the design problem. This necessary design data feedback met veto players, who could not or would not, for whatever reasons, relay the information to cognitive control in the years prior to the disaster.

Cognitive control had no knowledge of how the record-breaking Arctic blast would affect the designed system, i.e., the Shuttle Stack. Human Folly #4: Misunderstanding of the nature of evolutionary forces (failure to understand nature, Marie and Pierre Curie Folly) and Human Folly #3: a failure to understand weaknesses in the intelligent design of the artefact or system.

Assumption that the sharp increase in the number of flights per year would lower the costs per flight. In other words that a greater quantity of flights produces lower costs per flight (Human Folly #3). The STS programme had only twenty-four flights under its belt when the number of flights was to be sharply increased to more than one per month. In reality, it turned out to be a case of false economy: there was no international market for space shuttles, and therefore, there was no market for the parts, systems, and personnel. Since everything was custom-made-to-order, market forces could not play any significant role in lowering the costs per flight; instead, the increased schedule led to increased pressure on available parts and labour, producing an artificial scarcity that was felt even in the training time for crew members. From the Dr. Sally Ride interview:

> **Q.** Dan Goldin, the NASA administrator from 1992 to 2001, had a mantra, 'Faster, better, cheaper.' Was that a mistake?
>
> **A.** 'Faster, better, cheaper,' when applied to the human space program, was not a productive concept. It was a false economy. It's very difficult to have all three simultaneously. Pick your favourite two. With human space flight, you'd better add the word 'safety' in there, too, because if upper management is going 'faster, better, cheaper,' that percolates down, and it puts the emphasis on meeting schedules and improving the way that you do things and on cost. And over the years, it provides the impression that budget and schedule are the most important things.

MONUMENTS & PRIORITIES

President Ronald Reagan announced his National Space Policy on 4 July 1982, in front of a huge audience at Edwards AFB in California: 'Beginning with the next flight, the Columbia and her sister ships will be fully operational, ready to provide economical and routine access to space for scientific exploration, commercial ventures, and for tasks related to the national security.'

The evidence points to a situation where the go / no-go decision process prioritised competing goals and monuments above the safety and ensured success of the mission (Human Folly #3). President Reagan, or whoever was driving the launch schedule, was blind to the iceberg by choice and by default.

The Challenger launch was originally scheduled for 22 January 1986, and was postponed multiple times due to bad weather or mechanical problems. Christa McAuliffe, the charismatic High School teacher who was the first civilian selected for the TISP, was scheduled to conduct televised lessons from space. If the launch had been delayed yet another day, her lessons would have fallen on a Saturday due to the scheduling of the experiments to be conducted on board, and thus the lessons could not have been viewed live by students. Further, President Ronald Reagan, who announced the TISP in 1984, was scheduled to deliver his State of the Union Address, which had never before been postponed, and, as a president who was politically active during the Cold War period, would have wanted to tout the fact that the United States had put a teacher successfully into space. Christa McAuliffe's two lessons were to be broadcast on live television coast-to-coast. There was a media frenzy associated with this particular mission, and the source of the frenzy was not the safety of the mission but, of course, the TISP.

Delaying the mission yet again could be detrimental to NASA's public image, and the accompanying disappointment could derail and deflate the media frenzy which was cultivated to be a public-relations bonanza for

NASA. Therefore, the evidence points to a situation where the go / no-go decision process prioritised these competing customer goals above the safety and ensured success of the mission. The United States, as a competitor in the space race with the Soviet Union, was set for a propaganda coup. The news of this accomplishment would undoubtedly have made its way into the Kremlin and around the world. This was classic Blue-Sky Monument Building. A news article from the era puts the run-up to the launch into perspective:

TEACHER IS FOCUS OF SPACE MISSION

McAuliffe to Be First Private Citizen on a Shuttle Trip
By William J. Broad, Special to the *New York Times*

The flight of the first private citizen into space, scheduled to begin Sunday, has filled the Kennedy Space Center with crowds of teachers and tourists in what promises to be a public relations bonanza for the National Aeronautics and Space Administration.

...

Last year, after President Reagan announced that the first private citizen in space would be a teacher, 11,400 educators applied for the flight, and that number was narrowed to 114 state finalists. The teacher-astronaut and backup were selected from this group. A similar competition is under way for journalists. Today a televised celebration of Mrs. McAuliffe's impending flight began as Barbara Morgan, the backup teacher-astronaut, broadcast a live "Mission Watch" from the Kennedy Space Center. It was carried nationally by the Public Broadcasting System.

"There's the famous clock that helps us count-down to lift-off," she told her viewers, mostly children in elementary schools across the country, in a televised tour of the Kennedy Space Center. Starting Monday, the "Mission Watch" is to be broadcast daily. On Wednesday, Mrs. McAuliffe, who was born in Boston and teaches high school in Concord, N.H., is scheduled to broadcast two live lessons from space to the nation's schoolchildren. According to space agency officials, more than 800 reporters have requested credentials for this mission, a huge surge.

In the last several missions the number of reporters at the launching site has dwindled.

New York Times, *25 January 1986*

Earlier in the chapter, I pointed out that organisational factors must be operating correctly to maintain control over the 'assembly line,' the assembly of all the components that must come together in the correct order at the appropriate time to produce a safe flight, the first step in the value stream. If we look at the Space Shuttle Programme in the light of manufacturing and assembly lines, the first question that comes to mind is: who is the customer? This is a very good question to ask, especially in terms of national monuments. When you approach a manufacturer and ask them about manufacturing a product, one of the first questions you will get from them is, 'who is the customer and what do they expect from the product?' Considering America's oldest holiday, Independence Day, commonly known as July 4th, is a day that simultaneously belongs to everyone, yet nobody 'owns' it; it is a signifier of national identity, a collaborative national Cultural Monument that all Americans have inherited through their enculturation, often by birth, but not necessarily so. Anyone can inherit a national Cultural Monument and identify with those who hold that monument dear.

In the case of the Space Programme and the Cold War in the 1950s, one could say that for the Soviets, Sputnik was a Blue-Sky Monument: a monument to the technical achievements of the Soviet Union. On the other hand, Americans did not (with very few exceptions) inherit the Soviet system and all the Soviet monuments: like Lenin, Marx, and Engels, Sputnik could be said to be the antithesis of a Blue-Sky Monument for Americans, which I call a Dark-Sky Monument. A Dark-Sky Monument for the A-Team can be, and often is, the competition's Blue-Sky Monument.

Going back to the first sentence on NASA's web page – 'The Cold War between the United States and the former Soviet Union gave birth to the space race...' – I do believe, ladies and gentlemen, that we have identified the American Space Programme as a national Blue-Sky Monument. Therefore, we should consider the Space Shuttle Programme as another American National Monument like Independence Day. The Space Shuttle had its day, and is no longer held up as a participant in the geopolitical battleground. As a product, the Space Shuttle is now obsolete and there are no more orders being placed. But if we are to investigate the Value Chain, that is the sum of the processes which produced value for the primary customers of the Space Shuttle Programme, we will need to identify the customers who had influence within the operations of that programme in its day. That is beyond the scope of this inquiry, but I would like to name a very prominent customer of the Space Shuttle Programme and identify the product this customer most likely requested. As we know, monuments can mean many things to different people, but to Ronald Reagan, the Space Shuttle was indeed the technological masterpiece designed not only to carry items to orbit, but to bury the competition in the space race, especially the Soviet Union. In 1982, President Reagan announced a national goal for the US Space programme to accomplish in the next decade: 'The first priority of the STS program is to make the system fully operational and cost-effective in providing routine access to space.'

When a product fails to meet the expectations of the customer, it is often helpful to examine the Value Chain from start to finish to uncover veto nodes within the feedback mechanism that controls various aspects of the product, including how much of the product to produce, what properties the product should have and what standards it should meet before being forwarded on to the customer. This has been referred to as a Value Chain Inquiry. Let us next have a look at the Concorde disaster using what we have already learned and adding a Value Chain Inquiry.

Understanding Value Chains helps organisations to understand the full range of processes that produce the product or service they were designed to produce. Through error, these processes cannot produce a 'better' product than that which they were designed to produce. Often, unless the Value Chain process is tightly controlled and well adapted to its environment, errors will produce a worse outcome, sometimes far worse than intended.

The past can be a dangerous thing. In this case, the STS programme's past had a series of twenty-four successful missions, and as you now know, the Trojan Horse Folly applies. This was likely due to the fact that there had been no serious accidents up to that point, and therefore there was no obvious internal threat to act as a unifying call to action. Just as Nokia's continued success became its golden handcuffs, Morton Thiokol and NASA had twenty-four successful previous missions. Ongoing success fosters a deep attachment to the existing operating practices. Primates as a group are naturally quite conservative. This is summed up by the maxim of the Three Wise Monkeys, and nobody, or almost nobody, wants to hear about O-rings or lifeboats or other safety issues when the flags are flying high.

If the Value Chain is diverted by a powerful leader primarily to boost his personal brand and to inflate the pride of a nation, these implied goals may conflict with the safety of the passengers and crew, and often these processes will be somehow maladapted to one or more aspects of the environment, setting the stage for a disaster. Each step in the Value Chain of a human design is analogous to an iteration of evolution: each version of a plant or animal either lives or dies in its habitat – either it can account for its environment or it cannot. Design by evolution is design by brute force. Those who had the power to scrub the Challenger launch were unaware that they were players in a much wider system: a system in which human lives were involved, a system dependent on judgement, and that judgement constituted the difference between intelligent design and the brute force of design by nature. Ultimately, due to overarching geopolitical priorities, chance or randomness, which are the tools of evolution, was allowed to enter a designed system and disable the ability of that designed system to account for its very cold environment – a point of weakness in that designed system.

PILOTING A [FLAWED] NATIONAL MONUMENT: THE CONCORDE DISASTER

/ TO SQUANDER A FORTUNE IN PUBLIC MONEY, BILLIONS AND BILLIONS, STUBBORNLY CARRYING ON WITH A CONCORDE WE CAN ONLY SELL TO OURSELVES.

Jean-Jacques Servan-Schreiber

It was to be the trip of a lifetime. A group of mostly German tourists, forty-nine of them from the German State of North Rhine–Westfalia, had boarded a Concorde chartered to ferry them from Paris to New York, where they planned to join the cruise ship MS *Deutschland*, which would take them through the Panama Canal to Ecuador, ultimately arriving in

Sydney two days ahead of the start of the 2000 Olympic Games being held there that summer. But after rotation and lift off, their Concorde suffered a loss of two engines and was unable to gain altitude. A huge flame was visible to witnesses on the ground, some of whom said that the plane was actually on fire before it left the runway. The combination of a deceleration and overloaded tail of the aircraft produced a nose-up stall, a roll-over, and a crash. The plane slammed into Hotel Hôtelissimo, an establishment serving budget-conscious travellers and businesspeople, killing four of its workers, one of whom was a French–Algerian youth on her first day of work. The hotel owner, Michèle Fricheteau, barely made it out alive, suffering burns during her escape from the fireball engulfing the hotel lobby. In total, 100 passengers and nine flight crew were killed, alongside the four on the ground. The French Transport Minister, Jean-Claude Gayssot, grounded Air France's Concorde fleet until the accident was fully explained. Though British Airways continued with its Concorde service up until mid-August, it soon followed suit when ordered to do so by the Civil Aviation Authority. It was the only fatal crash involving the Concorde over its twenty-seven years of operation.

CONCORDE: FAR MORE THAN AN AEROPLANE

An aerospace project that cost over a billion pounds could never just result in the aeroplane equivalent of the pretty-girl-next-door. The project, financed by French and British taxpayers, cost many times the original sticker price of £170 million, and after a long, expensive, and painstaking gestation period, Concorde supersonic passenger service became a reality in January 1976. Always controversial, the Concorde project needed fans. It was the product of a transactional relationship, an arranged marriage between historic enemies France and Britain with no escape clause. The progeny of this marriage needed eternal glamour, and the worldwide wonder-and-admiration-driven fan club supplied that in ample quantity.

The Concorde was the world's only supersonic commercial passenger jet to attain regular service. It was also arguably the most famous and glamorous aircraft the world has ever known, producing a value stream that is difficult to quantify, since it was the only reliably and continuously operating source for supersonic passenger transport in the history of the world. Economic sustainability aside, it became exactly what it was intended to be: a great monument to the technical achievements of France and the United Kingdom. The design and power of the aircraft allowed it to fly 800 mph faster than any other transatlantic passenger jet. People around the world came to regard the product of this massive collaborative effort as an icon of the twentieth century. Captain Mike Bannister, Chief Concorde Pilot for British Airways, said that 'Concorde was born from dreams, built with vision and operated with pride.' Michael Heseltine, the British government's former Minister for Aerospace, said that Concorde's creation was the second largest project ever undertaken by man after the American Space Programme. Though he noted that some would always view the Concorde programme as a misuse of resources, he countered: 'Now the dream has come true. Flying on the Concorde is like flying in any other plane – until you step off and look at your watch.'

DID THE WORLD NEED CONCORDE?

Looking back on the Cold War period, it is clear that the United States was well on its way to becoming a world power. The Americans were becoming conspicuous with the memory of their contribution to the Allied victory of World War II, technical achievements in aviation and the American Space Programme, their pending domination of the unfolding passenger jet market, and of course with their very American mass consumption. The British and French political elites, therefore, needed some sleek materialistic one-upmanship, but mostly their own market to dominate, without playing second fiddle to the American aerospace industry.

Like Coca-Cola and Pepsi dividing the American soft drink market, the appearance of the US Boeing 707 and the Douglas DC-8 in 1958 quickly dominated the international marketplace supplying airlines with passenger aircraft. The world's first commercial jet airliner, the British de Havilland Comet, suffered two 1954 breakups over the Mediterranean in mid-flight that killed all on board. After a two-year grounding that served as a cautionary tale to both Boeing and Douglas, de Havilland found itself behind the eight ball and never regained its initial momentum. Independently, both France and Britain understood their aircraft industries would fare poorly in the struggle for a share of the subsonic aircraft market, leaving long-range supersonic passenger transport as the obvious means of taking on American aerospace. Neither historical nor natural allies, the French and British views of the Concorde differed slightly based on, one could argue, national character. The British seemed keenly aware of the economic and political pitfalls of spending taxpayers' money to build a supersonic passenger jet with limited seating and cargo capacity. To the French, however, Concorde was much more than a money pit; it was a French National Monument, a symbol of French achievement, and to both countries, the Concorde project represented a challenge, on an international scale, to American technical and manufacturing prowess. Concorde was never really about pure business practicality or pure consumption, but an object of consumption, a totem of national pride and admiration which depended on the flying business and political elite for financial vindication. Concorde was simultaneously a combination of elegance and speed, a vision of a united Europe and a beautiful symbol of national achievement, the sum of which did not depend on economic viability, public utility, or genesis in the distant past to gain authenticity.

A STAR IS BORNE

Concorde flew for the first time on 2 March 1969. It was televised the next day, becoming one of the most watched events in British television history. The event marked the beginnings of a glamorous career narrated by hyperbole: *ground-breaking, technological marvel, supersonic marvel, superb technical achievement, metal monster, aviation wonder, supersonic giant, national treasure, the most glamorous aircraft ever built.* But while Concorde was typically viewed as exclusively for the rich and famous, the plane's movie-star quality gave a vicarious thrill to the public when it flew overhead. A transatlantic ticket aboard Concorde could put you in the company of the likes of Paul McCartney – said to have once sung Beatles songs on a flight – Joan Collins, Naomi Campbell, Eric Clapton, and Elton John. For pilots, flying Concorde was not only glamorous, it was a 'magical experience.'

Concorde came out-of-the-box as a star. Its maiden passenger-service flight from Heathrow to Bahrain on 21 January 1976 was validated by a crowd of 50,000 onlookers assembled just to catch a glimpse of the take-off. Journalists noted that a superstar had left with 100 passengers and nine crew aboard. The news coverage fed the public interest, and the public, in turn, consumed the news coverage in a near-perfect, circular feedback loop that they seemed to never tire of; however, the number of everyday Britons and French who would ever set foot on a Concorde as a passenger was a tiny fraction of the population. Concorde was rarefied air indeed, just dripping with luxury, a tantalising glimpse into a supersonic, glamorous, utopian future.

Concorde became an enormous shared goal on a national scale in both France and Britain. For engineers, it was the equivalent of today's young computer scientists longing to work at Apple or Microsoft; it was the project everybody wanted to work on. It had a certain prestige factor. But like almost any monument handed to the people of a nation, Concorde was not free of controversy. The flying equivalent of a 1970s gas guzzler, Concorde entered service in the wake of the 1973 oil embargo and subsequent crisis. Concorde thus became less attractive to airlines as projected operating costs skyrocketed, with multiple orders and options being cancelled – including Pan Am, Continental, TWA, Japan Air Lines, and American Airlines.

In 1980 it was established that around 8 million Americans lived close to airports where noise pollution was considered disruptive and possibly harmful. The Federal Aviation Administration (FAA) established noise standards in 1969, and in 1976 required that older aircraft not in compliance with those standards be retrofitted with noise reduction equipment. Concorde, with its high take-off speeds using reheat (afterburners) and the sonic boom produced at supersonic speeds, was a potent noisemaker, and studies conducted at the time found higher incidences of birth defects and death rates in areas within a six-mile radius of LAX and London Heathrow, and further, psychiatric admission rates were significantly higher around busy airports than in rural control areas. Still, Concorde backers pressed for landing rights in US airports.

The US Congress refused to finance America's own Supersonic Transport, dubbed the SST project, leaving space for the French and British governments to double down on lobbying to get the Concorde into US airports. With only one airport directly under the control of the Federal Government, Washington Dulles, Concorde finally had a home base in the New World, the result of a hard-won battle with opponents, including President Jimmy Carter. After a sixteen-month probationary period, Concorde landing rights were made permanent, and the aircraft went on to procure landing rights in other airports, despite the noise concerns. Initially refusing Concorde, the Port Authority of New York was taken to court by Concorde's ultimate sponsors, the French and British governments, and the Supreme Court eventually ruled against the Port Authority. Court challenges significantly delayed Concorde landing rights in other airports under the control of state and local governments.

There was a joke about Concorde: no aircraft had ever caused as much discord. Of course, the name was meant to symbolise, at least figuratively, the cooperation between the British and French that made such an endeavour possible. The technical cooperation was not seamless, but it was probably the aspect of the joint venture that had the least turbulence associated with it. There was scarce a doubt that Concorde, as a technological marvel, could achieve regular operations, but the questions remained: what would the final cost of the project be, and exactly what was the real purpose of Concorde? What were the real needs of Britain and France, and how did Concorde's economic performance serve those needs? Journalists pointed out that Britain's share of the Concordes was 'actually sold back to the same taxpayers who have paid for their production, through their national airlines, all so that a few businessmen could pay [a large sum per round-trip ticket] to arrive in America four hours earlier, a first class fare, plus a 20% surcharge ...' It was predictable that as Concorde ushered in the age of supersonic passenger transport, there would be endless optimism and fanfare, or at least sufficient to drown the concerns of the doubters. But cost overruns pushed the final tally up to the £2 billion range, split between the French and British governments, paid by taxpayers, and written off and never recovered in any tangible manner. Concorde ended up costing more than nine times the original sticker price, a sign that Concorde was willed into existence almost as if by brute force, without regard to the cost of the venture. A British columnist joked that he had been aboard the world's first supersonic aircraft to make a profit, and it cost him only two dollars. He had paid a visit to the Boeing 2707, intended to be much larger and faster than Concorde, flying at about Mach 3, which was only at the prototype stage when it was cancelled by Congress. When the programme was scrapped, the physical prototype was bought by entrepreneur Bill Magruder and put on display, with tickets selling for $2 each. While Concorde struggled, the Boeing 2707 raked in cash, but the latter never left the ground.

THE 'CONCORDE EFFECT'

On Concorde's first flight to California in September 1986, about 40,000 people waited, some having camped overnight, for its arrival at the Ontario, CA airport about fifty miles east of Los Angeles. The sleek, other-worldly Concorde was thoroughly lapped up by a gobsmacked public, whether in France, Great Britain, or the United States. Concorde's appearances at air shows, first at Farnborough and then at Coventry, were associated with throngs of fans, many of whom arrived early to catch a glimpse. At the Coventry Air Day in August 1981, for example, the crowds yearning to gawk at the Concorde flyover were estimated at 85,000. The organisers described the event as a £15,000 gamble which paid off, thanks to the 'supersonic crowd-puller.' Headlines described Concorde as a 'supersonic tonic for city air day' as 'cameras clicked, eyes popped and mouths opened in awe as the giant white delta-winged bird skimmed 100 ft above the crowds.'

Concorde clearly had star power, a less tangible value for those who could not shell out the required £10,000 for a transatlantic return flight. Over Concorde's years in service, however, many fans had an opportunity to take a short pleasure flight on the Concorde at affordable ticket prices.

BUILD IT, AND CONCORDE WILL COME

They called it a white elephant.

Humberside International Airport's future lay in the hands of the County Council. The old Royal Air Force bomber runway, nestling in rural Lincolnshire near the village of Kirmington, was too short to accommodate a modern passenger jet fully loaded with holiday travellers and their luggage. There were two larger airports within seventy miles of the diminutive airport which had a distinct advantage over sparsely-populated Lincolnshire: both were in more densely populated areas, and due to the higher numbers of passengers, could offer a much wider range of scheduled flights than Humberside, threatening it with obsolescence. Airport closures due to a decline in demand for aviation services were an outcome within the realm of possibility.

But someone had to carry the flag of aviation for the region. Humberside County Council had resisted the pressure to sell off the airport, and had instead worked hard to earn the airport's 'International' designation, a rarity in the region. What would happen to the historical airfield in the hands of outsiders? Lincolnshire, in the East Midlands, has deep roots in aviation going back to the Great War. During this period of conflict, around 6,000 people were involved in the manufacture of 3,500 aircraft and at least 3,000 aircraft engines, and on 1 April 1916, the first military air academy opened at Cranwell, near Lincoln. During World War II, Lincolnshire became known as bomber country due to the number of RAF bases located there, with nearly fifty airfields, more than anywhere else in the United Kingdom. These airfields covered approximately 30,000 acres of the county and accommodated 80,000 RAF personnel, their importance rooted in their geographic proximity to Northern Germany. Redundancy and possible closure of the region's only link to the wider world was unthinkable. The little airport needed a survival plan.

It was well understood in the 1980s and 1990s that a great deal of airport traffic was actually generated in the north of England, but those passengers had to travel down to London to board flights to European capitals. Newly published forecasts showed that regional airports could grow much faster than Heathrow, Gatwick, or Luton, which, it was forecast, may be approaching saturation by 2005. Humberside International Airport Ltd, wholly owned by the County Council since 1986, formulated its plan not only to survive, but to thrive and take advantage of the new potential. In 1989 they hired Bill Savage, originally from Liverpool, as the new managing director. The ambitious go-getter had been brought in to mastermind the runway extension process at Humberside since he had already been through the same process at Leeds–Bradford Airport in Yorkshire. The Humberside budget constraints cut final plans to a paltry £8m, in contrast with £22m for the Leeds–Bradford extension project. But Mr. Savage remained optimistic, as the Civil Aviation Authority said the region within a forty-five-minute drive of Humberside Airport had generated 750,000 air travel passengers in 1987, the vast majority holidaymakers to the Mediterranean and North Africa. It was 'good news for Humberside,' and 'a market just waiting to be tapped,' according to Savage.

AN ACE IN THE ATOL

While at Leeds–Bradford, Savage noted the huge crowds drawn to the airport to catch a glimpse of the Concorde. An estimated 70,000 people arrived on 2 August 1986 when an Air France Concorde charter flight landed for the first time. Savage saw first-hand the publicity and tour operator profits generated by the Concorde. This gave him an idea for Humberside. Rather than wait for outside companies to charter flights into Humberside, an Air Travel Organisers' Licence (ATOL) from the Civil Aviation Authority would enable Humberside International Airport to charter its own flights. Humberside became the first airport to have this license.

As the summer of 1991 rolled in, work on the runway extension had started, and was complete by about twelve months later. Plans began to take shape for the Concorde extravaganza scheduled for the 14 June 1992. Newspapers announced the event:

A dream comes true

> THE visit of Concorde is the final seal of approval on what started as a dream in 1968 and has now become Britain's fastest growing regional airport. The first prototype Concorde was less than a year away from its first flight when the old Lindsey County Council first sat down to consider a plan to turn the old bomber airfield at Kirmington into an airport. ...] the airport has steadily grown ... There have been some setbacks, but those in charge of the airport's affairs are still blessed with the foresight of their predecessors ... It was this faith in the future which led the present county council to invest £8million in the lengthening of the main runway. And it is because of that runway that today we are celebrating the visit of the world's favourite aircraft to the country's brightest airport.

Grimsby Daily Telegraph, *13 June 1992*

[A caption to a photo of the Concorde rotating upward:]
WE HAVE LIFT-OFF: Concorde is set to put the final touch to Humberside Airport's growing importance. This year the airport has become Britain's newest departure point for Mediterranean holidays. *Hull Daily Mail*, 18 March 1992.

The Concorde made two landings at Humberside on 14 June 1992. Headlines declared a 'Fascination for a metal monster.' News coverage of the event described an estimated crowd of 20,000 gathered to see the Concorde, which was chartered for seven hours. Ticket prices were affordable, and there were several excursions to choose from. All in all, 300 passengers flew on the Concorde that day from Humberside. The Concorde Extravaganza became a recurring event at Humberside International, with repeats in 1993, 1994, 1995, 1996, and 1997, with reported attendance up to 37,000.

CONCORDE DESIGN AND OPERATION: ADAPTING UNUSUAL CHARACTERISTICS TO TYPICAL CONDITIONS

One could argue that the origin of Concorde began with the earliest powered human flight in 1903, or even with man's earliest dreams of powered flight. Each stepwise aeronautical improvement yielded information that could be used as a basis for the improvement of the following generations of aircraft through a continuous improvement process. Half a century after the Wright Brothers took to the sky, the earliest concepts for a British supersonic passenger service were discussed in a 1954 study group involving the Royal Aircraft Establishment under the control of the British Army, concluding that more research into supersonic aerodynamics was needed. The British government formed the Supersonic Transport Aircraft Committee (STAC) in 1956, and the Concorde programme started in earnest with a treaty between the unlikeliest of partners, France and Britain, to jointly develop the supersonic transport which was signed on 29 November 1962. It was the first significant cooperative aircraft design venture.

A major design hurdle with Concorde was the type of wings to use. The wings needed both to produce sufficient lift at subsonic take-off speeds attainable on existing runways and to be stable enough for flight at the planned Mach-2 cruising speed. 'Delta' wings not only optimised speed by reducing drag, but provided sufficient lift for take-off and landing at subsonic speed. This design exhibited sufficient but not excessive lift at supersonic speeds and reasonable handling during landing, but necessitated special pilot training that included instruction on compensating for ground-effect handling characteristics unique to this wing design upon landing. Delta wings also required take offs and landings at steeper angles. Another design peculiarity was due to the lower lift characteristics of the delta wing configuration: practically the entire loaded weight of the aircraft was borne by the landing gear and tyres until rotation and take off. Pilots and engineers were aware that Concorde was particularly hard on its undercarriage. This design compromise would require the tyres to be essentially marvels of engineering. On Concorde's first ever landing in North America in 1976, inspectors found a tyre which they felt was excessively worn, and insisted upon its replacement. The unusual take offs and landings also needed a visibility engineering hack: the nose piece was thus designed to tilt to facilitate vision during taxiing, take off, and landing due to the sharp angle of attack.

The validation of the Concorde design took 5,000 hours in wind tunnels, large capacity computers, and other research. A specific aluminium alloy was selected as the basic structural material, chosen after evaluation of many thousands of available alloys for mechanical properties, fatigue strength, resistance to corrosion, and 'creep,' the deformation of metal caused by interaction between mechanical loadings and high temperatures.

The Concorde fuel tanks were designed to take on sufficient fuel for taxiing to the runway, typically two tonnes (4,400 lbs) of fuel due to the extreme inefficiency of jet engines operating at low speeds. Concorde's engine intakes were also modified to control engine efficiency at subsonic and supersonic speeds. This gave Concorde's pilots more control over power surges and allowed power to remain level throughout the different temperatures, airspeeds, and air pressures the aircraft would encounter during its ascent from ground level to its cruising altitude of 60,000 feet (18,300 metres). The engines were fitted with reheat (afterburners) that could provide a power boost of up to 20% without additional bulk to the engines. This feature was key to Concorde's ability to take off on existing runways, reaching a V2 (take-off safety speed) of about 214 knots (nearly 250 mph) within the maximum runway length requirement of 3,600 m/ 11,800 ft for maximum load. The initial climb out speed for Concorde was 250 knots and accelerating from there. A point to note here is that the typical V2 for a jumbo jet is 188 knots (airspeed). The decision speed, V1, is the speed at which the aircraft probably cannot be stopped within the runway length after an engine failure. The V1 for a jumbo jet is approximately 160 knots, whereas the V1 for Concorde was 165 knots; but due to the very fast acceleration of Concorde, that speed was reached relatively quickly, and a decision to abort would necessarily have to be made very quickly, a response time that pushed the limits of human decision-making.

The required training of a Concorde pilot was well beyond that of a typical passenger aircraft. For an existing licensed pilot candidate, it took six months to prepare for Concorde, as opposed to two months to qualify on other aircraft. The first two months were technical in nature, capped off by a qualifying exam. Those who passed would spend the next two months in the simulator, learning normal and emergency operation of the aircraft. This was followed by a series of practice take-offs and landings before supervised passenger flight training with an instructor. Certification was followed by continuing education and more practice on simulators to stay current on emergency procedures. The overall design and operation of Concorde was characterised by a great deal of time, effort, and expense. As a supersonic passenger transport, the Concorde programme needed to establish, from scratch, the additional requirements above and beyond those of subsonic passenger design and operation. Additionally, the pilots, flight crews, and maintenance and ground crews needed extra training above and beyond the preexisting requirements for subsonic aircraft.

A RED FLAG EMERGES

Concorde Blows a Tire

BRISTOL, England, April 7 (UPI) – The British version of the Concorde, the supersonic jetliner built by Britain and France, blew a tire while on taxiing practice today. Officials said further tests would be made and the plane would make its maiden flight Wednesday. The French version has already been flown. *New York Times*, 8 April 1969.

The NTSB is an independent federal agency in the United States responsible for investigating accidents involving transportation of goods, fuel, and passengers within the boundaries of the United States and incoming traffic from outside those boundaries. After a series of four incidents over a twenty-month period involving Concord tyre blowouts, in 1981 the NTSB issued a letter to the French bureau responsible for accident investigations.

In June 1979, at Dulles International Airport, a Concorde experienced the blowouts of two tyres on take-off, resulting in flying debris which punctured a fuel tank and resulted in a two-square-foot hole in the left wing, and ruptured hydraulic lines involving the left side braking system. The Concorde returned to Dulles and was safely landed by the pilot, Air France Capt. Jean Doublaits. An Air France spokesperson said that the tyre incident was unprecedented for Concorde. The NTSB letter stated that 'tire debris and wheel shrapnel resulted in damage to the No. 2 engine, puncture of three fuel tanks, and severance of several hydraulic lines and electrical wires.' A second similar incident at Dulles occurred in July 1979, and the Concorde landed safely at Kennedy International Airport. Two more incidents were outlined in the letter, one in October 1979 and another in February 1981. The letter described 'serious concern' about the blowout problem and stated that these incidents were 'potentially catastrophic' and could result in a fire or an explosion which could be caused by overheated parts such as tyre rims skidding on the runway. Air France responded that they were planning to install 'flat tyre detection systems' on its seven Concordes.

But despite these apparent precautions, incidents involving Concorde's tyres continued. In early August 1981, a Concorde piloted by Captain David Brister was taking off from Kennedy International Airport when multiple tyres burst and rubber debris flew into an engine, rendering it inoperable. Further, broken landing gear was flung up and ripped a hole in the fuselage. A British Airways official remarked that the pilot 'would not have had time to abandon the take-off if the plane had been going ten miles an hour faster.' The supersonic jet came to a halt just twenty-five yards short of the end of the runway. It was thought that the tyre bursts were caused by runway debris. In 1993 a tyre-burst incident not only broke a water deflector on the undercarriage, but debris punctured a fuel tank. Concorde pilots had for years complained about the problems with burst tyres.

A CASSANDRA APPEARS

In 1987, after a ten-year stint at Arthur D. Little Inc., a world-renowned chemical safety consulting firm, Dr. Albert Moussa started BlazeTech, a company formed to investigate fire and explosion risk in aviation systems, including aircraft vulnerability and accident survivability. Dr. Moussa consulted for the FAA regarding the vulnerability of aircraft fuel tanks to explosion, initiated by the TWA flight 800 crash in July 1996. Dr. Moussa investigated the potential for fuel tank damage caused by foreign debris, and the results of this study were published in 1997 under the title 'The Potential for Fuel Tank Fire and Hydrodynamic Ram From Uncontained Engine Debris.' While the study did not replicate the events which occurred three years later in the Concorde disaster, it did show how the process of 'hydrodynamic ram' can occur: as the debris from an engine breakup or Concorde tyre blowout impacts the fuel tank, the tank experiences an increase in pressure within, and the forces can be released through the weakest part of a tank wall, thereby causing a rupture in the tank wall matching or exceeding the size of the penetration or near-penetration. With a string of tyre-fragment-impact events causing fuel leaks and structural component failure, those who had the authority to pause Concorde passenger service would have had adequate impetus to call for tyre re-engineering, fuel tank structural reinforcement, and rupture risk abatement measures.

THE CRASH AND THE FIRST CLUES

On a hot summer day in Paris, Air France Flight 4590, scheduled to depart on 25 July 2000 and serviced by Concorde F-BTSC en route to New York, crashed just minutes into flight. The French Transport Minister, Jean-Claude Gayssot, grounded Air France's Concorde fleet until the accident was fully explained, and British Airways soon followed suit.

On 16 August 2001, the Bureau Enquêtes Accidents (BEA) determined that a tyre blowout caused the crash and recommended suspension of Concorde's certificate of airworthiness. France's equivalent of the FAA (the DGAC) and Britain's Civil Aviation Authority followed through on the recommendation.

The runway used by Flight 4590 was quickly isolated from further air traffic and thoroughly investigated and photographed from a helicopter. As sections were combed through, the first clue was a piece of fuel tank no. 5 that was found lying on the runway. This piece was determined by analysis to have been pushed out of the aircraft by a hydrostatic force resulting from an impact. A bent metal strip was found nearby, which was later determined to be a part from another aircraft. Also recovered from the scene was a 4.5-kg piece of rubber tyre, whose condition suggested that it had been sliced into by an object. This tyre fragment is thought to have been the projectile that slammed into the body of the aircraft, setting off a chain of events that eventually caused the crash. It should be noted that both the metal strip (not part of the Concorde) and the large chunk of rubber tyre (from the Concorde) were located on the same runway slab.

THE DNA OF DISASTER DIAGNOSIS

When considering designed disasters, it is quite helpful to approach the event as a product of a factory. As I have said earlier, designed processes typically cannot produce a product better than that which they were designed to produce; flawed processes often produce a product which is far worse than intended. Like the *Titanic* and the Space Shuttle, the Concorde was a very well designed and constructed passenger transport machine into which the designers put years and conducted thousands of tests to verify prior to construction. These designers and builders embedded their knowledge and skills into the physical structure of the vessel. But, like the *Titanic* and the Shuttle, the intelligent design of the operation of the aircraft was altogether another matter. If you think of each flight in the way an object is made in a factory, i.e., the Value Chain, you can start to understand how the 'factory' made errors concerning the quality of the final product.

THE CONDITION OF THE PASSENGER VESSEL

Undercarriage

Human Folly #3, Trojan Horse.
The Concorde's physical condition was poor at the outset of the flight. Concorde's undercarriage used a unique spacer arrangement designed to keep the wheels supporting the aircraft straight and true. Concorde is the only passenger aircraft that used a design requiring a spacer and there was no external indication that would alert an inspection team that the spacer was absent. The Air France ground crew undertook a maintenance procedure for the first time ever on the day prior to the flight, and upon reassembly, inadvertently left the spacer in the aircraft hangar, meaning the spacer was left out when the undercarriage truck was reassembled. According to John Hutchinson, a British Air Captain who flew the Concorde from 1977 until his retirement in 1992, the spacer was required to maintain alignment

of the wheels on the landing gear. Without the spacer, the wheel may not have run straight and true, being able to spin at a range of motion of about three degrees on a vertical axis, similar to a shopping trolley wheel. The BEA accident report also noted that this was the first time a change of landing gear bogie had been undertaken on Concorde at Air France.

Fuel Tanks

The aircraft's fuel tanks were overfilled. Human Folly #3, Trojan Horse. Essentially, the aircraft took on a minimum of 2,000 kg of taxi fuel. The fuelling system was designed to stop at 82 or 83% full, leaving air space in the tank. However, for the flight in question, the quantity of fuel loaded into tank no. 5 was around 94% of the total tank capacity. Fuel tanks are routinely designed to function with an airspace since fluids are not compressible. Impacts to the fuel tank can be absorbed by the air bubble, similar to the function of a pneumatic shock absorber. From the BEA report section 1.16.7.3, The Fuel in Tank 5: 'It has been established that the aircraft began taxiing with tanks completely full.' This fuel was not burned off completely during the short taxi run. The amount of fuel burned off was closer to just 800 kg.

Loaded Weight of the Airframe

The aircraft's airframe was significantly overweight. Human Folly #3, Trojan Horse.
Concorde's stated maximum take-off weight for the conditions is said to be 185,070 kg. However, according to the BEA report, the total weight of the aircraft at the beginning of the flight was 186,900 kg. But this may not have accounted for the extra taxi fuel taken on by Captain Christian Henri Marty, as well as the luggage of late-arriving German tourists. According to Captain John Hutchinson, Captain Marty authorised Flight 4590 to take on additional taxi fuel beyond the normal two tonnes (2,000 kg). Fuel tank no. 5 was overfilled, leaving an imbalance owing to a heavy left side. Further, after the refuelling process, Captain Marty allowed the luggage from the German tourists to be loaded, even though the aircraft would

certainly be well overloaded. In all, there were nineteen pieces of luggage allowed on-board that were never weighed.

Again, according to Capt. Hutchinson:

> About half an hour or 20 minutes before it was due to pushback, up comes the dispatcher telling the captain that he's leaving nineteen bags behind. "Why?" asked the Captain. "Because you're overweight," said the dispatcher, "and therefore I'm not putting them on." Captain Marty: "Oh, no, no, no, these passengers are joining a cruise ship, they need their baggage."
>
> And you can imagine this is not lightweight baggage. These are people going from New York, through the Panama Canal to Sydney for the Olympics, so this was the trip of a lifetime, and they were going with their dinner jackets, their ball gowns and the whole shooting match.
>
> Then the Captain said "Is there physical space to put those bags on?" And the dispatcher said "yes, we can actually put them on, but you're going to be way overweight and your centre of gravity is going to be out."
>
> Captain: "Oh, just stick them on, it won't matter. So now 19 bags were put into the baggage hold at the rear end of the aeroplane."

Captain Hutchinson explained that the taxi time to the take-off position at Runway 26R was only a few minutes. This short time did not allow them to burn off more than 800 kg of taxi fuel. This, combined with the nineteen bags of luggage that were unaccounted for, put the aircraft approximately three tonnes overweight, with the centre of gravity slightly to the rear. This contradicts the BEA report, which suggested that the aircraft was only 810kg over the maximum safe take-off weight. The report also claimed that any loss of performance due to this excess weight was negligible. However, it did mention that: 'The maximum structural weight on take-off being 185,070 kg, it appears that the aircraft was slightly overloaded on take-off, regardless of the hypotheses used to make the calculations.'

THE ENVIRONMENT OF THE 'FACTORY FLOOR'

We will consider the environment of the Concorde as the factory floor. By considering the factory environment this way, we can easily identify potential problems.

Weather conditions: the planned runway had an 8-knot tailwind at take-off.

Human Folly #3, Trojan Horse, and Human Folly #4, Marie and Pierre Curie Folly.
We now understand that an intelligent design, i.e., a passenger vessel, must interact with its environment. If the operators of the vessel misunderstand how their vessel will interact with natural phenomena present in the immediate environment of the vessel, we categorise it as Human Folly #4. Often, however, Human Folly #3 also applies, since the accompanying misunderstanding is misinterpreting the true nature of the human-designed passenger vessel.

The flight operations manual for Concorde specifies that the tailwind limit for a take-off is 20 Kt. The procedure to avoid this problem would be to taxi to another runway in the opposite direction, to enable taking off into a headwind. The 8-knot tailwind lowered the maximum safe take-off weight to 183,300 kilograms due to a tyre speed limitation. By various calculations intended to determine the possible extent of overloading, Flight 4590 was at the minimum 600 kg, but possibly as much as 2,951 kg, or almost three tonnes, overweight. According to section 2.5.1 of the BEA report, the fact that the crew protested neither the captain's announcement that the aircraft would be taking off above the structural weight limits nor into a tailwind, which would further reduce the maximum safety take-off weight, is telling.

Carrying a quantity of fuel as a fixed taxiing allowance which was clearly higher than the estimated quantity required for the real taxiing time and the anticipated wait on the ground does not appear to be a satisfactory practice. This does, by and large, appear to have been a common practice on flights which were critical from the fuel perspective. This excess fuel did not attract any comment from the captain, apart from his remark that they were going to take off at the aircraft's structural limits. Equally, the controller's announcement of a tailwind did not lead to the slightest comment from the crew, which is, as we have seen, surprising.

The same report mentions that 'it was impossible to discover whether the crew took possession of the flight dossier, even though it had become redundant. The load sheet, including the fuel loading sheet and the captain's signature, was not found.'

Presence of a foreign object on the runway.

Human Folly #3, Trojan Horse. Essentially, this is a man-made iceberg in the path of the vulnerable passenger vessel.
One of the cardinal rules of the DNA of Disaster Methodology is that all intelligent design MUST account for its environment. The factory floor contained an obstacle the Concorde design was demonstrably vulnerable to, a miniature 'iceberg.' The infamous strip of metal that fell off of a Continental Airlines DC-10 was mentioned in the BEA report summary in the first sentence of the summary. What is known about this event is that this DC-10 departed about five minutes prior to the departure of Flight 4590. This strip was found at slab 152, 1,740 metres from the point of origin of the Concorde. In reconstructing the mechanism of the fuel tank puncture, the investigators concluded that the strip of metal scalped a large chunk of rubber, weighing about 4.5 kg, off the right front tyre of the left side undercarriage (tyre no. 2) when the aircraft was travelling at 240km/hr (173 knots). The investigation concluded that this large chunk of rubber was flung up into the underside of the Concorde at an estimated speed of 140 metres per second (310 mph). The kinetic energy was transferred to the fuel tank (no. 5). The report also stated that:

At the time of the accident, there were no national regulations relating to surveillance of the movement areas on French aerodromes, such as those derived from standards and practices recommended in Annex 14 to the Chicago Convention. For an aerodrome the size of Paris Charles de Gaulle, Annex 14 recommends carrying out inspections at least twice a day in order to monitor the condition of the movement area and to communicate information relating to operations or concerning aircraft performance.

A hole in fuel tank no. 5 appeared, and caused the release of fuel from the aircraft.

The report said that the rupture of fuel tank no. 5 was caused by a mechanism that had never been seen on civil aircraft before the accident. The physics of this mechanism is theoretical, and the outcome was never fully reproduced under controlled conditions. Therefore, it is difficult to determine the precise process by which the debris on the runway led to the fuel tank hole and subsequent flame, and the mechanism is thought to be indirectly related to the piece of rubber scalped off the landing gear tyre. It did not puncture the fuel tank, but instead created a shockwave inside the tank. Since this tank was completely full, there was nowhere for the energy from the impact to be absorbed. Essentially, the shockwave was reflected off the opposite side of the tank and focused on a small and possibly weak section of the fuel tank. The focal point of this wave was likely a 32x32 cm piece of the wall of the tank. This piece of tank was found lying on the runway in about the same location as the chunk of rubber tyre. This tank fragment upon visual examination was found to have been petaled outwards, and the conclusion was made that the forces that displaced this fragment came from within the tank.

The stream of fuel from the fuel tank ignited, causing a blowtorch of flame emanating from the underside of the left wing. As the fuel came pouring out of this hole in fuel tank no. 5, it became atomised and ignited. The source of the ignition is not completely without controversy, but according to the BEA report, the most likely sources were one of three possibilities: an engine surge, an electric arc, and contact with the hot sections of the engine and/or reheat/afterburners. The engine surge was eliminated due to the temporal findings that the fuel leak and flame occurred just prior to the first engine surge. Of the two remaining possibilities, investigators concluded that the most likely source of ignition was from arcing of the cables in the landing gear wiring harness.

The Concorde started to veer off the runway toward the left.

Human Folly #3, Trojan Horse.
Concorde veered off the runway, toward an Air France 747, carrying President Chirac and his wife. This event is poorly explained in the BEA report. What is known is that the Concorde veered to the left about eight metres from the centreline. This phenomenon in cars is attributed to uneven tyre pressure and improper wheel alignment.

What is also known comes from a photo that was taken from inside the Air France 747. This photo shows that the Concorde came very close to a collision as the 747 was waiting to taxi across the Concorde's take-off path on its way back to the terminal. In the final few seconds before rotation of the nose of the aircraft for departure, the flight officer exclaimed, 'watch out!, 'as the left side engines suffered their first loss of thrust. By then, the captain had already begun to deflect the rudder to the right to correct the aircraft's pull to the left. According to the investigation, significant damage was absent to engine no. 2 (left side, inside engine). This leads to the conclusion that the surges and loss of power on engine no. 2 were due to the ingestion of hot gases emanating from the flaming fuel leak, whilst the loss of thrust on engine no. 1 was likely caused by ingestion of hot gases and/or tyre debris.

Vr (Velocity of Rotation) was at 183 knots, 11 knots under normal speed. As the Captain pulled back on the control column to lift the nose, the flame was noticed by observers while the first engine surge occurred. For a brief moment, engine no. 1 recovered to 80% of nominal thrust and the calibrated air speed reached 196 knots. In the next ten seconds, the aircraft continued to veer off to the left side of the runway, and an edge light was smashed by the Concorde's wheel no. 6 as the path deviated

22.5 metres from the runway centreline. Within two seconds of this, the aircraft departed from the ground at a speed of 205 knots. This early rotation at low speed could have been a response by the pilot to avoid a collision with the 747. The famous photo of the scene, taken by Japanese businessman Toshihiko Sato, a passenger on the plane carrying President Chirac, showed that the Concorde was already aflame upon lift-off. This image would become the 'public face' of the disaster.

The flight engineer shut off engine no. 2 without permission from the captain.

Human Folly #3, Trojan Horse.
About two seconds from effective take-off, the flight engineer said, 'Failure, engine two,' followed by an engine fire gong. The flight engineer then said, 'Shut down engine 2,' and in the same instant, the captain ordered the engine fire procedure. This breached all embedded cockpit procedures for an engine fire during take-off. Concorde engines had a built-in fire extinguishing system, but the procedure stipulates that a 400-foot altitude and stable flight must be achieved prior to initiating the engine fire procedure, and then only upon the Captain's command. The engine fire sensors were unable to determine the difference between hot gas intake and an actual engine fire, so the flight crew had no discernible information to base a decision upon other than procedural algorithms. The aircraft was already tail-heavy, and becoming rapidly more so due to the fuel loss close to the midline of the aeroplane. The centre of gravity should normally be at about 54% of the total length, but was at a minimum of 54.2% aft. The tendency of the Concorde design to stall and rear up if the centre of gravity was too far aft was a known phenomenon. The test pilots were well aware of this, and it was included in the training for Concorde pilot qualification.

The landing gear would not retract.

The cockpit voice recorder examination revealed that the crew struggled to get the landing gear up so the aircraft could gain speed and height, but the gear was stuck and would not move. The BEA report concluded that the origin of the non-retraction of the landing gear could not be determined. As the fire destroyed the wing and the left landing gear, the fate of the aircraft was sealed. The combination of the excess drag, the lack of thrust, an overweight airframe, and the continuous blowtorch of flame consuming the underside of the aircraft caused the Concorde to stall, roll over, and crash into a hotel in Gonesse.

Normally, the folly which would apply here is Human Folly #3, Trojan Horse. But the events at this point are beyond the crew's human decision making. The designers of Concorde embedded their designs during the planning and prototyping phase of Concorde's development, but they could not anticipate the exact events which caused the crash, and could not account for this exact sequence of events in the embedded design of the aircraft. We acknowledge that a designed system has a dynamic range of function, that is, the ability of the system to account for events of novel complexity presented by the environment. But when the system is presented with conditions that exceed the dynamic range of the embedded compensation mechanism(s), the possibility of a failure enters the scene. In this case, the embedded systems could not compensate for the combination and severity of the 'factory defects' and the final product was far worse than the system was intended to produce.

The BEA Report Summary:

> During take-off from Runway 26 right at Roissy Charles de Gaulle Airport, shortly before rotation, the front right tyre (tyre no. 2) of the left landing gear ran over a strip of metal, which had fallen from another aircraft, and was damaged.

CRASH ANALYSIS

As discussed in the *Titanic* chapter, while Concorde was a remarkable achievement for its time, both the design and operation of Concorde showed a lack of understanding of the basics of intelligent design. That is, as I have written in earlier chapters, *all* aspects of the intelligent design must account for *all* aspects of the environment within which the design will function. This includes the local environment on the ground when the aeroplane is in operation. The Concorde crash exposed a major flaw in the operation of movement areas of airport runways prior to the accident. When the Concorde crashed, there were no international standards regarding clearance of foreign-object debris from the traffic surfaces of airport runways. Aviation experts remarked that a 'teaspoon in Concorde's path' would have been enough to cause a tyre burst. After the crash, the first continuous runway monitoring system was launched at Vancouver International Airport in 2007.

According to the DNA of Disaster Methodology, the designers neglected feedback from the early operation of Concorde and failed to adequately adjust the design for limited runway space and high tyre speeds and loads. Just like the *Titanic*, the Concorde hit an 'iceberg' placed there by the environment. Just like the *Titanic*, the Concorde operation team was blind to its existence in the span of time just prior to impact, and the crew was unable to avoid collision with this iceberg. Again, the catastrophic potential was derived mainly from the speed of the vehicle upon encountering the iceberg. In contrast, however, the runway of the Concorde was more like that of a railroad or just a road, rather than the open ocean. The embedded design present in the runway was much the same as any road or railroad and accounted for obstacles that would have been present prior to the construction of the runway. Tragically, there was no runway at CDG or any other airport designed and constructed specifically for Concorde, with its quick acceleration, high take-off speeds, and tyre vulnerabilities. The runway should have been much longer and much more vigilantly inspected. The time for decision-making in the cockpit shrunk to mere seconds in the event of a mishap, and the lack of adequate runway length to slow the speeding Concorde safely in the event of a tyre blowout or other catastrophe did not exist.

Designers of the runways were unable to account for an aircraft design which did not yet exist at the time of the runway design and construction. Therefore, Concorde was, by design, maladapted to the existing runway design and management. An optimal Concorde runway would have had more length to handle the stretched-out Concorde requirements safely in the event of an aborted take-off. Further, the operators of Concorde were unwilling or unable to demand runway foreign object detection and removal prior to take-off. In this regard, the airports where Concorde would be taking off and landing would need to screen for foreign object debris on runways each and every time a Concorde used them. This would have been impractical, slow, and expensive, but anything less would be leaving safety to chance. Of course, runway inspections take time, exactly what the Concorde was expected to save.

A COMMERCIAL FLIGHT: A QUALITY PRODUCT PRODUCED IN A TIGHTLY CONTROLLED ENVIRONMENT?

One can think of each passenger flight as a performance of an assembly of different parts to come together and produce a product, i.e., a safe flight. To produce value for the customers, who are mostly the passengers on board, the 'factory' starts out with a well-designed vessel, in this case a Concorde, which must be maintained, checked, and loaded properly, must function properly, and all environmental obstacles and conditions must be accounted for by the pilot or piloting systems and software. If a designed system is giving off noise, that is the system sometimes produces an unexpected result, the conditions that produce this unexpected result should be thoroughly investigated.

The Concorde tyre blowout problem was a known problem and had a recorded history prior to Flight 4590. As stated earlier, it was established during legal proceedings that during Concorde's time in service, there had been seventy tyre-related incidents resulting in fifty-seven runway tyre failures. This system was clearly producing noise but there was no internal effort to address the corresponding problems. This was likely due to the fact that there had been no serious accidents up to that point, and therefore no obvious threat to act as a unifying call to action. Continued Concorde success fostered a deep attachment to the existing operating practices, even though the system was obviously producing spurious results. The DNA of Disaster Methodology suggests the existence of a cognitive bias produced by the past success of the Concorde programme and the additional cognitive bias produced by the aircraft being a National Monument of both France and Britain. The 'factory' producing the product had to function within this environment.

Flight 4590 showed a sloppiness from the outset, beginning with the incorrect assembly of the landing bogie on the left side of the aircraft by the Air France technical team two days earlier. One flight crew member's medical clearance had expired nine days prior to the flight. Then there was the overfilling of the fuel tanks, the addition of the nineteen unweighted tourist bags, and the request for the use of the entire runway, an indication that the flight crew was aware of the overloaded airframe. In addition, there were no protests from the co-pilot or other crew members regarding the overweight take off with a tailwind. To top it off, the runway had not been checked for twelve hours prior to the Concorde take off. This factory was out of control and delivered a product so riddled with defects it was doomed to crash with no way out. This fecklessness left entirely too much to chance. Safety of operations begins deep within an organisation; in this international effort, no one was really in charge of the entire programme. Evidence of this was as simple as the lack of any defined method of updating the design or operation of the Concorde fleet as new information became available throughout the years of passenger service. Like the *Titanic* and the NASA Challenger disasters, there were precedents to the catastrophe in question: new information became available during the early operational years that called into question the assumptions made during the design and construction process. Re-engineering tyres and shielding or reinforcing of the fuel tanks could have been demanded had there been accountability.

If we consider a typical automobile or smartphone factory again for comparison purposes, those products are produced by a long series of steps from initial design, prototyping, supplier coordination, and assembly and quality control. The Toyota production system taught the world that best practice is that any person on the factory line can stop production when they spot an error. This may seem counterintuitive, since the part or unit with an error can be corrected at the end of the line. However, this does nothing to stop future cars and smartphones from having the same error built in. It is much better to solve a quality problem when it first becomes known than to rely on 'rework' at the end of the line. The notion here is that a process to produce a car or smartphone is optimised to produce that particular car or smartphone. Value for customers consists of a

product that functions as intended, a product which fulfils its promised purpose. A factory error will never produce a product variation that is better; the best-case scenario is that a fully functional car or smartphone is produced, and hopefully only a very small number of non-functional smartphones or defective cars. The similarities and differences to evolutionary design are evident here, where evolutionary design sometimes, over many generations, produces a variant that has an advantage.
A smartphone factory can only make fully functional units or paperweights. This implies that errors in designed processes will likely never spontaneously produce a better outcome by chance; errors are far more likely to produce a worse outcome. Rework at the end of a crash means recovering the pieces to find out what happened.

In the end, Captain Marty was piloting a National Monument. There had been so much glamour and admiration heaped upon Concorde as well as hopes and dreams of a futuristic utopian supersonic age that the operators and public were misled into a fool's paradise. The French newspaper *Le Monde* recognised it for what it was in 1969, after the first Concorde prototype 001 went airborne with test pilot Andre Turcat in the cockpit. *Le Monde* presciently observed that Concorde 'was created largely to serve the prestige of France ... [it was] the expression of political will, founded on a certain idea of national grandeur.' Unfortunately for the safety of the passengers and crew, nobody wanted to look too closely at such a revered national treasure to find flaws and 'stop production,' preferring instead the fostering of a form of supervised neglect. The safety of a designed system hinges on the availability of a veto player – someone who is in a position of authority to stop operations Toyota-style when a major defect is discovered on the factory floor. Thus, the factory floor, by design, was certain to reproduce the defect over and over again until a crash occurred.

The purpose of Concorde was to boost national pride with a challenge to American commercial aviation supremacy. As we discussed, the United States of America had a trophy programme of its own, a National Monument known as the Apollo Programme which was not much different than the national pride heaped upon the *Olympic* and *Titanic* superliners of the early twentieth century or the US's installation of the Space

Shuttle Programme which followed Apollo. As I have said before, there is a tendency to overlook safety concerns when national pride is at stake. Nobody, or almost nobody, wants to hear about tyre problems, O-rings or lifeboats when the parade flags are waving.

LESSONS FROM DESIGNED SYSTEMS PRODUCING UNEXPECTED OUTCOMES (AKA NOISE)

A component of the DNA of Disaster is that when a designed system starts to throw off noise, it is prudent to find its origin. Concorde had a burst tyre incident before its very first flight, while taxiing on the runway. By 1980, there was sufficient evidence that a redesign of the Concorde undercarriage was warranted, and a shielding of the fuel tanks should be considered. Another related lesson: tightly-coupled event cascades leave little room for error. The *Titanic* disaster taught us these two principles many years before. The inability of ships to avoid objects such as underwater rocks, reefs, icebergs, and other ships was a glaring indicator of the designed system's inability to account for its environment and the entrance of chance into the system. The O-ring problem with the Shuttle's SRBs, the Shuttle's External Fuel Tank foam-shedding problem, and the tyre problems with the Concorde show us that a designed system producing noise can go unnoticed and uninvestigated for years. Sunken or lost-at-sea ships that are not amenable to inspection can hide the failure(s) in their design and provide little in the way of design feedback. Reusable components available for inspection are a valuable constituent of designed systems, as are easily inspectable components. A critical component that requires disassembly for inspection is clearly a design choice, a potential problem, and must be accounted for.

Iceberg

A strip of metal was struck by the speeding Concorde tyre. While this iceberg was man-made, it was thrown at the Concorde by the environment. While Concorde tyres had, in the past, shown the tendency to shred spontaneously and fly upwards towards the aircraft underside, the sequence of events leading up to the crash indicated that the tyres were vulnerable to both small runway debris and to spontaneous shredding. Either way, directly or indirectly, the tyres produced the iceberg which brought about the crash.

Randomness and the Designed System

The Shuttle design displayed a similar weakness: the operators of the system failed to consider the factory floor when deciding whether or not to assemble the parts within the factory and produce the intended product – a shuttle flight.

In order to function properly in the design, the shuttle booster O-rings were required to be supple and freely able to move into their sealing position. Since cold O-rings lack this ability, the pressurised gases from the solid rocket motor got past the seal and compromised the ability of the O-rings to maintain a seal throughout the burn of the rocket. Chance (a component of evolution) entered the designed system, leading to unpredictability, providing a random path for the escaping hot gases to emerge from where they did. Had the blowby (by chance) started 180 degrees away, on the other side of the rocket, there may have been no accident. The game of Russian Roulette NASA was playing was leaving things to chance, that is, a partially controlled instead of a fully controlled release of energy. The factory floor delivered a product somewhere between a completely controlled burn and a volcano, somewhere between intelligent design and evolution.

Our original question at the beginning of this section was this: what blinded those who had the power to adapt these designed systems to their respective environments? In other words, what blinds the operators of a system to the 'iceberg' in the environment? We can now better answer this question with the understanding that cognitive control requires feedback from the environment. The small child learning to ride a bike must also learn to avoid potholes.

Feedback Authenticates the Designed System

Markets provide feedback in the form of the Chain of Tribute, i.e., payment for products or services. The Chain of Tribute follows the Value Chain, in which the production of value to the customer is accompanied by a reverse Chain of Tribute, a direct transaction. This reward for producing value becomes the basis for further production. If the Chain of Tribute dries up, production dries up as well. In a centrally planned economy, there is no Chain of Tribute which directly accompanies the Value Chain, hence the legendary scenes of huge surpluses of boots of the wrong size and the shortages of products actually needed inside the Soviet Union.

Those who operated Concorde could easily measure the transactional Value Chain by the Chain of Tribute which accompanied ticket sales. But the Value Chain of a Cultural Monument is altogether another matter. Those who look 'under the hood' of Independence Day celebrations and find slaves indifferent to the suffering of their masters at the hands of the British Crown will not find many inheritors of Independence Day willing to acknowledge the hypocrisy at the origin of their beloved Cultural Monument. In the same way, one could argue that Air France, along with Captain Marty and his crew, did not look too closely at their beloved symbol of French technical genius to find flaws. A Blue-Sky Monument may only be blue on the surface. Discovery and familiarity with regard to an imperfect Cultural Monument may indeed breed contempt, or at the minimum, disillusionment.

The Challenger disaster taught us that the NASA of the 1980s suffered from the same blindness as a Soviet-style planned economy. A product was designed, prototyped, and put into production, but it was poorly adapted to the changing environmental conditions (the field-joint design) and did not completely meet the customers' needs. An imbalance between expected production and actual production capabilities began to take shape. The successes, all twenty-four of them, gave the customer a false sense that their future needs could be met by the current product, while the feedback information containing evidence that the designed system was throwing off noise (O-ring blowby) did not make the journey back to cognitive control (NASA upper-level management) or, further, another customer, President Reagan, who, like the Concorde passengers, was completely divorced from any environmental feedback until the disaster. Unlike the Concorde passengers, who had no control over their situation, the Gipper was free to impose a cognitive bias onto NASA management in the form of geopolitical priorities. This could, in turn, place direct pressure on NASA management to suddenly disregard any information indicating there may be a safety problem with the SRBs. This is the force which caused a pivot from normal operations: pulling information needed to justify a launch from those on the production line to pushing the justification upon those same Value Chain workers. Much of the Challenger has been recovered, as has the Concorde. Even the *Titanic*, lying at the bottom of the ocean, has been found and recorded. But the designed system which produced the Challenger disaster has been scattered into the shadows. I argue that the hidden component unavailable for inspection is actually Reagan's directive to move the TISP forward and launch the shuttle regardless, which, if I am correct, has remained classified up to today, and constitutes what blinded NASA managers to the warnings from Thiokol engineers. NASA managers placed themselves in the veto player position, formerly occupied by contractors such as Morton Thiokol or Rockwell. Those NASA managers were always veto players, but now, instead of preventing an unready vehicle from launching, they were blocking any feedback information from the engineers who were right next to the production line (the origin of the Value Chain or Value Stream) and were preventing this feedback from reaching cognitive control. Cognitive control was thus handed over to an entity (the Gipper), who was completely unaware of the environment and did not even know to look for the binoculars in order to check for icebergs. Therefore, the process which was designed to produce a successful mission at best, produced a far worse product than it was designed and intended to produce. Intelligent Design must either account for or control its environment (or both). Any design that fails to do so will be considered semi-intelligent design, subject to evolutionary forces, i.e., survival or extinction. Monuments, especially politicised Monuments, can create the conditions for disaster by reshuffling priorities, handing over cognitive control to agents which have neither information about the physical environment containing the designed system, nor the ability to control the environment that the designed system operates within.

Looking back on the Challenger disaster, it is now apparent that with the increased shuttle flight schedule demands, NASA would need to launch year-round, in colder weather as well as in typical Florida weather. Had any person the power to stop production, Toyota-style, to force engineering to solve the O-ring problem, the resulting pause for reengineering would have greatly helped to make the entire system less sensitive to environmental conditions, and would have allowed NASA more flexibility to meet the additional flight requirements from customers. Unfortunately for the astronauts aboard the Challenger, the penalties for doing so would be tantamount to career suicide. Like the Concorde system entering a state of post-engineering supervised neglect, the Challenger entered this phase after only twenty-four flights.

The Challenger disaster also highlights inherent deficiencies in hierarchical control structures. One veto node controlled by a veto player is capable of inducing a specific blindness in cognitive control. Further, these governmental agencies or military types of hierarchical structures with clearly defined reporting boundaries are very susceptible not only to veto nodes, but also to individuals with higher rank or status diverting the processes for their own ends, such as an American President and his geopolitical ambitions. This, I argue, is what appears to have happened with the Space Shuttle Challenger Disaster.

Likewise, the design, engineering, and manufacturing prowess of France and Britain were embodied and celebrated by Concorde. Captain Marty played the part of Captain Smith of the *Titanic*: he allowed himself and his flight crew to be lulled into a fool's paradise and they were blind to the Concorde's weaknesses. When the Concorde disaster occurred, we had seen it before. Perhaps the iceberg was a little different; the path taken by the vessel was of course a runway rather than the ice field in the North Atlantic, or the Challenger launch pad in Florida which was about to be pummelled by an ice storm the night before the planned launch. The Concorde suffered from a vulnerability – the tyres were too sensitive to speed, load, wear, and small obstacles on the runway. It was not determined whether each tyre blowout was due to an obstacle impact or a tyre defect. The differences between these two causes are worth mentioning, though. If the blowouts were due to speed, wear, and load, it would be akin to the Space Shuttle Challenger disaster fourteen years prior and the Columbia disaster that occurred three years later. In Challenger's case, a blowby problem, under just the right set of conditions, allows escaping burning gases to breach the containment of the cryogenic fuels in the External Tank. In Columbia's case, it is the ongoing presence of an External Tank foam-shedding problem where chunks of foam enter the environment and may impact and damage the Orbiter during launch. In Concorde's case, the tyre chunks flung off at high speed become debris, enter the environment, and become analogous to a manmade iceberg impacting the vulnerable underside of the Concorde – the area of the fuel tanks. In the other scenario, the tyre is vulnerable to existing debris on the runway and sets a cascade in motion, placing the aircraft structure at risk. It seems perhaps that both scenarios were true, not investigated prior to the crash, and very troubling.

The Human Follies were also the same as in the Space Shuttle disasters: Human Folly #3, the Trojan Horse Folly, which is misunderstanding the true nature of an intelligent design, applies to those involved in making judgements about the safety of the flight and the vessel. They were unaware of the actual condition of the vessel, completely unaware of the iceberg, and also unaware of the effect any 'iceberg' would have had on their vessel. This lapse in judgement ultimately meant that the intelligently designed vessel could not account for its operational environment. Chance entered the scene in just the right conditions, and brute force overwhelmed the vessel, its passengers, and crew.

The design weaknesses in Concorde were swept under the rug throughout almost its entire passenger service career. These weaknesses were an open secret, but not dealt with until there was a catastrophe. If the Value Chain is distorted by a need to inflate the pride of a nation with the success of a passenger vessel which doubles as a Cultural Monument, the continuous improvement of that passenger vessel and the systems and processes that support it may be interrupted by the need to carry on with the operations of that passenger vessel. This implies a need to keep up the appearances of success, since the vessel is intertwined with the pride and identity of a people and a nation. This implied priority hierarchy may conflict with the safety needs of the passengers and crew, and often these processes will be somehow maladapted to one or more aspects of the environment, setting the stage for a disaster. Each step in the Value Chain of a human design is analogous to an iteration of evolution: each version of a plant or animal either lives or dies in its habitat – either it can account for its environment and thrive within it, or it cannot. Design by evolution is design by brute force.

Those who had the power to pause Concorde passenger service failed to recognise the need and the urgency to do so, even though Concorde represented a designed system in which human lives were at stake. Concorde was a system dependent on judgement, and that judgement constituted the difference between intelligent design and the brute force of design by nature. Ultimately, the change in priorities – i.e., the need to swell the pride of a nation – blinded the operators of the system and allowed chance or randomness, which are the tools of evolution, to affect the designed system. Further, the distorted priorities disabled the technical improvement of that designed system to improve its ability to account for runway debris in its environment and other problems affecting the Value Chain.

> "History is a constant race between invention and catastrophe. Education helps but it's never enough. You also must run."

Frank Herbert, *God Emperor of Dune*

The Shuttle Disaster of the 1980s and the Concorde Crash of 2000 had happened before – the scene had already played out in 1912 when the Titanic, piloted by the undaunted, guided by the unseeing straight into the unknown, grazed the side of an iceberg in the middle of the North Atlantic at full speed. Will we ever learn?

THE WORLD'S ONLY CARBON-FIBRE SUBMERSIBLE

Startups are a lot like cults. They are centred around a belief held by a wise or charismatic founder and impressed upon a core group of early adopters. Ideally for the founder, those who are somehow 'caught' by the startup are more than just employees working for a pay packet, but true acolytes who align with the sense of mission, belief set, and direction of the startup as prescribed by the visionary. This little cadre of disciples must be handpicked and easily written into the storyline of the visionary's dream. It is well understood in Silicon Valley that for this reason start-ups take on the personality of their founder. Two well-known examples of this phenomenon are Steve Jobs of Apple and Elizabeth Holmes of Theranos, who adopted a persona that emulated the former. Initially a reluctant cofounder, Jobs helped shape the rules and norms of the tech industry with his focus on design aesthetics and minimalism, obsession with detail, and a relentless pursuit of perfection, while Holmes broke those rules in pursuit of building her startup, investing a lot of attention and effort into hiding the fact that she was breaking those rules, flying under the radar, out of sight of potential critics. Holmes' Edison machine, a printer-sized device supposedly able to run a battery of tests on a single drop of blood, never functioned well enough to run an actual test and produce a usable, reliable result. That's the point where Theranos had a run-in with fundamental science: batteries of blood tests cannot be run on a single tube of blood by current technology, let alone a battery of tests on a few drops. Theranos needed to first develop the fundamental testing technology before it had any hope of miniaturising those tests. Elizabeth Holmes, almost never seen out of her Steve-Jobs-like character, was extremely effective as an evangelist for her startup, but she had no Steve Wozniak counterpart creating miracles in the laboratory. She did have some scientists working on the problem, but the basic science had not progressed significantly beyond existing testing technologies, and the laboratory methods were well-established, where best practices were already standard in the industry. Like most fields of science, the biological sciences plod ahead, with each laborious advancement hinging on prior understanding, thorough vetting, and demonstrated reproducibility. The science Theranos needed was not nearly ready yet, but the business deals were way ahead of the non-existent tech. Her genius was in parlaying her dream into a small empire of invested dollars before inviting anyone who had the slightest inkling of the diagnostic sciences into the fold. Holmes, a nineteen-year-old Stanford dropout who had grown up steeped in the family's hereditary ties to the Fleischmann's Yeast empire, had just the right amount of pixie dust to be believable, and she founded Theranos in 2003. By 2013 Holmes had raised more than $700 million from venture capitalists and investors, giving it a valuation of around $9 billion. During this incredible ramp-up, nobody bothered to look under the hood to see if the technology actually worked as advertised, until the wheels fell off the whole venture. Another startup with an element of pixie dust was OceanGate, owner of the world's only carbon-fibre submersible, which was also the world's only five-passenger sub capable of reaching the *Titanic*. Its swashbuckling designer and builder, Stockton Rush, continually boasted that he was breaking the rules. While Holmes dodged transparency and accountability for most of the years Theranos was in operation, Stockton Rush had critics. Lots of them.

Like most people, I was completely unaware of the existence of the *Titan* submersible prior to its disappearance. By the time I knew anything about OceanGate or its CEO, Stockton Rush, he was already dead. But the moment I had learned about the *Titan* submersible as a one-of-a-kind deep-sea passenger vessel, I immediately knew he had taken paying passengers on board an unproven prototype vessel, the exact capabilities of which turned out to have been deftly marketed but also strongly disputed. This I had seen before; this, we had all seen before. Yet another example of a passenger vessel pushed beyond its limits by an operator who did not understand those limits. Who, exactly, was Richard Stockton Rush III, and why was he taking himself and paying passengers to 2.4 miles under the ocean to view the wreck of the *Titanic* in an experimental, unproven, carbon-fibre submersible?

IN SEARCH OF STOCKTON RUSH

The deep ocean entrepreneur was born on 31 March 1962 into a wealthy and well-connected family. He was a direct descendant of two of the signers of the Declaration of Independence on his father's side, a mythos which reflected in his given name, Stockton, a name that also functioned as a marquee, so that all would know the true legitimacy of the actor strutting and fretting his hour on the stage. Relatively unknown, he had a modest career as an American businessman and engineer, but is now best known as the co-founder and CEO of the defunct deep-sea exploration company OceanGate, which had only a handful of manned submersibles. Not only was Stockton Rush the leader of this startup, he was a member of a much smaller subset of startup leaders, describing himself in this rarefied group as a 'daredevil inventor.' This appetite for risk revealed itself at a young age when, already a licensed pilot, he built his own fibreglass plane from a kit while still an undergrad at Princeton. Rush took upon himself a daredevil narrative that he probably invented and encouraged, or at the very minimum embellished, since there was nothing cutting-edge about fibreglass plane kits by the late 1980s, even if assembled and flown by such a young person. After graduating from Princeton University, Rush began his career in aerospace engineering and then worked for McDonnell Douglas as a flight test engineer on their F-15 programme. But his dreams of being an astronaut were dashed with his first setback: his eyesight was not adequate to be accepted for Air Force pilot training, the well-established fast-track to NASA. He later transitioned to venture capitalism and moved to the Pacific Northwest in 1989, and in his free time began scuba diving in nearby Puget Sound, an enthusiasm dating from his teenage years. But the freezing temperatures in the local waters put him off, as he was used to diving in more southerly locations such as Tahiti and the Cayman Islands. Still with a lingering interest in space, he attended Richard Branson's 2004 launch of SpaceShipOne from the Mojave Desert, which demonstrated that a privately designed, financed, and operated civilian craft was capable of reaching space. Branson proudly declared the beginning of the age of space tourism, and revealed his plans to offer wealthy passengers the chance to travel to the edge of space and experience weightlessness while viewing the Earth from eighty miles high. The ticket price for this history-making venture was planned to be $190,000 in 2007; by 2023, it had a waiting list of around 800 individuals, some of whom had paid the current price of $450,000. Upon learning this, Rush said that his interest in space tourism suddenly vanished, telling the Princeton Alumni Weekly in 2019 about how this early obsession with space was fed by pop culture, but then he had a sort of epiphany: 'I realised, it's all in the ocean.' This would be his only genuine pivot, but not the only pivot he would need.

Journalist Tony Perrottet visited OceanGate headquarters in Everett, Washington in 2017 for a test 'dunk' of the *Cyclops-1* submersible in Puget Sound. Describing Rush's quest for innovation, Perrottet observed that 'in his zeal for innovation, Rush stands out even in the elite manned submersible community, which attracts wealthy and eccentric individuals willing to risk their fortunes on wildly uncertain endeavours.' But Rush started out a bit on the conventional side, with existing operational submersibles, again nothing approaching the cutting-edge. In 2006, two years after the first flight of the Branson rocket reached the edge of space, Rush said he developed an interest in underwater tourism after a transformative experience on a submarine in British Columbia. He attempted to purchase a submersible but was unsuccessful, discovering that only a very limited number of privately-owned submarines existed worldwide. Rush came upon the same problem that would confront Branson: there was no existing market for commercial space travel, so Branson himself was forced to develop the vehicle he would need to take paying passengers to space. In the absence of any Hertz or Avis for submersibles, Rush constructed a miniature submersible he called 'suds' using blueprints provided by a retired US Navy submarine commander. The feeling of immersion into the sea teeming with life from the inside of a submersible elated him. Rush was hooked. 'I wanted to sit in a submarine and watch crabs fighting to the sound of Mozart for two hours,' he said. He told Perrottet that he recognised a wide-open business opportunity, the result of a quirk of history that the ocean tourism market was not being served, partly due to the ongoing perception that underwater exploration was inherently dangerous, and partly due to the strict regulations regarding manned submersibles: the Passenger Vessel Safety Act of 1993, which specified how passenger vessels must be constructed and tested, and prohibited passenger vessels from diving below 150 feet. Rush believed that behind these barriers was a huge untapped market and need for exploration, noting that funding for ocean research expeditions is a tiny fraction of the resources given to NASA. Rush presented himself as a visionary who saw in the oceans what others did not see, or perhaps refused to see, and he had it all wrapped up in a tidy little narrative. His lines were well rehearsed, a world of little stories and explanations for his pivot to the deep oceans, and pat answers to common questions regarding his approach to safety or reliance on innovation. His direct connections to America's foundational generation, a story in itself that he had probably repeated a thousand times, his Princeton degree, his father's Princeton legacy, and the inherited intergenerational wealth combined to form a veneer of credibility which allowed him access to a world of possibilities which may have otherwise eluded him. But none of this would have mattered if Stockton Rush were not a storyteller. These stories gave him the most credibility with the general public, carefully, craftily conjuring an explorer mystique that would come to deflect some very good questions about his operations.

Around 2007, Rush made plans to found a company that would make and deploy submarine passenger vehicles. The long-term thinking was that the commercial success of the passenger trade to the wreck of the *Titanic* would fund the development of submersibles intended for use in undersea resource extraction and disaster mitigation, which Rush projected to be a huge market he could exploit with manned submersibles; an effort to capture some of the deep-sea work that was currently fulfilled by remote underwater robots. In 2009, OceanGate Expeditions was founded by Stockton Rush III and Guillermo Söhnlein with the purchase of the *Antipodes* submersible, a craft built in 1973 and which had made more than 1,000 dives. After a 1999 refurbishment, the *Antipodes* was capable of supporting five individuals for up to 72 hours, and was certified to dive to 1,000 feet. OceanGate began operations on the West Coast, focusing on providing manned deep-sea submersibles, and by 2010 began transporting paying customers in leased commercial submersibles off the coast of California, in the Gulf of Mexico, and eventually in the Atlantic Ocean. Two years later, OceanGate expanded its operations to Florida and the Caribbean, collaborating with the University of The Bahamas and focussing on the development and execution of submersible expeditions and research-based programmes. 2013 was a pivotal year for OceanGate, which announced a collaboration with the University of Washington on Project *Cyclops I*, a proposed new 3,000-metre-qualified five-person submersible. However, the collaboration abruptly ended after completing about $650,000 worth of work on a $5 million collaborative research agreement. The details on the parting of ways are sketchy, but cofounder Guillermo Söhnlein left OceanGate that year as well, although he retained a minor stake in the company. The collaborative effort resulted in OceanGate gaining a steel-hulled, oblong submersible with a large viewport capable of diving to 500 metres, a significant departure from the original plan for a sub rated to 3,000 metres. An innovation of sorts, the *Cyclops-1* was very conventional, able to seat five passengers, made of typical materials, and sticking to the known operational envelope for these types of submarine vessels. *Cyclops-1* took paying passengers to the wreck of the *Andrea Doria* off the coast of Nantucket. But Rush had the *Titanic* in mind: he needed a vessel capable of diving to 4,000 metres or 2.4 miles under the ocean's surface. 'There's only one wreck that everyone knows,' he told Perottet. 'If you ask people to name something underwater, it's going to be sharks, whales, *Titanic*.' A nod to the gravitational power of a nearly universal Cultural Monument such as the *Titanic*. Yes, this we had seen before.

Rush certainly had no hopes of beating the first three billionaires into space. In light of the undeniable evidence of a designed disaster, we must examine his motivations. What could have driven the need to redirect his ambitions to the deep? It's now clear that Rush entertained plans to do for deep ocean exploration what Richard Branson, Jeff Bezos, and Elon Musk are currently doing for space travel; he wanted to open up the deep-sea to tourism. 'I was exploring space, but [now] I'm exploring inner space,' he explained. But Rush was already wealthy through inherited money, so was the attainment of more wealth his end goal, or was it something else? He was clearly obsessed with the deep sea, but was there potential for a really huge expansion in deep-sea tourism? It would amount to creating a whole new industry, passenger excursions to the deep, on a scale that has never been done. He needed something big to engender investor buy-in, a magnet to get tourists to shell out the kind of money Branson was poised to rake in. While we do not know exactly when or how Rush decided to take tourists to the *Titanic*, it seems to have been a clear goal before 2017, since he was recorded speaking to the Explorer's Club in NYC in June of that year stating that the best-known site in the ocean is the *Titanic*, referring to it as 'the goal,' and mentioning that all of the current subs capable of reaching it were government-owned, and not available for commercial purposes. Rush explained that in the past, there was a commercial tourist operation contracting two three-person Russian Mir subs by a company called Deep Ocean Expeditions, where the service ship would set out for the *Titanic* site, and the two subs would take turns bringing the tourists down to the *Titanic*, two at a time, about twenty-four tourists per two-week expedition. He added that the portholes on those subs were quite small, not purpose-built for tourism, and the interior was very utilitarian and not at all photogenic, which he considered necessary for sharing on social media. The location of the *Titanic* wreck lies in international waters: the jurisdiction of the Passenger Vessel Safety Act extends to about 230 miles beyond the coast out in open waters, but the *Titanic* wreck is far beyond that boundary. There is no enforcement checking the safety of passenger vessels in international waters, and so regulation would not hinder Rush in his quest. Rush just needed a passenger sub, and the first carbon-fibre sub, the *Cyclops-2*, was already in the finishing stages by 2017, and OceanGate was already planning the first dive to the *Titanic* in the summer of that year. It would be the deep-sea equivalent of Branson's 2004 flight to space.

By late 2017, OceanGate had completed its prototype of the *Cyclops-2*. Carrying passengers was the goal which, by Rush's calculations, dictated the oblong design of the original *Cyclops* sub. This shape was conserved in the *Cyclops-2*, which was renamed the *Titan* in 2018. Rush needed to keep the weight of the five-person sub down to reduce the need for buoyant syntactic foam, he reasoned, which is expensive and bulky. Conventional titanium or steel subs weigh substantially more per passenger than *Titan* – for example, the *Alvin*, the first submersible to carry human beings to the *Titanic* wreck, has room for three persons, and weighs in at 45,000 lbs. But *Alvin*'s thick titanium pressure hull allows an operating range of up to 4,500 metres. Launched in 1964 and regularly refurbished, *Alvin* has made more than 4,700 dives. In contrast, the steel-hulled *Cyclops-1* weighs 18,600 lbs, and the titanium-and-composite-hulled *Titan* sub about 23,000 lbs.

Load cycling of the steel-hulled *Cyclops-1* was expected to be comparable with ordinary submarines which have the cigar shape that everyone recognises, along with characteristics and capabilities that are well understood. The US Navy operates its submarines down to a typical depth of 450 metres, or about 1,500 feet, with a maximum depth in the range of 700 metres. Those subs are typically hulled with high-tensile steel, which is very resistant to deformation and corrosion, and also capable of rebounding from repeated pressure cycling like a spring. Submersibles, small and dependent on a mother ship for support and transportation to dive sites, also have characteristics and capabilities that are well understood. Speaking on the state of innovation in submersibles in 2017, Rush called the *Alvin* the 'premier US submersible,' adding: 'there are not a lot of pieces of high tech equipment that celebrate a fiftieth birthday.' While the *Alvin* was government-owned and mostly unavailable for most commercial operations, the *Cyclops-1* and *Titan* were not the first deep-diving privately-owned passenger subs, and certainly not the only ones in operation by 2017. Rush had a colleague who had built and operated a submersible for about twenty years by this time; a three-passenger vessel which operated out of a natural harbour in Honduras, operated by an American submersible pilot, and the two had been communicating for years.

Karl Stanley, founder of the Roatan Institute of Deepsea Exploration (RIDE), is a self-taught engineer who has built two underwater vehicles, one of which he still operates today out of his home base in Honduras. Stanley knew at age 9 that he wanted to build his own submersible and take it down for a dive. At the age of 15, he started working on his very first sub, and actually took passengers aboard once it was finally finished. It was small and cramped, so he set out to build a larger version, a unique vessel which he assembled in the town of Idabel, Oklahoma. For about two decades, Stanley's submersible was the only place where those who wanted to personally dive 2,000 feet under the ocean could actually do so. By the time Rush had the *Cyclops-2* built, Stanley had already made over 2,000 dives in his submersible. Stanley took a conventional approach to designing and building his steel-hulled submersible. Taking advantage of the accumulated knowledge and experience within the established submersible community, which had a long history of operations without accidents, Stanley said he consulted with as many people as he could with expertise in designing and building for safety, and used the examples of other submersibles to construct his submersible *Idabel*, named for the town where it was built. Stanley said that he knew Rush for around ten years, communicating by email and meeting occasionally at marine industry events. Rush was familiar with Stanley's business operations in Honduras, and knew that if he played by Stanley's rules, his deep-sea business would resemble that of his friend. While an expert operator with a clear safety record, Stanley's single-vessel business model could not readily scale up to bring in millions of dollars of revenue each year, and his submersible could not reach the *Titanic* depths. Taking tourists to the *Titanic* was an altogether different proposition, but would have the potential to bring in ticket sales approaching the price of a ride on Richard Branson's rocket. Since the *Titanic* wreck is in water 2.4 miles deep (5,280 ft) and in the North Atlantic, far from the coast, the engineering challenges were on a different level, and Rush understood this as necessitating some serious rule-breaking.

'THIS IS NOT YOUR GRANDFATHER'S SUBMERSIBLE'

Rush's stated vision for OceanGate was to make the oceans more accessible to the general public. He repeatedly condemned what he considered excess safety regulations as an impediment to growth in the industry. But his heterodoxy seemed to be accompanied by a simple wish to provoke his listener, using nonsensical, even startling phrases, referring to the safety record of current submersibles as 'obscenely safe.' Was it really 'obscene' that they were so safe? Provocative indeed. This dissonance seemed to imply that this excellent safety record was mutually exclusive to the concepts of cutting-edge design and operation; if no red flags were going up, there was a dull, rote, mechanical quality to deep-sea exploration that was stifling his sense of adventure. His use of a gaming controller, for example, was not unprecedented, and actually made sense, given that the controllers were nearly ubiquitous, and in case of emergency, the chances that someone on board would be familiar with the controller were relatively high. Also, the small size of the controllers made them easy to have an extra as a spare, and he relished the surprise of the observer in the juxtaposition of such a commonplace item, found in practically every American teenager's bedroom, with a deep-sea pressure chamber which was the physical embodiment of the boundary between life and death. 'Stockton Rush: The Swashbuckling Adventurer' was flashing on the marquee, with a hint of an appearance by a modern-day Indiana Jones.

The conventional wisdom of submersible construction was dictated by available materials, such as steel and titanium, and the physical conditions present at the great depths and pressures the *Titan* intended to explore. Rush was constantly repeating his base assumption for why, in the face of incredible odds, his submersible design was the only one actually capable of accomplishing the feat of ushering in a commercial solution to *Titanic* exploration: 'carbon fibre is three times better than titanium on strength-to-buoyancy.' Not only did Rush choose an unconventional material with which to construct the hull of the submersible, but he also broke the mould of traditional submersible shapes. He aimed to create submersibles that were oblong rather than spherical, which he believed would provide more room for passengers and scientists. The spherical pressure chamber was a mainstay of the deepsea submersible design in order to load the hull evenly, and this 'last man standing' was the result of years of design and testing. The distribution of external force by the even loading of a spherical pressure hull allows the hull to withstand repeated cycling of pressurisation and depressurisation without the accumulation of stresses along the long axis of a loaded wall. Under load, one would expect the axial loads of an oblong wall to bow that wall inwards, combined with the intense pressure produced by the titanium endcaps, which do not appreciably flex under the enormous pressure at the depth where the wreck of the *Titanic* lies. The resulting loads on the *Titan* at maximum depth would tend to push the carbon fibre into a slight hourglass shape, thereby concentrating the forces perpendicular to the long axis of the composite walls, and more so as you got deeper. When you think a bit about geometry, a sphere does not have any walls. Any section of the surface of the sphere is basically an arch in every direction, and when you load that section, that load is distributed evenly to the rest of the structure, since it has no true walls. When you cut the sphere in two, you get two domes: simple, but able to hold an enormous load from above. Suddenly, with a dome, the direction of the force matters. A cigar shape is a sphere cut in two, essentially two domes, within which walls are added. If you compare structures that use arches, such as bridges, those structures are designed to withstand loads with a gravitational orientation – a top-down distribution of forces. But if a barge comes along and rams the wall, the magic of the arch shape is lost; the applied force is from the side and buckles in the whole structure as if it had been hit with a wrecking ball. This is what happened to the Key Bridge in Baltimore when it was struck from the side by a huge container ship.

'IT'S A NEW TYPE OF TRAVEL'

Stockton Rush seems to have told his stories whenever he could. He often mentioned that we know less about the world's oceans than we do about the surface of the Moon, citing that amongst the vast resources spent on exploiting the oceans for resource extraction, the percentage dedicated to submersible exploration is disappointingly low. As he was identifying his target market, Rush would explain that the number of private subs available to rent is rather small, and none are capable of diving below 2,000 metres, making it nearly impossible to explore the ocean bottom, where the average depth is 4,000 metres, and he was not wrong about this. He also frequently took aim at two myths that he claimed were pervasive and responsible for the failure to allocate resources to the cause. His most frequently-quoted myth was that people believed manned exploration of the oceans was dangerous. He often rebutted this myth, stating that classed, manned submarine vessels had transported fifteen million passengers, mostly in tourist submersibles, over a thirty-five-year period with no major injuries, thereby making it the safest mode of travel. His other favourite myth about the submersible industry was the assumption that submarines and submersibles are expensive, and this is why most of the current deep-sea subs out there are built by research institutions where cost efficiency is not a limiting factor and the focus is rather on capability. He also mentioned that the largest fixed cost for expeditions is that of the ships that carry the submersibles to the dive sites, noting that the larger and heavier the submersible, the larger and more expensive the support vessel needed to be.

Although Machiavelli presciently observed the difficulties and resistances in establishing a new order of things, to expend a great effort and expense to bring something new into the world and then leave its welfare to chance would seem to be the height of foolishness. Rush was certainly ambitious for change but what he carefully cultivated was not the actual safety of his submersible, but the perception of safety. This perception was directed externally to potential customers- laypersons who were not part of the submersible community. His efforts were aimed squarely at wealthy *Titanic* enthusiasts, individuals who would be unable to evaluate the true nature of his intelligent designs. Stockton Rush turned to social proof; he knew enough to bring on some team members who could lend authenticity and credibility to his operation- but this begs the question: how were these OceanGate insiders kept in the dark? One such person was Paul-Henri Nargeolet, also known as 'Mr. Titanic,' a Frenchman who had joined the French Navy as a youth and had spent a lifetime at sea, becoming more than familiar with the dangers involved, and had made thirty-seven successful dives to the *Titanic* wreckage. As a great storyteller and *Titanic* expert on board, he was present to enhance the shared customer experience, and could explain to the passengers what they were witnessing. Another was the physician–astronaut Dr. Scott Parazynski, a veteran of five shuttle missions who had reportedly 'committed' to OceanGate's mission for more than a decade. Scott referred to Rush as a 'real pioneer,' and as a former NASA astronaut, he lent great credibility to OceanGate. But there was one expert who saw what was being hidden, who would tell Rush the truth about his ideas and submersible designs as he saw them. His insight, you will not be surprised to hear, was not welcome.

TITAN'S CASSANDRA

David Lochridge was an expert submarine pilot with years of experience going back to his time working with the British Navy and the oil and gas industry. He was hired by OceanGate, and moved his family to Washington State to begin his employment, initially as a contractor tasked with 'ensuring the safety of all crew and clients.' As he became more familiar with the operations, he experienced mission creep, as his job shifted to independently certifying the sub, rubber-stamping it as fit for service without ever having put the *Titan* through rigorous testing or close inspection. As the *Titan* began to take form, Lochridge became more wary as he witnessed potential safety issues: design and build problems, flaws including air gaps in the hull material, O-rings (them again) groove errors, the viewport, which was rated to only 1,300 metres, a litany of other problems. In January 2018, when Lochridge was refused close inspection of critical components, including an ultrasonic hull scan and review of the oxygen system and the viewport among other items, he decided to create a quality control report to list the problems and requests for inspections, submitting it to Rush.

Rush's response? Lochridge was fired on the spot, and he and his wife were both served with a lawsuit claiming that he was trying to get fired. But, as a foreigner in the US on a work visa, Lochridge was almost defenceless against a far wealthier plaintiff pursuing legal action against him in a foreign country. Lochridge countersued for wrongful termination and submitted his concerns about safety lapses to OSHA, claiming whistleblower status. During this period, Patrick Lahey, cofounder of Triton Submarines, sympathised with Lochridge's efforts to bring the *Titan* up to standards, and assumed Lochridge's legal expenses as he defended himself against his OceanGate founder. Meanwhile, former OceanGate employee and deep-sea expert Rob McCallum attempted to mediate and persuade Rush to reconsider his plans. According to emails obtained by CNN, McCallum wrote to Rush in March 2018: 'As much as I appreciate entrepreneurship and innovation, you are potentially putting an entire industry at risk, I implore you to take every care in your testing and sea trials and to be very, very conservative ... In your race to Titanic you are mirroring that famous catch cry: "She is unsinkable."' But Rush ignored the pleas and responded that he had 'grown tired of industry players who try to use a safety argument to stop innovation and new entrants from entering their small existing market.'

After back-and-forth legal wrangling between Lochridge and Rush, Lochridge agreed to withdraw his claims and settle. He did not disclose any terms and has not disclosed the entire contents of the ten-page report he submitted to OceanGate back in January 2018. There were other Cassandras with warnings as well. The Marine Technology Society (MTS), which was incorporated in 1963, describes itself as an organisation which 'promotes awareness, understanding, and the advancement and application of marine technology.' The society became aware of OceanGate's activities and members were immediately concerned that OceanGate was ignoring existing safety standards, which had come about after decades of maritime experience and knowledge. MTS drafted an informal letter to Stockton Rush dated 27 March 2018, which appeared online, but was never formally delivered to Rush. The letter expressed concern that OceanGate's activities were ignoring 'best practices for the safe development and operation of new submersible technologies,' reflecting Rush's failure to have the *Titan* certified and classed. The letter stated that the manned underwater vehicle industry had:

> earned itself an enviable safety track record over the past 40 years. This is partly due to the diligent engineering discipline and professional approach exercised by members of the industry, but also due to the collective observation of (and adherence to) a variety of safety standards. This reputation is solid because it was hard won over many years of diligence application and has resulted in a safe and successful record of operation.

The letter also requested that since OceanGate had made claims on its website that the *Titan* meets or exceeds current safety standards, the submersible should therefore be submitted for independent, third-party validation and classification by a marine certification agency. The letter was signed by a number of the members of the MTS society. OceanGate never certified the *Titan*, and Lochridge, McCallum, and Patrick Lahey were unable to stop OceanGate from accepting paying passengers on its expeditions. After Lochridge's departure, Rush, who employed young engineers just out of school for $15 an hour, turned to his young finance and account administrator, offering her the role of head pilot. As she told *The New Yorker*, 'It freaked me out that he would want me to be head pilot, since my background is in accounting,' adding that she soon found a new job and quit OceanGate since she 'couldn't work for Stockton' because she 'did not trust him.'

Karl Stanley, the aforementioned expert submersible operator, was invited by Rush to dive with him in the Bahamas in April 2019, plunging to more than 12,000 feet or 3,760 metres. During the dive, Stanley heard 'gunshot like' noises emanating from the hull as the sub went deeper. Later, Stanley told Rush, in an email obtained by CNN, that he thought the sounds were indicative of hull breakdown and that 'what we heard, in my opinion ... sounded like a flaw/defect in one area being acted on by the tremendous pressures and being crushed/damaged,' and that on the return to the surface, 'from the intensity of the sounds, the fact that they never totally stopped at depth, and the fact that there were sounds at about 300 feet that indicated a relaxing of stored energy would indicate that there is an area of the hull that is breaking down [and] getting spongy.' In the email Stanley attempted to persuade Rush to reconsider his sub design and his intent to carry paying passengers on board, telling him:

> A useful thought exercise here would be to imagine the removal of the variables of the investors, the eager mission scientists, your team hungry for success, the press releases already announcing this summer's dive schedule... Imagine this project was self-funded and on your own schedule. Would you consider taking dozens of other people to the Titanic before you truly knew the source of those sounds??

In another interview, Stanley said he told Rush that he 'didn't have a marketable product,' but Rush wanted to continue with his present design, and pulled another story out of his hat. The acoustic monitoring system, another of Rush's innovations whose patent was filed in 2016, was intended to detect the breaking of carbon fibres within the submersible's hull. This system, according to Rush, was intended to alert the crew to potential structural issues before they became catastrophic. The utility of this alarm was, of course, based on his assumption that there was a remedy available to mitigate the hull's imminent implosion. It's like the time it would take the *Titanic* to clear the iceberg as it was speeding ahead. The approach happened far too quickly; the warning was too late to avoid the impact. Slowing the *Titan*'s descent and resurfacing takes considerable time, time which was not available in the event of a sudden catastrophic implosion. 'We can hear small things, like air pockets in the resin or the resin collapsing or fibres buckling … If the sounds are different than they were on previous dives, at 1,000 metres or any other depth, the pilot can abort the dive and return to the surface so crews can check the pressure vessel.' Another empty story Rush used to fool himself.

Rush also used his stories as a pacifying agent, telling David Pogue during a 2022 interview inside the *Titan*:

> We only have one button. It should be like an elevator, it shouldn't take a lot of skill.
>
> **Pogue:** And yet I couldn't help noticing how many pieces of this sub seem … improvised.
>
> **Rush:** We can use off-the-shelf components.

Later, David Pogue told the BBC: 'There's no back-up, there's no escape pod. It's get to the surface or die.'

Rush made a new hull in 2020, which is the one he claimed to have taken down to 4,000 metres. In a Geekwire summit talk in 2022, he described the layup of that hull, which made a 'lot of noise, which is a sphincter-tightening experience, we brought it back, and it wasn't getting quieter on the second dive, it should have been dramatically quieter.' He mentioned the Kaiser effect, which describes acoustic emissions from rocks or laminar composites undergoing cyclic loading. He said that particular hull was scrapped, and there was a change in direction. A new hull was made, citing Boeing, Janicki, and other firms. This new *Titan* hull was taken to the *Titanic* wreck site six times in 2021 and seven times in 2022, finishing out that season. It wouldn't finish another.

THE TITAN DISASTER

Sunday, 18 June 2023. In international waters, on its first dive of the season, the *Titan* submersible suffered a catastrophic implosion about ninety minutes into a dive to the *Titanic* wreck with five people on board, simultaneously losing communication with the mother ship after less than the full descent time. Later that day, OceanGate contacted the US Coast Guard when the submersible failed to resurface. An international search and rescue operation ensued, with a search area of up to 26,000 square kilometres. An underwater deep ocean robot was deployed to the dive site on 22 June, and the remains of the *Titan* sub were spotted approximately 1,600 feet from the *Titanic* wreck, which was determined to be consistent with the implosion of the *Titan* upon descent to the *Titanic* wreck. These findings were announced by US Coast Guard Rear Admiral John Mauger:

> This morning, an ROV, or remote-operated vehicle from the vessel Horizon Arctic discovered the tail cone of the Titan submersible approximately 1,600 feet from the bow of the Titanic on the seafloor. The ROV subsequently found additional debris. In consultation with experts from within the unified command, the debris is consistent with the catastrophic loss of the pressure chamber. Upon this determination, we immediately notified the families.

Plenty of questions remain unanswered as of the one-year anniversary of the *Titan* implosion. The most interesting question is: what were the assumptions made by the designer of the *Titan* that became the DNA of the disaster, and what was Stockton Rush thinking as he went about constructing and operating a submersible that had obvious weaknesses? Did he pivot from his original startup idea?

What strikes me most about this startup is the need for multiple innovations. I think most of us understand intuitively that for a new thing in this world to gain widespread acceptance, it must at least somehow fit into the existing framework of knowledge and understanding, in this case, deep-sea submersibles. There also has to be a problem and people who will stand to benefit from the solution to that problem, i.e., customers. Is it possible that someone who invents a great new product can also invent a great new way of distributing it? Or, develop a new medicine and simultaneously a way of delivering it precisely to the area of the body where it is needed? It is possible, yes, but not probable that both innovations will turn out to be best practices in the long run. A novel method to deliver an existing and useful drug is far more within the realm of probability. How many miracles do you need to make a dream come true? I think Perottet overestimates the undertakings of those wealthy eccentric individuals he was writing about; those adventurers like Victor Vescovo and James Cameron used the same methods that were used by the creators of the *Alvin* more than fifty years ago: a nearly indestructible metallic orb large enough to fit two or three people, with an attached buoyant foam capsule to compensate for the enormous weight of the hollow metal ball protecting the occupants on their journey to the abyss. Those individuals were not piling on innovations to the point of needing a wing and a prayer; they were using known materials combined with known designs, all under the watchful eyes of industry experts. Before they put human passengers into their new vessels, those vessels underwent test after test, such as pressure-testing the hulls 20% beyond their intended envelope of function – the maximum expected pressure during normal operations. This is the algorithm that submersible designers rely on, with a fifty-year history of passenger transport without a single fatality, and despite a significant increase in submersible traffic. This hazing process is something Rush simply failed to accomplish. One must consider that the carbon-fibre hull was a design and development choice, made by Rush himself under limitations, some of which he himself determined and others he ignored. Whether by financial limitation, hubris, or fear of being wrong, Rush tested the limits of his design with passengers aboard, an anachronistic, unnecessary approach. While Lochridge has been mainly silent since the *Titan* disaster, Karl Stanley has been quite vocal about the part he played in his attempt to avert disaster, sending Rush multiple emails asking him to reconsider and rethink his plans to innovate on the wrong things. Stanley hit the nail on the head, telling Rush the unexplained noises were the fibres of the hull breaking down under the enormous pressure. He said in an interview that he thought Rush had a new hull made after this exchange, perhaps at a cost of $1 million, and that Rush never told him exactly how many model tests he had done and where or how they failed. In another interview Stanley alleged that:

> Stockton was designing a mouse trap for billionaires ... He definitely knew it was going to end like this. He quite literally and figuratively went out with the biggest bang in human history that you could go out with. Who was the last person to kill two billionaires, at once, and have them pay for the privilege?

THE FOLLIES

As we now know, the Human Follies as I refer to them are within the realm of the human mind; Follies help to categorise the misunderstandings and biases which reside within a person's cognition. Since disasters are designed, we look closely at the thought processes and assumptions which give rise to the conditions that create a disaster. In the case of the *Titan* submersible, there are parallels with prior disasters to consider. The first and most obvious, is that the *Titan* had mirrored eighteenth- and nineteenth-century shipbuilding, in that each new prototype ship was tested with passengers aboard. In that period, sailing ships and steamships were very labour intensive, requiring at least a crew. While it would have been impossible back then to test ships without anybody aboard, the *Titan* development phase occurred in the era of robots, computers, and bench testing. It was clearly a step in the wrong direction. There were facilities available for hull prototype testing, and Rush never had any pressure chamber successes with the miniature models, with the one-third size model that had carbon-fibre domes imploding at 4280 psi, the pressure equivalent of a 3,000-metre depth. The failure point was the carbon-fibre dome, leading to the design choice of titanium endcaps. But there was no published evidence that pressure hulls with titanium dome endcaps were ever bench tested. Further, there was no clear testing phase that could reveal weaknesses in material and design in the full-size model without passengers aboard. Rush had relied largely on the track record of composites used in the aircraft industry and prior design work done by Steve Fosset and his team, as well as in pressure chambers used in scuba-diving tanks, for example. In those internal pressure use-cases, lightweight composites have few weaknesses, but there was no lengthy track-record of composite use in deep-sea pressure chambers that were directly transferable to the *Titan* submersible use-case. Pressure testing was done only on the 1:3 scale models, which were not exactly the same design as those that actually carried passengers.

Stockton Rush's base assumption: a carbon fibre hull is the lightweight, buoyant equivalent of a titanium hull.

1 Intelligent design must account for its environment.

Intelligent design which cannot account for its environment can be called semi-intelligent design. The less perfect the fit of the design to the environment, the closer and more vulnerable the design is to the forces of evolution (pure chance, thrown to the randomness of the universe). The *Titan* deep-sea submersible could not account for its intended function, that is, to make multiple dives carrying occupants to the incredibly hostile environment found at the depths of the *Titanic* wreck. The lack of adequate testing before commencing commercial operations opened up the whole venture to chance and led the designer and operator to the misunderstand the true nature of an intelligent design (Folly #3, Trojan Horse Folly). The innovative design and construction of the pressure hull of the *Titan* turned out to be unable to withstand the repeated application of intense pressure at the depths of the *Titanic* wreck. Unfortunately, there were passengers on board. Like NASA and the shuttle disasters, Stockton Rush and his associates accepted escalating risk apparently because they 'got away with it last time.' This is a once-good, always-good bias. The information contained in prior events, mainly the cracking noises from the hull, was not investigated. Rush was essentially handling a loaded gun, ostensibly unaware of the live bullet in the chamber, or at the minimum, was playing Russian Roulette: chance entered a designed system.

2 Tightly-coupled event cascades leave little room for error correction and evasive manoeuvring.

The real-time 'acoustic monitoring system' was based on a non-existent window in time that was assumed to be sufficient to alert the operator that a hull breach was imminent, abort the dive, and return to the surface. According to observers, the hull of the *Titan* sub made considerable noise when it encountered significant water pressure. The 'noise' was never quantified and correlated with a specific depth, making it difficult to assign any meaning to the interpretation of any noise alerts outside of qualitative changes to the hull's structure. The encounter of the designed submersible with the 'iceberg' was a requirement of the intended operation of the vessel, and while it withstood a number of prior 'collisions' with the hostile environment, the condition of the hull had deteriorated so that it could not withstand yet another encounter, leading to a sudden, catastrophic failure, rendering the warning system irrelevant. Another case of the Trojan Horse Folly. During each descent to the *Titanic*, the little submersible was surrounded by the iceberg of enormous water pressure, and the installed acoustic hull warning system was unable to give the occupants sufficient time required to surface and escape the 'iceberg.' Further, the thinking was marred by Human Folly #4 (Marie and Pierre Curie), a misunderstanding of the forces of nature. The 'ship' was intended to operate within an Iceberg Alley of sorts. While the operator was aware of the 'iceberg' directly below the submersible in the abyss, the operator did not fully understand the impact that these forces of nature would exert on the human-designed submersible in the deteriorated condition it was in at that time.

3. Rush assumed that the carbon fibre hull was robust and static, therefore undamaged and unaffected by the incredible pressures at the working depth.

In reality, though, the damage to the hull was cumulative, and each carbon-fibre hull could only have been taken to depth a finite number of times. This, of course, negated the economic feasibility of the *Titan* submersible. Prior to the implosion, Stockton Rush never fully understood the mechanism causing the hull breakdown, another example of Human Folly #3, and could not appreciate or quantify the extent of any observable compromise in the integrity of the hull. Further, there was no ultrasonic survey of its original condition, so it could not be meaningfully monitored for progressive degeneration. The design of the *Titan* submersible was more suited for repeated use at shallow depths, and may have had better economic viability in a business case which was based on this limitation.

NOISE GIVEN OFF BY THE DESIGNED SYSTEM

The *Titan* submersible was literally giving off noise during dives. Despite this persistent and obvious flaw in the designed system, dives were still permitted, as there were no veto nodes embedded within the human systems operating the submersible; that is, there was nobody there to say 'no!' Further, the conditions under which any installed veto node mechanism or algorithm should trigger a stop, i.e., a 'no-go,' were completely unknown with respect to the hull condition. There were red flags all over the place, noise being thrown off by the designed system which signalled faulty assumptions, extensive cost-cutting, and embedded design flaws, particularly in the carbon-fibre hull layups, according to Paul Lochridge. There were numerous safety incidents which resulted in interrupted dives, weather vulnerabilities, and the lack of an Emergency Location Transmitter or ELT, which would have allowed rescuers to locate the submersible in case of an emergency. The *Titan* was also never certified by any regulatory body, raising safety concerns among experts who were familiar with the sub. OceanGate could have performed some testing of the *Titan*, but its design, systems, and construction were never limit-tested or certified on an actual functional unit, which is standard practice for submersibles, submarines, and similar vessels. This was similar to Morton-Thiokol's methods of developing and testing the Shuttle's Solid Rocket Boosters with putty packing in the joints. As Allan McDonald told his boss: 'we did not fly the vehicle in that condition, so we needed to test in the exact same condition' [that we flew in]. Unfortunately for those who were lost on the *Titan*, OceanGate never bothered to test the limits of this passenger vessel under the same conditions in which it was operated. Another NASA parallel was the crackling sounds made by the hull. Like the SRB O-ring soot problem, and the External Tank foam-shedding problem, which was investigated post-mortem with the now-famous chicken-gun experiments, the continuous cracking sounds given off by the hull as it dove were never quantified or qualified, and nothing was actually known about the physical process giving rise to the noises. Rush simply pulled a story out of his hat as an explanation. Further, as we understand, there was a mating process using a luting cement between the carbon-fibre hull and the titanium ring, which was never investigated or assessed during the operation of the submersible. This constitutes a major structural component which was, by design, unavailable for inspection. This was similar to the use of spacers in the landing gear of the Concorde – a crucial system that was not readily accessible for observation and assessment by the pilot. I surmise that many of these concerns were presented to Rush by Lochridge in his quality control assessment document, but were rejected and ignored by him.

Stockton Rush made a typical startup mistake – that of trying to innovate on the wrong things. He conflated two concepts: he was observing a potential unserved and ignored market, but he used techniques more suited to exploiting a market which was already ripe for disruption. He successfully identified a market: selling expeditions to wealthy thrill seekers he called 'Titaniacs,' which is, in itself, difficult enough. But disruptive tactics enter an existing market by offering very low performance at low cost. The fatal mistake here is the assumption that the carbon-fibre hull was the low-cost equivalent of a typical metal hull. But, if the hull had to be replaced after, say, five dives, then the assumption is wrong, and the cost is actually much higher over time than the much higher initial cost of the titanium sphere with foam ballast. The lower initial cost of the carbon fibre hull allowed him to get his product into the customers' hands as quickly as possible, which is the basis assumption behind Mark Zuckerberg's famous motto, 'move fast and break things.' But we know that when this involves the safety of real people, the innovation must be much more carefully done. Stockton fancied himself a visionary, a real technological maverick who was destined to open up the deep seas to tourism and grant *Titanic* enthusiasts their wishes. He 'broke things' by getting mostly wealthy Titaniacs to the *Titanic* wreck as fast as he could, telling all who would listen that 'If you're not breaking things, you're not innovating.' When the supply of Titaniacs ran out, as it predictably would, he planned to pivot to supplying subs to the oil and gas industry. As a former venture capitalist, Rush was familiar with startups, but he forgot just how difficult real innovation actually is, and he broke a cardinal rule of startups: only one innovation at a time. This means that a startup founder should not try to innovate on every problem the startup encounters. Rush identified a market, Titaniacs, a material, carbon fibre, and a shape, oblong as opposed to a sphere, and he also innovated on cost: the *Titan* was built on a shoestring budget compared to existing, proven vessels which could dive to comparable depths. Did Rush consider whether or not all these innovations are compatible? Rush assumed so. Conventional submersible vehicles are made of very strong and durable materials such as steel and titanium. We have established that this is due to the intense hydrostatic pressure at these depths. The submersible industry, which has had an impeccable track record for decades, has already established best practices, which include pressure hulls that are spherical in shape and composed of titanium or steel, components capable of withstanding thousands of deep-dive cycles. The drawbacks to these materials are expense, weight, and the need for a buoyant material to counteract the weight. A five-passenger submersible would be huge, requiring a large spherical ball and a huge amount of syntactic foam. The advantage would be durability – there is no argument that this type of submersible would be extremely robust against the incredible pressures at working depth. But this is also a limitation: only the largest, most expensive ships would have the capability to bring this deep-sea tourist vessel to its dive location. This may actually have required a completely new, purpose-built ship, all prohibitively expensive for a startup on a shoestring budget.

His other option was to use a slightly larger sphere than the three-passenger *Alvin* to allow room for a fourth passenger, and design the pressure vessel to a working depth of no more than 4,000 metres. This would place financial constraints on his business model, but it would be honouring best-practices that have already been established, requiring only two innovations: just a larger sphere geared towards larger crews, and perhaps a larger mother ship to carry the extremely heavy vessel, and of course, a little private restroom wouldn't hurt.

What Rush did prove is that five inches of carbon-fibre composite is remarkably strong, even with its flaws. But, as we now know, he did not have any testing done on his full-sized vessel, and he tested it to failure mode with passengers aboard. There were millions of pounds of pressure on this cigar-shaped vessel over repeated dives. This means that he was actually defining the limits of this innovation; we know that it held well for two or three dives to 12,000 feet. We also know that where he cut costs, that is, using a viewport rated to only 1,300 metres rather than paying for a 4,000 metre-rated viewport, actually worked, but the question pops up again: how many miracles was he counting on? Since we know that stresses to carbon fibre are cumulative, this means that each hull is only good for a few dives to that depth. At a cost of $1 million per hull, this leads us to the true price of a ticket: closer to $1 million, instead of $250,000. Rush would still need to resist industry pressure to certify his sub design, even though each new sub could not undergo the certification process due to the cumulative damage to the hull, and it would be cost prohibitive. But this is the true cost of innovation. Stockton Rush was absolutely correct about the strength of carbon fibre, but he was also wrong in his assumptions that it could provide him with the functional equivalence of a spherical titanium pressure hull over the long term.

INNOVATION: CARBON FIBRE

From the video published by OceanGate, one can see that the pressure cylinder was wound with carbon fibre in only a single orientation, and was five inches (12.7 cm) thick. Unfortunately, this single orientation of the carbon fibre does not appear to be optimal for resisting axial and transverse loads. This means that the end caps, which at depth will be pressing in on the tube from the ends (axial loading), will only have the composite portion to resist the inward forces, and not the carbon fibre itself. This is due to the orientation of the fibres, which have their greatest strength in resisting tensile forces. It remains to be seen if carbon fibre which had been laid longitudinally along the long-axis of the tube could resist the transverse forces that tend to push the walls into the hourglass shape, but this work was not done, and the design question is still not answered. The use of carbon fibre in a submersible presented OceanGate with several design compromises which were ultimately the DNA of the *Titan* disaster. Carbon fibre is very suitable for pressurised containers – for example, the material is very good for use in scuba diving; it is lightweight and can contain the pressurised gas with very high reliability. Further, carbon-fibre pressurised vessels are a use-case that allows the tensile strength of the fibres to shine. The use of carbon fibre as a barrier against extreme pressures from outside the vessel is a use-case that pits the weaknesses of carbon fibre against the extreme environment. When the extreme pressure is outside of the carbon fibre balloon or tube, the disadvantages of both the carbon fibre and the resin composite come to the forefront and are at risk of failure from infracture by buckling. The carbon fibres can bend prior to resin hardening, but the combined, baked, and finished material is very stiff and brittle compared with unprocessed carbon fibres. The deformability of a carbon fibre part is largely dependent on the resin properties and the bond of the carbon fibre to the resin matrix. Carbon fibre is not known for its ability to repeatedly bend like a spring; the material does not have a significant ability to be deformed and spring back to its original shape; therefore the fibres will fracture or delaminate from the resin during extreme load cycling, and these flaws accumulate within the material – quite the opposite of modern alloys, which can both spring back to their original shape after bearing heavy loads and will significantly deform well before sudden failure, even in the presence of cold water. Another difference between metals and carbon fibre is that metals are isotropic – that is, their strength properties are equal in all directions. Carbon fibre is quite different – its strength is dependent on both the direction of the fibres and the direction at which the force is applied. Engineering.com estimated the pressure the end caps were placing on the hull was up to 20 million pounds, with a total force being exerted on the entire capsule of the *Titan* at somewhere in the range of 127 million pounds. For comparison, the fully loaded Space Shuttle stack on the launchpad was 4.4 million pounds. As we discussed, the *Titan* was overly innovative to the point where innovation did not add value to the final product: it was a false economy.

In summary, the Titan submersible used materials not entirely suited for the environment in which they were intended to function. Like so many vessels that had come before it, the *Titan* submersible was a system which had entered a state of post-engineering supervised neglect at the point when passengers were boarded. Despite what Rush had been saying about the carbon fibre, his design of the sub used the carbon fibre in its weakest orientation with respect to the forces being applied – that is, a unidirectional spool orientation, yet significant crushing forces would be applied to the cylinder from the titanium end caps. This end-crushing pressure would be applied to the tube in a direction perpendicular to the orientation of the fibres, a force against the Achilles Heel of the carbon-fibre composite hull. Thus the designer and operator of the *Titan*, Mr. Stockton Rush, was displaying a typical combination of Human Follies #3 and #4 – misunderstanding of the true nature of an intelligent design, and misunderstanding the natural environment the submersible was intended to operate within and how that environment would impact his design, respectively. Rush had his critics who tried to help him understand more about what he was doing – these were industry veterans with ample accumulated wisdom. Instead, Rush, like Elizabeth Holmes, preferred to surround himself with individuals who lacked expertise in the field and were thus unlikely to challenge his ideas. When confronted, he repeated his prior pattern, rejected well-meaning criticism, and fired the voice who told him the truth. Rush became a charismatic leader with a polished story line for every situation. We see it quite often in life; one can almost put a finger on the moment when the charisma takes over, replacing the hard work required to reckon with the actual truth. Charismatic leaders have less work to do; they get a hall pass so easily. They use their stories to generate assumptions in their listeners, handing them follies which are nothing but spackling to cover the ugly truth. So now the storyteller can get on with the grand filch that is his business. There was so much riding on that carbon-fibre hull. All the money sunk into it, the commitment to the idea of a lightweight, super-strong carbon fibre pressure vessel. When it was down to the brass tacks, Rush pulled out his officially accepted OceanGate Expeditions Entrepreneurial Creation Myth. David Pogue handed Rush a way out of his predicament, a get-out-of-jail-free card, right there on the ship in the North Atlantic, sitting face-to-face in the summer of 2022, a year before the fatal implosion.

> **Rush:** If I heard the carbon fibre go pop, pop, pop, then the gauge says, "You're getting a whole bunch of events."
>
> **Pogue:** So if you heard the carbon fibre creaking – Could you get three hours back to the surface in time?
>
> **Rush:** Yes. Yes, 'cause what happens is once you stop going down, the pressure, now it's easier. You just have to stop your descent. And so that's what we did a lotta testing on. You know, what kinda warning do you get?
> And as I said, the warning is about 1,500 metres. It's a huge amount of pressure from the point where we'd say, "Oh, the hull's not happy" to when it implodes. And so you got a lotta time to drop your weights, to go back to the surface, and then say, "Okay, let's find out what's wrong."
>
> **Pogue:** It seems like this submersible has some elements of MacGyver-y, jerry-riggedness.

In lieu of examining his actions and assumptions, Rush instead decided to save face and pulled out his invented chain of authenticity, telling Pogue:

There are certain things you want to be buttoned down ... The pressure vessel is not MacGyvered at all, because that's where we worked with Boeing and NASA and the University of Washington. Everything else can go, your thrusters can go, your lights can fail, you're still going to be safe.

There it is, the OceanGate Expeditions Entrepreneurial Creation Myth: the pressure vessel is not MacGyvered at all, because that's where we worked with Boeing and NASA and the University of Washington. It's the original story, the story that gave birth to the same grand filch, which is designed to plug-into an existing chain of authenticity: Boeing and NASA and the University of Washington. The plugging-into of institutions of repute, more or less. By holding the hand of Boeing, NASA, and the University of Washington, OceanGate and Stockton Rush received the benedictions they imparted upon him and his organisation. Nothing useful needs to have sprung from those loins. All one must do is just believe.

Stockton Rush seems to have had an unspoken retort to every question regarding the safety and survivability of his invention: 'Who needs proper certification when you have carbon fibre and raw, unadulterated brilliance?' As we look for signs of his motivations, there are aspects to this story which colour my understanding of Rush aside from his casual relationship to safety and the laws of physics. As a genetic and cultural White Anglo-Saxon Protestant, whose ancestors also go back to British Colonial America, I see him as a fellow descendant of the group who arrived in North America as strangers, a group which, due to the wildness of the land they left the comforts of their British homeland for, was a group given to the illusion of cohesiveness on the basis of a shared origin story and raised on a steady diet of cultural myth. But over time, this society had devolved into the same power hierarchy they were subject to in the old country, the power structure from which they escaped. My parents also looked to the ancestors for my given names, but Rush's parents gave him a name that reveals his double sprinkling of pixie dust, a direct plug into the chain of authenticity leading back to the founding fathers. But the pixie dust can also act as a burden, and one so burdened must live up to the accomplishments of his storied pedigree in an age of tech-bro billionaire worship, and also within a society which still remembers the old heroes, but now kneels before a different altar. How would he, with his modest accomplishments and allotment of inherited wealth, keep his chin up amongst his fellows at Bohemian Grove, many of whom were undoubtedly extremely wealthy, some of whom he perhaps asked to invest in his startup? Did he have the nerve to tell them that his carbon-fibre-hulled MacGyvery, jerry-rigged contraption was failing, and his assumptions were off, and he would need to pivot, or at least redesign his submersible and with it his entire business model? If you've been projecting raw, unadulterated brilliance, it may be difficult to admit to everyone you were wrong, and the *Titanic* flybys that put you on the map were now a thing of the past, and there is no carbon-fibre free lunch after all. It was all so perfect. His wife and partner in OceanGate, Wendy Rush, is the great-great-granddaughter of the retailing magnate Isidor Straus and his wife, Ida, two of the wealthiest people to die aboard the doomed ocean liner *Titanic*. The pair refused seats on a lifeboat since there were mothers and their children still waiting to flee the doomed steamer. A direct connection to the Founding Fathers and to the *Titanic*. Almost too good to be true.

Even darker, Rush changed the name of the *Cyclops-2* to the *Titan* somewhere around 2018, spawning post-mortem comparisons made to the title of a novella that preceded the sinking of the *Titanic* by fourteen years: *Futility* by Morgan Robinson, revised as *The Wreck of the Titan* in 1912. It features a fictional British ocean liner named *Titan* that sinks in the North Atlantic Ocean after striking an iceberg, with only two survivors. But this would imply that Rush knew *Titan* was doomed back in 2018. Doubtful. But Rush's stories about the hull noises were the most revealing. Karl Stanley told him in 2019 what they were, and while Rush, an engineer, also knew what those noises meant, he pulled out his prepared narrative, telling David Pogue in the 2022 interview:

So the key on that one is, we have an acoustic monitoring system. Carbon fibre makes noise. There're millions of fibres there. There are 667 layers of very thin carbon fibre in this five-inch piece. It makes noise, and it crackles.

When the first time you pressurise it, if you think about it, of those million fibres, a couple of 'em are sorta weak. They shouldn't have made the team. And when it gets pressurised, they snap, and they make a noise. The first time you get to, say, 1,000 metres, it will make a whole bunch of noise. And then you back off, and it won't make any noise until you exceed the last maximum [depth]. And so when, the first time we took it to full pressure, it made a bunch of noise. The second time, it made very little noise.

Rush told so many stories that he practically narrated his own demise. He was also in the hole financially. While he identified an underserved, neglected market, he could not, just like Elizabeth Holmes, accomplish all of the innovations which would allow him to serve that market sustainably. I think he was unable to invest the enormous resources that it took to accomplish the multiple innovations his startup required. Like the Challenger O-ring problem, Rush's vessel had limited opportunities to launch due to weather or systems failures; the ratio of scrubbed or aborted launches was at least 3 to 1. Also, we must assume there is a limit to the number of 'Titaniacs' who would plunk down such a price for a ticket to see the *Titanic*, and fewer still who would be willing to leave their $250,000 ticket on the table if the attempted launch was unsuccessful for the season. Eventually, Rush would need to come to terms with the true cost of each adventure. Had he done the testing on the full-sized hull, he would have known the boundaries and could have planned around the limitations enforced by those boundaries, thus eliminating Human Follies #3 and #4, taking control of the situation, which would otherwise be left to chance. Instead, Rush left the entire operation to a familiar battle of forces, that of man against nature; he pitted his flawed, off-the-shelf, cobbled-together hodgepodge of a vessel against the iceberg, and lost.

CONCLUSION: CATASTROPHE BY DESIGN

/ WHEN YOU INVENT THE SHIP, YOU ALSO INVENT THE SHIPWRECK; WHEN YOU INVENT THE PLANE YOU ALSO INVENT THE PLANE CRASH; AND WHEN YOU INVENT ELECTRICITY, YOU INVENT ELECTROCUTION ... EVERY TECHNOLOGY CARRIES ITS OWN NEGATIVITY, WHICH IS INVENTED AT THE SAME TIME AS TECHNICAL PROGRESS.

Paul Virilio

Behind every disaster we have discussed, the actions of humans are the most significant common denominator. As our analysis draws to a close, we must seek to understand the intentions of those actions.

DESIGN ENABLES FUNCTION

Human-designed objects or systems have a purpose or function, and they have embedded design to enable that function. Therefore, the object or system displays two types of design: basic embedded design and operational design. Each designed object or system contains features which constitute embedded design, and the manner in which the object or system is used or implemented constitutes the operational design. When a human designer creates a design, we can call that intelligent design. We have yet to categorise and name the designs created by intelligent systems. But for human-designed systems, the designed objects or systems have been designed according to function; the assumptions held by the designer are, in a way, frozen in time. In contrast, the operator of that design must use decision-making in real-time during the function or use of that intelligent design. Predictably, the embedded design assumptions made by a designer are not always completely understood by the operator of that designed system or object, or by those who could be affected by it.

The chief lesson of this study is that, like organisms, human-designed systems must function in the environment within which they were intended to function, and when those systems display embedded flaws, the flaws will manifest as noise, that is, an unexpected output, a result which was (hopefully) not intended by the designer or operator of that system.

Knowledge about the natural world is obtained through intelligent observation or experimental observation of that world. Systems that are not capable of accurately observing the world in real-time are also not capable of adapting to the world in real-time. The *Titanic* is our model system, designed and built by a group of experts who were using the best technology available for its time. The *Titanic* was operated by a different set of experts led by Captain Smith, chosen for his experience and prior accomplishments. Smith relied on traditional navigation methods in use at that time, including available maps, which contained information on the location of various ice fields, determined by observation in the past. Real-time electronic surveillance of the environment was unavailable at the time, and a single set of binoculars was the intended tool for scanning the immediate environment for threats. Like almost any human-designed disaster, the *Titanic* disaster unfolded like a story, almost as if the actors were unwittingly following a script; each step revealed itself to the 'actors' until the entire scene was played out. Cognitive control, in the form of Captain Smith, for his own reasons, was blind to the immediate surroundings of his giant ship, and by the time the threat was spotted, the collision course could not be altered to avoid the death-dealing iceberg. Of course, the iceberg dealt death only because of the human-designed system in its vicinity, a very flawed, very human system, which was rendered helpless once the point of no return was reached.

As I was writing this manuscript, the *Titan* submersible incident occurred, and as I dove deeper into the sequence of the events, I found that it closely paralleled the *Titanic* disaster, and while it was not completely congruent, it was close enough to generate comparisons in the media and warrant its own chapter in this study. It's almost as if the *Titan* disaster happened just to serve as an example of a typical designed disaster. The moment I found out the *Titan* pressure chamber was constructed of carbon-fibre-epoxy, I knew what happened intuitively; that is, the design somehow could not account for the environment. The water pressure at the *Titanic* depths, about 4 kilometres below the surface, is 6,000 psi. Six thousand pounds, about the weight of a typical American SUV, per square inch.

The submersible's material was a carbon-fibre tube with two titanium end caps. One of these contained a viewing port that was manufacturer-certified to only 1.3 km in depth. But that may not be the worst of the problems. Dentists like myself work with composites in their daily practice, and the dental profession is well-versed in composite vs metal failure. Dental composites are very similar to carbon fibre and also subject to strain and elastic deformation. Most of the time, the stresses on composites are normal and the material recovers, bouncing back to its original shape, a bit like a rubber ball. Pushing a material beyond the elastic limit, which is deformation or distortion beyond the material's ability to spring back to its original shape, you can get fractures, debonding of the composite from the tooth or partial denture framework, or you can get spalling (pitting) or other types of wear beyond the elastic limit of the composite, and often there are tiny bubbles or imperfections in the material that act as stress accumulators. The patient may report an audible snap. This happens more often after many repeated chewing cycles. Repeated chewing cycles weaken composites, but dental composites, while getting better and better, just do not hold up in the oral environment as well as metals and ceramics do by and large. Composites are strong and have a little flexibility built into their structure. It's a desirable quality in certain instances. But when I heard about the carbon-fibre hull of the pressure vessel, I immediately thought of the weaknesses of dental composites, imagining a submersible constructed of reinforced dental composite. Just about any dentist would have told Stockton Rush that metals are stronger, more uniform in composition, and do not undergo delamination and sudden failure like composites typically do. I also got wind of rumours early on that prior passengers were reporting the hull making noises as the vessel descended. This is literally a designed system throwing off noise, opening up this human-designed-and-operated system to chance. As we now know, this is a big red flag. Obviously, the design could not account for its environment. The OceanGate CEO was testing prototype designs on actual passenger vessels, just as steamer companies were doing in the nineteenth century.

It seems like such a simple concept, doesn't it? Intelligent design must account for its environment. When it cannot do so, it is considered semi-intelligent design and will likely be throwing off noise when it is subjected to certain stresses from the environment. It is deceptively simple, though. Take for example the Boeing 737 MAX accidents. The Boeing 737 MAX is a reworking of the old stalwart 707 and 737 designs from the early 1950s, known as the workhorse of the skies. This design was ageing poorly in terms of fuel economy, range, and power compared to its main competitor, the Airbus A320, first designed from scratch in 1987 and updated with larger, more powerful and more efficient engines in 2010 which became known as the A320neo (new engine option). The A320 design accepted the more efficient engines without significant modifications to the airframe, cockpit, or operating procedures, and became very attractive to airlines. This option, combined with other offerings from smaller manufacturers from the US, Brazil, and China, threatened Boeing's ageing cash cow. Boeing decided to modify the old design instead of starting from scratch, adding the newer engines to the existing airframe. To accommodate the larger diameter, ultra-efficient engines, Boeing needed to mount the engines further forward and higher up in relation to the aircraft's body and wings, significantly changing the flying characteristics of the aircraft. The new forward location of the engines and the design of the engine nacelles (engine mounts and housings) caused the aircraft to have a strong forward lift with a tendency to push the aircraft nose up, creating a high angle of attack. An uncorrected nose-up tendency could lead to a stall and a crash.

Rather than a costly re-design of the aircraft, Boeing instead implemented a software system they called MCAS, for the Manoeuvre Characteristics Augmentation System. The intelligent design: the MCAS will automatically drive the stabiliser to force the nose down when sensor data indicate a dangerously high angle of attack. It is an active compensation system: an electronic system that corrects for a deep design flaw. Think back to the beginning of the Titanic chapter; I described the wooden schooner Wyoming: in heavy seas, the wooden ribs and timbers flexed so much that the hull planking flexed and allowed water to enter the ship. The builders installed a pump that could continuously pump out the water, an early 'version' of the MCAS, a hack necessary to compensate for a deep design flaw. It was also a single point of failure. According to Greg Travis, a software expert witness, the MCAS code, written by outsourced workers, relied on data from a single sensor on the aircraft, like the binoculars aboard the *Titanic* – had they been available. It is understood that external sensors are exposed to the environment and are vulnerable to failure from weather, airborne dust abrasion, ice, and bird strikes, and redundancy is therefore needed, but there was no redundancy built into the system. As we know, without redundancy in a critical system, a single point of failure is enabled. In the 737 MAX, there are two AOA (angle of attack) sensors, and the system reads from one of the sensors during a flight, switching to the other sensor on the next flight. But this places the aircraft and its passengers into a system which contains a single point of failure. An iced-up or otherwise malfunctioning AOA sensor sends the system into a dive. This system was implicated in two 737 MAX fatal crashes which occurred in October 2018 and March 2019, respectively, killing all passengers and crew onboard, a total of 346 deaths. Further, Boeing, at first, did not inform pilots of the existence of this system, placing them directly and unwittingly into Human Folly #3 territory – so that the pilot and crew did not fully understand the designed system they were operating. The aviation equivalent of Alec Baldwin being handed a loaded gun and not being informed of the live bullet in the chamber. In contrast, Airbus aircraft use four sensors, and the system reads from all four simultaneously and uses the data from the two sensors that most closely agree. In the Airbus aircraft, the ability of the system to get accurate, real-time input from the environment is much more secure. As I said before, systems that are not capable of accurately observing the world in real-time are also not capable of adapting to the world in real-time. A crash is an unexpected output of a designed system, and an indication that a system is producing noise. If a human-designed system is producing noise, this is a manifestation that the system either suffers from a severe design flaw, and/or is unable to account for one or more aspects of the environment that the system is operating within. On the other hand, as we have discussed, systems which are designed by their environment, that is, naturally evolved systems, are shaped by evolutionary forces, that is, the noise of the universe: survival or extinction, no judgement present, just simple, brute force.

Unfortunately, relying on evolutionary design for human-carrying passenger vehicle designs involves deaths. Designing a system to account for its environment before that system is implemented may not be completely possible, but I recommend that when we build something new, we should learn from past disasters, and build that acquired experience into the new system. The DNA of Disaster cardinal rule is that all designed systems should account for their operational environments in all ways possible, and when not possible, we should recognise this shortcoming and try to understand that part of the environment which goes unaccounted for or uncontrolled. At the very minimum – and I am talking to Boeing management here – the operators of that system should be informed by the builders of the system that an active design flaw compensation mechanism is present.

APPLYING WHAT WE HAVE LEARNED: HOW A DEATH FROM A SEPTIC MISCARRIAGE IN IRELAND PARALLELS THE SPACE SHUTTLE CHALLENGER DISASTER

Ireland's Eighth Amendment effectively banned abortion in Ireland. The DNA of this law, in effect from 1983 to 2018, lay in the Offences Against the Person Act 1861, which was an Act of the British Parliament when Ireland was part of the United Kingdom. This law declared that it was unlawful to 'procure a miscarriage,' which granted an equal right to life to the mother and the unborn. The law stated that the act of abortion, where there was no immediate physiological threat to the woman's life to continue the pregnancy, was a criminal offence punishable by life imprisonment. This law was placed on the books despite the knowledge that 10 to 20% of pregnancies end in miscarriage. Despite this fact, the harsh law provided no protection from prosecutorial discretion or overreach, no protection of bodily autonomy for the pregnant person, and perpetual legal jeopardy for the doctor and hospital providing care to pregnant patients, where a pregnancy can turn for the worse on a dime. It was a fraught system, where a 'landmine' could explode at any moment. This meant that every pregnancy in Ireland was affected by the Eighth Amendment while it was on the books. Even for individuals whose pregnancy was troubled, the Eighth Amendment removed the right of a pregnant person to uphold her decisions regarding medical interventions during her pregnancy. By becoming pregnant, Irish women were effectively waiving their rights to bodily autonomy. The enforcement of the Eighth Amendment was, over time, gradually shifted to Irish obstetricians and maternity hospitals, who naturally practised a very defensive form of medicine, where interventions were often 'necessary' to protect the hospital and physicians. Under threat of being taken to court for refusal of an intervention, many Irish women were forced to submit to procedures against their will and suffered emotional trauma from their maternity experiences. Unsurprisingly, many Irish women who wished to terminate their pregnancies sought this care abroad or, traumatised by denial of bodily autonomy during an initial pregnancy, went abroad for sterilisation to avoid future pregnancies. Estimates suggest that at least 170,000 women living in Ireland have travelled to Britain to access reproductive services since the Eighth Amendment was introduced in 1983. This implies that Irish women faced significant barriers to accessing the full range of maternity services in Ireland, barriers which were exacerbated by the need to travel, adding financial burdens and logistical challenges to what should be a modern, convenient and safe maternity healthcare system. While we cannot know the details of each case, there were 170,000 red flags going up, indicating a flaw in the design of the system, a system generating a great deal of noise. Further, immigrants to Ireland needing maternal services likely made assumptions about care in Ireland based on a standard of care they were familiar with in their home country. These individuals may have been unaware of the dire situation of Irish maternal services, and could be caught by surprise and wholly unprepared when confronted with a system designed to prevent pregnancy terminations altogether, the healthcare providers instead focussing their attention on a labyrinth of legal requirements they were ill-equipped to navigate in rarer cases. One of those immigrants was named Savita Halappanavar, at the time a 31-year-old dentist from India, living with her husband, Praveen Halappanavar, an engineer and also from India, in Galway, Ireland.

Saturday, 20 October 2012. After traditional preparations for the birth of her first baby, Savita, at seventeen weeks pregnant, had difficulty sleeping due to lower back pain radiating into the pelvic area. She was in and out of the toilet throughout the night as her pain worsened. In the morning, Praveen made a phone call to the Galway University Hospital maternity ward, and the midwife who answered the phone told him to bring her to the ward for examination. After an exam, urinalysis and vital signs were recorded, including the heartbeat of the foetus, and the couple was sent home without a diagnosis, assured by the midwife that everything was fine. Later the same morning, after having some breakfast, Savita became alarmed and told her husband, 'Something is wrong.' She had felt something hard starting to protrude through the birth canal. They went back to the hospital and were greeted by the same midwife who had seen her earlier that morning. An examination revealed that the gestational sac was protruding from her body, indicating an inevitable miscarriage. She was admitted to the hospital, and her condition was discussed with the physician on call over the weekend. Just after midnight on Monday morning, Savita's waters broke, but did not expel the foetus. An ultrasound determined the presence of a foetal heartbeat. Despite the unfolding miscarriage, Savita was not induced, and her condition continued to deteriorate. By Wednesday afternoon, it had been more than two full days since her waters broke, and there was still a foetal heartbeat present. A foul-smelling vaginal discharge became apparent, and the hospital staff came to the conclusion that Savita was in the process of a septic abortion, a condition that is medically very dangerous because it can turn into sepsis and organ failure without prompt treatment. Savita and her husband repeatedly requested an abortion, but their pleas were denied. As her condition continued to deteriorate, she was taken to the operating room, and there she spontaneously delivered the stillborn foetus. But her suffering was not yet over: as her condition continued to worsen, she was transferred to the intensive care unit. During the next four agonising days, Savita developed a severe antibiotic-resistant systemic infection, which progressed into sepsis and organ failure, and by the early hours of the morning of Sunday, 28th October 2012, Savita suffered cardiac arrest and died. Her death gave momentum to a growing impetus for change in Ireland's reproductive healthcare system. Yet another human sacrifice upon a very human altar built in the distant past.

On 25 May 2018, Ireland held a referendum asking voters if 'provision may be made by law for the regulation of termination of pregnancies.' With a turnout of 64.51% of eligible voters, the result was a resounding victory for the repeal side, with 66.4% voting in favour and 33.6% against.

This outcome effectively repealed the language of the Eighth Amendment, paving the way for the Irish Government to legislate for the full range of reproductive healthcare services, even if as of today, six years later, the full spectrum of maternity services has not yet been restored in Ireland. But at least now there is potential for the system to modernise.

Obstetricians in Ireland were faced with the same quandary that faced the engineers who tried to prevent the Challenger disaster. If you will now recall the scenario: NASA management had shifted the launch algorithm from 'prove that your hardware is safe to fly' to 'prove your hardware will crash and burn.'

But as we now know, this is quite difficult to prove. There was simply not enough data to convince a roomful of NASA managers that the Challenger launch in the cold weather was risky, with the Space Shuttle Programme having made just twenty-four successful launches. The engineers were aware that there was an element of chance being baked into the system due to the design of the rocket boosters, but their data was slow to accumulate due to two factors: 1. There had been only twenty-four launches, only a few of which were in cold weather, and 2. A Thiokol head engineer was personally going into the static test rockets and packing the joints with putty, masking the problem during cold weather test burns. Therefore, the engineers had a difficult time proving beyond any doubt that the Challenger was going to explode since the data was just emerging. I have read some assertions that there were actually enough data points to sway the management at NASA and at Thiokol, but I maintain there were not enough data points presented to overcome a desire not to disappoint a popular president. Had there been more instances of cold weather launches, the data would be much more difficult to ignore. Savita's doctors were faced with an almost identical algorithm: prove the foetus was doomed to die, and further, prove that the mother was also going to die, before being allowed, by Irish law, to perform a pregnancy termination. Proving that the mother was going to suffer harm was not enough; the doctors must prove the foetus would die while the foetus still had a heartbeat. The data points necessary for this proof were 1. Absence of a foetal heartbeat and 2. Development of a septic miscarriage. In Savita's case, the presence of the foetal heartbeat overlapped with the presence of a septic miscarriage. Are these two assumptions compatible? This is not addressed by the law, written in 1983, and was not legislated by case law, partly due to the absence of data points, which were made scarce by the hundreds of thousands of pregnancies treated abroad. Those data points were absent; thus, Irish case law was not readily available for immediate access to decision-making by obstetricians and their barristers working in Ireland.

The penalties for a perceived wrongful termination of a pregnancy far outweighed the penalties imposed for a maternal death. Which ball did Savita's doctors keep their eyes on?

Savita's doctors were forced to navigate legal landmines around the pregnant patient in Ireland. Taking control of the situation and terminating the pregnancy when the miscarriage was discovered could get them hauled into court, and could actually result in them facing life in prison. The membranes holding Savita's foetus had ruptured, and bacteria entered the area surrounding the foetus. The pregnancy was doomed. Yet, the foetus had a heartbeat, and her doctors felt they were forced to protect themselves at Savita's expense. Due to this heartbeat, they were unable to prove beyond a reasonable doubt, in an Irish court of law, that her foetus was indeed non-viable and a miscarriage was underway. Like the Thiokol engineers who could not prove a crash was imminent, Savita's doctors could not prove that Savita was going to die, and they could also not prove that her foetus was doomed, since there was still a heartbeat. It is clear that Savita did not get the best or even average care in Galway Hospital; it was substandard care, no doubt. But the presence of the very real legal penalties clouded the judgement of the doctors and interfered with optimal intervention, making her situation very dire, and quite possibly unsurvivable for most pregnant patients. Savita's physicians spent precious time consulting about legal questions rather than attending to her care, wrapping an already complicated pregnancy with even more complications. The Eighth Amendment prohibited abortions once the foetus had a detectable heartbeat, therefore it removed the judgement of the doctors due to the standard assumption which was controlling the sequence of events by law: as long as there is a heartbeat, the foetus is viable.

This is a very common assumption, and it is currently being implemented in the United States again after the defeat of Roe, a very troubling development. In Savita's case, the pregnancy was in crisis due to a rupture of the membranes supporting the foetus. Even as her uterus and the membranes became infected and septic, the placental blood supply to the developing foetus remained intact, therefore the foetal heart had a supply of oxygen and could keep pumping. Essentially, the patient with a troubled pregnancy is headed towards the iceberg. How close must that patient get to the iceberg before the doctors can comfortably make the recommendation to abort the pregnancy? If they do indeed save her, they will always be at risk of being second-guessed in a court of law. No doctor wants to be in front of a prosecutor and a jury of laypersons with an obligation to 'prove that the patient, mother or foetus, was going to die.' In medicine, there are indications that a patient is headed in a certain direction, but those indications in no way constitute proof. The only way to prove beyond any doubt that the patient will die under certain conditions is to indeed let her die. This brought the decision-making algorithm down to the presence of Irish case law, decided by courts on the basis of priors. Savita's case was atypical, constituting an edge case, so rare that case law was either absent or not readily available for consideration in decision-making. In Savita's case, the silver bullet was legal, not medical. The DNA of this disaster: the Patriarchy, which brought the Eighth Amendment into existence in 1983. In your mind's eye, you can almost visualise the bishops whispering into the lawmaker's ear as the text of the Amendment was being written. Cultural monuments, Cultural DNA. Again. Like an ancient, sacred, sun-baked rock in central Australia, the church became not only the school, but also the law clerk, the judge, the jury, and had become the face of reproductive care in Ireland. Difficult pregnancies in Ireland always ended in hospital, the place where medical care was the most abundant, but somehow, it was not fully available to them and instead they resorted to a wing and a prayer. The ancient mariner encountered the same problem when he spoke the words: 'Water, water everywhere, nor any drop to drink.'

The State of Idaho is just one of many states in the United States which are treading very close to the same scenario Ireland just rejected. After the defeat of Roe, State Law will be taking precedence, and Idaho now has one of the strictest abortion bans in the United States. Idaho's new law allows physicians to terminate pregnancies only to save the life of the mother, but not to preserve her health. Again, how sick must the patient get before doctors are allowed to initiate termination? Instead of giving the troubled pregnancy a wide safety margin, the Idaho law will push these pregnant patients right up to the iceberg, and attempt to pull them away at the last moment; or, now more likely, patients with crisis pregnancies will be airlifted out of state. Doctors simply do not want to put themselves or their careers into the position of being at the mercy of prosecutorial discretion, and will instead refer these patients out of the system for care. Just the fact that Idaho women are now being airlifted out of state for maternal care is a red flag: the designed system is undisputedly throwing off noise. Instead of quality, timely, and safe medical care in-house, Idaho's designed maternity care system will be generating life flights out of the state in all kinds of weather. Instead of caring for women with crisis pregnancies, Idaho's maternity wards will become triage centres for these pregnancies featuring a built-in delay for urgent treatment. Nice going, anti-abortion fanatics. Your system, by design, will place an excess burden on these pregnant patients and their families, and these incidences will come at a much greater cost to boot. If this human-conceived and fabricated system were fair, this excess cost would be paid for by the Idaho fanatics who designed and implemented the system. But, as we know, religion always gets a hall pass. Someone will fall through the cracks, and Idaho Republicans will have blood on their hands. Independently, the State of Idaho will start to lose their ob/gyn doctors, affecting the system at its deepest level. Placing your difficult patients on a life-flight out of state is the ultimate in defensive medicine, a tactic which is topped only by refusing to practise in the state altogether. It's the law of unintended consequences. Will we ever learn?

NATURAL DISASTERS

The February 2023 earthquake and aftershocks on the Turkish–Syrian border region are amongst the most severe natural disasters of the last century. More than 52,000 people were killed and more than 100,000 injured when many very new buildings collapsed, alongside other structures which did not collapse, in a seemingly random fashion. Almost immediately, Turkey's Justice Ministry produced a list of over 600 people suspected of construction negligence contributing to the disaster. Building engineers witnessed countless pancake-type collapses, where the supporting structures holding up the elevated floor and roof portions of a concrete multi-storey building completely gave way, creating difficult conditions both for survival and search and rescue teams. This is a clear example of noise being thrown off by a designed system. According to the *New York Times*, after the last massive earthquake hit a region near Istanbul in 1999, Turkey implemented a plan to upgrade building codes to prepare for future quakes. Turkey's new construction codes resulting from this effort were considered world-class. Despite these valiant efforts, there were systemic problems with implementation and enforcement.

Construction amnesty, also known as reconstruction peace and zoning reconciliation, is a set of Turkish laws that register and legalise structures that do not comply with Turkey's strict building code. The amnesty came into use by the government to deal with the many unapproved building modifications that occurred, and has been very popular with voters. There have been a total of nineteen building amnesties since 1948, most recently in May 2018, just weeks prior to the Turkish Presidential Election. There have been prior spontaneous collapses in buildings with illegal extensions, with one dating to early February 2019 where the owners put three extra floors on the top, ostensibly to get extra rent money, but did not add any additional support below. There have even been cases where the ground floor owners or tenants may have had a supporting column removed to open up space and were eligible for amnesties. Further, construction companies were able to create subsidiaries that were purposed to inspect that company's own construction works. The fox was guarding the henhouse indeed. These accumulated violations could be wiped clean on amnesty day; all the concerned parties needed to do was to pay a fine. In many cases the fine would absolve the offender from fixing the code violations. The government has an incentive to conduct a building amnesty programme, given that the 2018 amnesty was said to have brought in $3.1 billion in property taxes and fees to government coffers. Another example of a Trojan Horse, in which the embedded design – in this case the shantytowns and other substandard Turkish properties – could not account for their direct physical environment, i.e., an earthquake-prone geographic area. Looking at the history of this disaster, it appears that in Turkey, the easy part was the passing of the strict building codes. The difficult part was overcoming the temptation inherent in a popular government programme that hauls in generous resources.

CLIMATE NOISE

There is no judgement involved in an earthquake, a meteor strike, an ice storm, a tornado, or a flood. There are no gods punishing us; these natural phenomena have been a part of the Earth's environment as long as it has been in existence. One has only to glance at the pockmarked surface of the moon to see the accumulated effects of meteor or asteroid strikes over billions of years. As a larger body with eighty-one times the mass of the moon, the gravitational pull of the Earth has undoubtedly invited more object strikes than its satellite. The atmosphere and biosphere of the Earth either prevent impact altogether or conceal the traces over time. Much of the ocean water has probably arrived via icy asteroids over billions of years. Drought or floods do not mean there is more or less water on Earth, only that there is a distribution problem. It is the same with carbon in the atmosphere. The Otto cycle engine proved to be very reliable and efficient, and the effect it had on civilisation was unprecedented. In the age of mass manufacturing and mass consumption, when millions of fossil-fuelled engines are used on a daily basis, they annually pump millions of tons of carbon taken from deep within the Earth into the atmosphere. Again, a distribution problem. As any college chemistry student knows, when you change the composition of a mixture of gases, the physical properties of the mixture of gases will also change. It is analogous to polluting the oceans with vast amounts of rubbish or radioactive industrial waste products. The dumping ground will change somehow, we just are not always sure how. What we can do is look for noise generated by the system involved.

Are areas with historically mild climates experiencing repeated, extended droughts or floods? Are there suddenly many more hurricanes, tornadoes, or other severe weather phenomena, or is it a gradual increase with occasional drought or flood spells? Are there longstanding climate phenomena such as the AMOC (Gulf Stream) showing signs of reaching a tipping point? Are certain sea creatures experiencing bioaccumulation of radioactive substances which were produced in a nuclear reactor? By pumping our industrial waste into the atmosphere or oceans things will change; we are just not aware of what those changes will be in toto. We are throwing our human-made monkey wrench into Earth's biosphere. Radioactive waste from accidents like Fukushima going into the oceans and the carbon being dumped into the atmosphere is very likely a Trojan Horse Folly (#3). Our training data does not include future events, but before the environmental systems start throwing off more noise, we had better start looking for solutions in earnest.

FUTURE CATASTROPHES

My parents used to remind me the only things that are inevitable are death and taxes. I think we can add disasters to this list. Human beings have always dealt with disasters: some minor, some major; some natural events, the vast majority man-made. The future will contain disasters, some of which are undoubtedly already in process. I can make my predictions, but the point of this study is not only to help humanity avoid disasters but also to deal with those disasters that are unavoidable by identifying and characterising the cognitive processes at work in designed disasters. It is this cognition that enables us to separate ourselves from the noise of the environment and rise above the forces of evolution. This embedded cognition, part of our birthright as members of humanity, can be found everywhere man has been: churches, farms, factories, stories, narratives, laws, deterrents, cities, towns, cars, roads, books, and communication systems, as well as social structures. It helps protect us, prolong our lives, feed us, clothe us, and keep us warm at night, separating us from the elements. Cultural Monuments that helped us make quick decisions were powerful because they required little thought or consideration; they are repositories and transmitters of cultural knowledge and have functioned as a superpower for humanity. Cultural monuments form the basis of customs and traditions handed down through the ages, they were vital to our survival; allowing us to learn from our ancestors at a time when pen and paper were unavailable to store knowledge for future generations. We must learn to identify not only those monuments that help us maintain and conserve our world for future generations but also understand how they can be used to isolate us from our fellow human beings or manipulate us. Flawed thinking as well as flawed systems and processes can lead us to disaster, but the embedded, stored cognition that appeals to our tribal urges can also work against us if we are unaware. We should learn from the past to help predict the future.

MY BIGGEST WORRIES

The total amount of water on the planet, as climate change slowly melts polar ice to liquid form, will squeeze the world's population into ever-smaller plots of habitable land. There was no intelligent design that determined the amount of water present on our planet in our favour. Some significant amount of water was probably here in Earth's beginnings, but then water was added through random icy-body impacts over its four-billion-year history. As we now know, many bodies in our solar system contain large amounts of water in liquid or solid form. Much of that water on Earth has been in solid form for millennia, giving humans plenty of dry, habitable land. Therefore it is folly to assume the amount of dry land we have now will remain dry; we will permanently lose large swathes of coastal land, and likely much arable land, which will be an enormous disruption to humanity. We can expect the future to produce more disasters with a climate component due to our changing of the atmosphere's chemical and physical properties, which in turn will drive the solid water to liquid form. This liquid water has the ability to store vastly increased amounts of solar heat energy, while the same water, piled up in polar ice caps and vast glaciers, could store essentially no energy in comparison; the white sheen of the ice reflecting solar energy back into the atmosphere and then to space. This excess energy in our oceans can power ever more destructive weather events, some of which we are now experiencing. I predict that climate change will produce large numbers of refugees, who will likely not be welcome in the habitable northern locations to which they will flee.

There is a concept in manufacturing known as six-sigma. It represents a process that reduces the errors contained in a product to only 3.4 defects per million opportunities. Current nuclear technology produces a waste product that is so dangerous it must be kept isolated from the environment essentially forever. Human beings commonly display violent power struggles or poor regulatory design and implementation that may ultimately compromise the containment of this dangerous material. As we know, intelligent design must account for its environment. But due to the very long half-life of these radioactive materials, the intelligent design separating nuclear waste from its environment must operate perfectly for millennia. Knowing what we now know about human-designed systems, the success of this seems improbable. We now have many large, Ukrainian nuclear power stations situated in or near a conflict zone. I fear accidental release of dangerous nuclear material, for the simple reason that the Fukushima and Chernobyl disasters show us how easily human-designed containment systems can fail. We do not know if current nuclear technology will be compatible with climate change, and since nuclear technology is extremely resource-intensive, I fear that the constant feeding of the nuclear monster will lead to future subsidy fatigue, and as other future crises seem to be more urgent, they could take priority over nuclear safety, setting the stage for supervised neglect.

SUMMARY OF WHAT WE HAVE LEARNED

The universe produces unplanned events that may impact the Earth, such as solar flares and meteor strikes, while the Earth itself, as a product of the universe, can produce earthquakes, volcanoes, or catastrophic weather events. These were some of the forces that contributed to evolution in the biosphere, which we can refer to as evolutionary forces.

We've learned that all human-designed systems must account for or completely control the environment they operate in. If they cannot do so, these systems will begin to produce unexpected or unplanned results, which we call noise. These unplanned and unexpected results will have characteristics similar to the forces that produced evolution, that is, life or death.

This leads us to the first rule of the DNA of Disaster:

Intelligent design must account for (or control) its environment

If a designed system lacks the ability to account for its environment in one or more ways, it will most likely throw off noise in the form of unexpected events prior to its total failure or collapse. This can be viewed as the forces of evolution creeping into the designed system. As we have established, the forces of evolution can cause stresses in ecological systems, which can, in turn, stress the life forms inhabiting the ecological systems. Some of these life forms can withstand and adapt to the stresses and will emerge from the catastrophic events alive and able to reproduce, while other life forms will be unable to withstand these stresses and die off. When a designed system encounters these same stressors, the system will likely produce unplanned and unexpected events which may hazard the viability of a company such as Nokia, or human lives in a passenger vessel such as the *Titanic*, Concorde, or Space Shuttle, or scatter radiation into the environment as with a nuclear power plant built on the edge of the ocean as in the case of Fukushima Daiichi or within a war zone such as Zaporizhzhia Nuclear Power Station in Southeastern Ukraine.

A Cultural Monument can be a human artefact or it can be a naturally occurring event in the universe, such as the sun, the moon, stars, or even a giant sandstone formation as in Uluru. The culture itself generates the monument, whether it is a ritual, a statue, a carving, a law, a leader, or a mountain. Not all Cultural Monuments are physical objects, as we now understand. In some cases, the artefact gains monument status; that is, it becomes a Cultural Monument elevated above the mundane; symbolic constructs which were at one time passed between generations within the family and tribal units, but now these ideas are scattered far and wide, bolstered by social proof, spread by propaganda and masquerading as absolute fact. Further, a rather mundane monument can gain followers and even achieve sanctified status, which gives that Cultural Monument the ability to withstand the withering effects of the aeons. Sanctification of a monument changes the nature of the way that monument is viewed by its believers and defenders; the human capacity for bestowing holiness upon a Cultural Monument or artefact elevates that entity above the mundane into the realm of the sacred. We have seen this phenomenon at work in the Uluru Cultural Monument, and we have explored how the consistent appearance of both Blue-Sky and Dark Sky Cultural Monuments in religious and cultural narratives mirror that society's embedded 'yin and yang,' acting as a cultural shorthand, producing predictable responses in members of that culture. But it is clear that Cultural Monuments can and always will be present, whether existing for millennia, like Uluru, or more recent, such as a mainstream religion. Cultural monuments can be constructed for the collective good, or hijacked for personal benefit, or even collectively constructed and defended for collective benefit. The Concorde disaster shows us how a Cultural Monument can be manufactured and harnessed for various ends, but can also create blind spots, where no one dares to 'look under the hood' and find flaws. To find hidden flaws, look especially for a system that has entered the dreaded state of post-engineering supervised neglect, such as the Space Shuttle Solid Rocket Boosters, the Concorde tyres, and even the lifeboat laws governing the very new, very giant passenger steamships of the early twentieth-century. As we can now attest, laws and regulations, like passenger vessels, are indeed designed, and as products of design, must account for the environment in which they actually operate.

The second rule of the DNA of Disaster:

Designed systems which produce an unexpected or unplanned result are likely throwing off noise.

Noise is an indicator of a design flaw: it's likely that one or more components of the designed system cannot account for its environment. This concept is best illustrated by the O-ring seals of the Challenger solid rocket boosters. The temperature sensitivity of the system was producing noise in the form of blowby, and this was actually recognised by the engineers closest to the rocket's design, however they were not in a position of power to actually prevent the disaster. If the leaking O-ring seals sprang up on the outward-facing side of the booster rockets, the giant External Tank and the structure holding the Shuttle Stack together would have remained intact, and we would have gotten fireworks from the Challenger launch, but there would not have been a breakup. Those who made the call to override the engineers' concerns were unaware that they were introducing the element of chance into their designed system, running right up to the iceberg, and were inadvertently setting the stage for a disaster of their own design.

The third rule of the DNA of Disaster:

Individuals and cultures can possess blind spots, usually beliefs or assumptions that obscure the true nature of naturally occurring phenomena, designed systems, biological systems, or historical events.

These blind spots are often created by Cultural Monuments and are the result of holes in knowledge; whether that ignorance is due to cognitive defects or manufactured blind spots, these blind spots in knowledge are either possessed by the designer of the system or the event, or by those who operate the system or are affected by the designed system or event. These holes in knowledge are described by the Four Human Follies:

1. Assuming the presence of intelligent design when merely semi-intelligent design or no intelligent design is present (The Divine Intervention Folly);

2. Assuming the absence of intelligent design where it is present (The Propaganda Folly);

3. Misunderstanding the true nature of an intelligent design (The Trojan Horse Folly);

4. Misunderstanding of the true nature of the universe, randomness, and evolutionary forces (The Marie and Pierre Curie Folly).

When we look at these Follies, the importance here lies in their applicability to modern life, but all of these follies have been encountered by humans in the past. Let us look at a few current applications:

Folly #1 can be predicted to affect us in the future by our reliance on technology, such as in the case of self-driving cars. The human driver may misappropriate the location or source of the intelligence. If we refer to technology as self-driving or having an autopilot feature, we are relying on a system that at present does not contain the full intelligence of an actual human driver, and the origin of the intelligent design was actually the designers and programmers of the system rather than the system itself. If we consider the number of accidents involving the Tesla self-driving system, with only a relatively small percentage of cars on the road having this feature, we can extrapolate what may occur in the future. This may be a significant number of accidents. Perhaps Tesla and other companies should instead focus on augmenting the highly variable skills of human drivers before claiming full autopilot ability. But this is not limited to Tesla. Just recently, in August 2023, a Cruise autonomous taxi got mired in wet concrete in San Francisco. This shows that the intelligent design (the autonomous vehicle) could not account for its environment (a road with wet concrete) by avoidance. Humans can easily detect the difference between a road construction area with clues that surround that zone, like traffic cones, workers in hardhats, and perhaps nearby clues such as cement mixers or heavy machinery. Further, undistracted humans can detect minor differences in reflectance or shade differences in wet concrete vs. set concrete. This level of detection may elude autonomous vehicles. A better idea might be to augment the traffic cones with indicators that are easily picked up by autonomous vehicles that signal 'do not travel here', but of course these signals could easily be copied and used by pranksters and those with more nefarious intentions. Perhaps the road construction area can receive a unique code from the municipality that signals to the autonomous car that 'here is the construction area you were expecting.' This will still need to be worked out, but these events prove the intelligence controlling the car is not quite up to par with real humans, at least not at the present time. When assessing the power of the AI we rely on, we should be asking an important question: is this AI a colleague, or is it an appliance or tool? At the time of writing, I know of no AI system that could be considered a colleague of the actual human being it would replace. If you consider the fact that autonomous vehicles must account for their environment, just look to other similar instances: airliners, ships, and trains still have pilots. Car drivers are subject to an infinite number of scenarios of novel complexity as they navigate public roads – the drivers are operating in a minimally controlled environment. Aeroplanes, trains, and cargo ships have far more structure in their movement – fewer degrees of freedom of movement. Trains stay on the tracks, and aeroplanes and ships have controlled paths as they travel, if less than trains on tracks do. Once the aircraft is away from the port, the large open spaces reduce the chances of collision should the craft veer off course. Cars, as we know, can easily run up onto a sidewalk, striking pedestrians, cyclists, and motorcyclists, hinder or block the numerous first responder vehicles that will have the right-of-way, or run straight into a work zone or other unmapped obstacle. A system dependent on preprogrammed prior situations at some point will be hard-pressed to account for the myriad number of obstacles which can be thrown into the path of an autonomous vehicle by the environment. Will it know what to do in each case? Does the system have real judgement? As we now understand, sentient human beings sometimes have difficulty in accounting for their own environment; therefore, why are we assuming the AI has this ability at present? Human Folly #1 applies. Is it a designed system that is misunderstood? Human Folly #3 also applies. We should not assume these systems are already capable of human-level judgement. These systems will need to exceed human-level judgement before they will attain universal acceptance.

Air traffic: The 2022 air travel season ended with a Southwest Airlines fiasco. Between 19 and 28 December 2022, Southwest Airlines was forced to cancel more than 16,000 flights, leaving thousands of people stranded for days. Early on in the event, inclement weather appeared to be the iceberg due to the fact that it affected all the other airlines. However, as time went on, the other airlines recovered, but Southwest continued to cancel flights. Planes were kept on the ground and passengers remained stranded. Eventually the CEO of Southwest was forced to come clean and reveal the true DNA of the disaster: outdated IT systems implemented in the 1990s had become inoperable. While Southwest's C-suite had plans to upgrade everything, nature threw an iceberg into their path and they were unable to account for the environment. This was a disconnect between cognitive control and the designed system. The IT system was the primary means of communication between cognitive control (the brain) and various other parts of the components of the system (the body) and it could not function to coordinate those various parts. This software type is called Enterprise Resource Planning (ERP) software. Due to the breakdown in this outdated system, the airline staff responsible for coordinating personnel and assigning flight crews to flights had no means of carrying out those assignments.

A similar problem is brewing in the air traffic control system. The FAA's NOTAM system, which is the system that updates pilots of safety hazards, stopped functioning on 10 January 2023 and ground to a halt, unable to process updates. This system was originally installed in 1993 and has been in continuous operation ever since. Further, there is a vast shortage of air traffic controllers today. According to CNN ('Ancient computers, too few pilots and air traffic controller shortages,' 13 June 2023), US air travel could be a rough ride in the near future. There are 1,200 fewer air traffic controllers in 2023 than there were in 2013, and there is no solution to the problem currently in place. In total the shortfall is closer to '3,000 workers, according to Transportation Secretary Pete Buttigieg.' The article's sources explain that hiring and training air traffic controllers is a time-and-resource-consuming endeavour, a problem that is exacerbated by spending caps in most of the departments of the FAA, which is chronically underfunded.

Close Calls: In a *New York Times* article dated 21 August 2023, it was revealed that 'Airline Close Calls Happen Far More Often Than Previously Known.' Many of these close calls happen near or within the area of airport runways and the immediate airspace surrounding airports. This, of course, is very similar to steamship ports, as we discussed in the *Titanic* chapter. The number of moving passenger vessels sharply increases the nearer one is to ports. What is disconcerting is the number of close-call incidents that have been reported. The *Times* article reveals that 'preliminary F.A.A. safety reports … not publicly disclosed – were among a flurry of at least 46 close calls involving commercial airlines last month alone.' The article also states that the *Times* has been analysing internal FAA reports and has found that the 'incidents often occur at or near airports and are the result of human error, the agency's internal records show. Mistakes by air traffic controllers – stretched thin by a nationwide staffing shortage – have been one major factor.'

If you look back into the history of the problem, it can be traced all the way back to the Reagan administration during the air traffic controllers' strike. Yes, the Gipper, our favourite culture warrior, strikes again. The administration fired all 11,345 strikers and barred them from federal service for life. Unfortunately, this has created a large wave of retirements, and the resulting vacancies have been difficult to backfill. A gruelling job, the FAA may face a tipping point where the scarcity is so vast and the remaining employees so overworked, that the air traffic controller career path gains a toxic reputation with catastrophic consequences. As we have discussed before, this system is teetering on the precipice of Human Folly #1, where pilots may erroneously assume that cognitive control (air traffic control) is present and aware of a situation, but in reality, cognitive control will be absent in certain cases, or it will be so distracted and its attention spread so thinly that it will be ineffective.

We could also predict that the skies may become so crowded that the communication between cognitive control and the airborne pilots may become broken, spotty, or functionally ineffective. Pilots flying into foggy areas have reported multiple near-misses as well as near-misses on runways, when aircraft are out of place. This could be how the next airline catastrophe occurs. At the very minimum, we should be regarding the increase in unexpected near-misses and IT failures to be signs that these designed systems are generating noise, an indication that a designed system is being stressed and is nearing the limits of its design basis, and in some instances the system cannot account for one or more aspects of its environment. When this happens, the designers should be looking for chinks in the armour, that is, defects in the intelligent design, and should implement corrective action immediately.

In these scenarios, we are often dealing with multiple follies and maladies, like in the Concorde disaster. The DNA of Disaster rule of thumb: catastrophes can have as many maladies as they please. For example, NOTAM failure: this is similar to the lack of binoculars in the *Titanic*; the lack of a hazard warning system limits cognitive control and blunts timely decision-making ability, so that the intelligent design (in this case cognitive control) cannot completely account for its environment due to a blindness induced by a fault in the system. An airborne pilot may assume that the NOTAM system is working when it is not. Therefore, Human Follies #1 and #3 apply to the pilot. This reflects not only loss of cognitive control, but also the assumption that a designed system (NOTAM) is functioning properly when it is not. Human Folly #3 applies to the FAA since they were assuming that their designed system (NOTAM) was functioning adequately when it failed and caught them by surprise.

Pilots flying into foggy areas and suddenly encountering a 'plane (or drone) that isn't supposed to be there': Human Folly #2 – assuming the absence of intelligent design where it is actually present. This is nothing more than another aircraft substituting for the iceberg. But the pilots also assume there is cognitive control from the air traffic control system when there is none or it is defective, disconnected or distracted, so Human Folly #1 also applies.

Southwest Airlines: thirty-year-old IT systems crashing when stressed
Human Folly #3; Misunderstanding the true nature of an intelligent design. Cognitive Control (the C-suite) was unaware that their creaky software and system would crash and cease operating when stressed. Did the C-suite misunderstand how their designed system would hold up as it encountered the iceberg, i.e., the winter storm? If yes, Human Folly #4 also applies.

CLIMATE CHANGE

If we look again at the first rule of the DNA of Disaster that intelligent design must account for (or control) its environment; we can immediately understand the risks of dumping greenhouse gases into the atmosphere. The change in atmospheric chemistry enables the earth to capture and store more solar radiation. These greenhouse gases remain in the atmosphere for long periods of time, leading to an increase in global average temperatures. The prior stability of the climate becomes disrupted, setting off the chain of events that will then cause the polar ice caps to melt, contributing to sea level rise and further disrupting the climate system. We and our progeny are going to be dealing with an environment that not only is out of our control, it will be throwing increasingly large 'icebergs' at our embedded intelligent designs: cities, suburbs, roads, transport systems, farming and supply chains. Inhabited places worldwide will face the prospect of being made obsolete or even dangerous by the new environmental conditions. Intense, increasingly common wildfires fuelled by climate change in areas where they had been more mild or predictable could become the new normal. The built environment in these areas, such as the western United States, may contain a majority of housing and commercial building stock constructed of combustible materials that are well-known, standard and suitable in the majority of climate zones- for example in the eastern or midwestern United States. This ubiquitous wood framing type of construction may have been perfectly acceptable if not slightly risky in the old conditions which included occasional earthquakes and wildfires, but will be increasingly incompatible with and even foolhardy to use in the new environmental conditions. A complete redesign of cities will likely become necessary in the western United States as the climate produces more extreme weather events leading to hotter, drier weather and more accumulated combustible vegetation surrounding the built environment. Building wood framed homes at the base of chaparral-covered mountains was always risky, but in the future it should be considered downright reckless. Coastal cities will be battered by ever-more-intense storms fuelled by the ever-increasing heat content of seawater. The accompanying storm-surges will likely make many of these areas uninhabitable. Extreme heat, drought, and water distribution problems will challenge our established infrastructures; wars may be fought over the ever-shrinking habitable land mass. As I write, there is a disconnect between the amount of water on the planet and the present proportion of habitable, dry land available for human dwellings. If all of the water on Earth exists in a liquid and vapour state, humanity will be dealing with an enormous, continuous catastrophe.

THE CULTURAL MONUMENTS OF THE HOME TEAM

As we consider how allegiance, loyalty, national pride and Cultural Monuments can affect decision making, it is a foregone conclusion that we, as team members, want our home team to be a source of pride. The same is true for our religion, political party, and other Cultural DNA. Cultural Monuments are indeed the building blocks of a society, built by society itself, spread around by propaganda and enforced by often self-appointed minders, at least in a democracy. Propaganda is very effective when the tribe understands who the enemy is – even when the 'enemy' has not directly attacked the tribe. In the absence of a direct attack, how does one firmly establish within the tribe the idea that the 'devil' is indeed bad?

National achievements become a source of pride in the same manner as team sports, albeit with potentially deeper reverence. Consider for a moment how Britain and the world came to regard the *Titanic* and its sister ship the *Olympic*: the ship's 'towering hills are moulded to battle against the seven seas.' This type of grandiloquence can be found wherever Blue-Sky Cultural Monuments are in the process of being constructed; bombast is the building material of myths and monuments, designed to nudge members to cheer on the tribe's chosen horse for the race; and like the yin and the yang, Cultural DNA often tells tribe members which horse to avoid. Cultural monuments are a survival mechanism, comprised of embedded knowledge that has been passed down through the generations to allow members of the tribe to operate almost instinctively, so that very little thought is required. Cultural Monuments become entrenched through immersion in cultural programming from infancy. Blue-Sky Monuments are a tribe's 'shining cities on a hill'; they are embedded, hard-wired, instantly recognised, requiring little to no individual judgement, since the founding fathers, tribal elders, and high priests have already passed judgement. Likewise, something so 'good' implies that there is also something not good. The original dichotomy requires there to be something not desired, something to be loathed, something bad. In America, it's the exact polar opposite of the 'shining city on a hill.' As a polar opposite, Marxism has been a consistent Dark-Sky Cultural Monument in the United States, and as such, has been deeply and consistently integrated into Cultural DNA so that Americans, by and large, require little or no deep thought about what Marxism actually means. It is therefore no surprise that such Cultural Monuments can produce a strong bias in judgement. The existence of these cultural über-biases can influence perception and decision-making in many hidden ways and on many levels of power. Cultural Monuments had purpose and meaning in our early history; they were part of the social contract, holding the ancestors and their land as sacred, conserving it for future generations unspoiled, unexploited, and intact. But our ancient monuments have been hijacked and are now being used as tools by social entrepreneurs. They have become the altars upon which the 'other' are sacrificed. What you hold sacred reflects what you value: Uluru is the church, the school, the law, and the land itself. When our land is not sacred, we tend to extract from the land to serve another god, a neon god. When we lose sight of the sacredness of human life, we tend to extract from it just the same – to serve yet another, more human, more avaricious god; hence the almost 400-year history of slavery in the Americas. With this recent history, America had to show a sceptical world not just that capitalism was indeed better, but that the American brand of capitalism was the right medicine for a world trembling at the sight of two atomic colossi malevolently eyeing each other.

In this inquiry we have learned how Cultural Monuments have contributed to disasters through the introduction of bias, whether cultural or deliberately manufactured. We have seen examples of Blue-Sky Monument Building in the case of the *Titanic*, and we have also seen how a collective manufactured Cultural Monument such as Concorde can escape scrutiny and even engender a lax mentality regarding maintenance and operations. We have also encountered a system that is liable to being co-opted by very powerful decision-makers in a strictly hierarchical control structure. These systems are vulnerable to powerful veto players who may steer the system to serve their own ends. Further, these individuals do not always possess the correct 'binoculars' to identify and understand the various threats to that designed system, but their power and position within that hierarchy may give them the illusion that they understand the environment and its threats, when they do not and cannot understand.

In the future, we need to discuss how Cultural Monuments are manipulated by populists in order for them to gain influence over large numbers of culturally similar people who share compatible, culturally embedded monuments. We should dive deeper into how Cultural Monuments come into existence – whether grassroots, top-down, or otherwise – and how they can be manipulated by populists, authoritarians, and dictators.

There is much to learn about how Human Folly #2, the propaganda folly, comes into view, especially during culture wars. Historical events are in the past, and any past event can no longer be changed by decision-making in the present. Hence the phrase, 'you can't change the past.' But how the past event is presented or remembered is subject to intelligent design, i.e., manipulation, and therefore subject to folly. Bias frequently enters the retelling of events as they occurred, even to the point that two people who were there and saw the event may have interpreted what they saw differently. Human Folly #2 will continue to play a large role in propaganda and populism through misinformation and disinformation as well as Dark-Sky and Blue-Sky Monument Building. The folly will apply to those who accept a manipulated version of past events. Unfortunately, the details of the actual event(s) can be carefully hidden and buried under the flooding of the zone.

In "Catastrophe by Design" we have peeled back the layers of some of history's most infamous calamities to reveal an unsettling truth: many disasters are, in fact, products of human design. From the hubris-laden voyage of the Titanic to the tragic launch of the Challenger, the flawed 'factory floor' that produced the Concorde crash to the outright intellectual fraud that led to the Titan submersible implosion, this study dissects the cognitive biases, Cultural Monuments, and systemic flaws that pave the way to catastrophe.

This book explores how our greatest achievements often carry the seeds of our most spectacular failures. We have identified and examined the "Four Human Follies" that blind us to impending doom, and how cultural and invented narratives can transform even the most glaring design flaws into accepted norms.

From the icy depths of the Atlantic to the skies above Cape Canaveral, "The DNA of Disaster" shows that behind every 'act of God' often lies a very human error. It's a cautionary tale for our times, reminding us that in our race to conquer nature, we might just be engineering our own downfall.

After all, those who don't learn from history are doomed to redesign it.

To my fellow humans, with my warmest regards,

Devin Savage

BIBLIOGRAPHY

INTRODUCTION

Darwin, Charles. *On the Origin of Species.* John Murray, 1859.
Lovelock, James. Gaia: *A New Look at Life on Earth.* Oxford University Press, 1979.
Malthus, Thomas. *An Essay on the Principle of Population.* J. Johnson, 1798.
Sagan, Carl. *Cosmos.* Random House, 1980.

ULURU

Adams, Micheal. "Pukulpa pitjama Ananguku ngurakutu – Welcome to Anangu land: World Heritage at Uluru-Kata Tjuta National Park." University of Wollongong. ro.uow.edu.au/sspapers/1753/. Accessed 17 April 2022.
"Australian dig finds evidence of Aboriginal habitation up to 80,000 years ago." The Guardian, February 14, 2018. www.theguardian.com/australia-news/2017/jul/19/dig-finds-evidence-of-aboriginal-habitation-up-to-80000-years-ago. Accessed 17 April 2022.
Beier, Ulli. *Aboriginal Myths: Creation of the World.* 1970.
Bradshaw, CJA, Norman K, Ulm S, et al. "Stochastic Models Support Rapid Peopling of Late Pleistocene Sahul." Nature Communications 12, no. 1 (2021): 2440. www.ncbi.nlm.nih.gov/pmc/articles/PMC8085232/. Accessed 17 April 2022.
Bush, George W. *Decision Points.* Crown Publishing Group, 2010.
Clendinnen, Inga. *Dancing with Strangers.* Cambridge University Press, 2005.
Dawkins, Richard. *The Selfish Gene.* Oxford University Press, 1976.
"Humans and Neanderthals 'Co-existed in Europe for Far Longer than Thought.'" The Guardian, May 11, 2020. www.theguardian.com/science/2020/may/11/humans-and-neanderthals-co-existed-in-europe-far-longer-than-thought. Accessed April 2022.

Jaireth, Subhash. "Knowing and Unknowing Uluru." Axon: Creative Explorations 9, no. 2 (December 2019). axonjournal.com.au/issues/9-2/knowing-and-unknowing-uluru. Accessed 17 April 2022.

Parks Australia. "Kata Tjunta/ Uluru National Park." parksaustralia.gov.au/uluru/discover/culture/tjukurpa/. Accessed 12 April 2022.

"Uluru and Kata Tjuta." Parks Australia, Australian Government. www.dcceew.gov.au/parks-heritage/national-parks/uluru-kata-tjuta-national-park#:~:text=Ulu%E1%B9%9Fu%2DKata Tju%E1%B9%AFa National Park is Aboriginal land, jointly managed, of Alice Springs by road. Accessed 8 October 2022.

"Uluru Climbing Ban: Tourists Scale Sacred Rock for Final Time." BBC News. www.bbc.com/news/world-australia-50151344. Accessed 8 October 2022.

"Uluru, Australia's Iconic Red Center." uluru-australia.com/about-uluru/aboriginal-uluru-dreamtime/. Accessed 12 April 2022.

"Uluru Statement from the Heart." ulurustatement.org/the-statement/. Accessed April 2022. fromtheheart.com.au/. Accessed 18 August 2022.

"Uluru's Significance to Australian Indigenous Culture." www.wayoutback.com.au/blog/ulurus-significance-to-australian-indigenous-culture/. Accessed 23 April 2022.

"UNESCO World Heritage Listing – Uluru-Kata Tjuta National Park. Outstanding Universal Value." whc.unesco.org/en/list/447/. Accessed 23 April 2022.

Tjamiwa, Tony. Quoted in: Australia National Park Management Plan, 1985.

TITANIC

Belfast News-Letter. "Post-Disaster Inquiry in the House of Commons." 19 April 1912.

Board of Trade. Merchant Shipping Act of 1894. Sections 427 and 428, outlining life-saving appliances and rules for British ships. Revised 1911.

The Bristol Mercury. "Compulsory Bulkheading." 23 June 1896.

Cialdini, Robert. Influence: Science and Practice. Harper Collins, 1993

Cork Examiner. "The White Star SS. Olympic: A Wonderful Vessel." 21 January 1911.

Daily Citizen (Manchester, UK). "The Titanic Disaster Destroyed the Legend of the 'Practically Unsinkable' Ship." 13 March 1913.

Gloucester Citizen. "A Shipbuilding Record Triumph for Belfast Skill." 19 March 1907.

Haidt, Jonathan. The Righteous Mind: Why Good People Are Divided by Politics and Religion. New York: Pantheon Books, 2012.

Harland and Wolff. Technical Reports and Correspondence. Estimates of water influx and *Titanic*'s structural vulnerability, attributed to Edward Wilding, Senior Naval Architect.

Herbert, Frank. *God Emperor of Dune.* Dune Chronicles #4. New York: Ace Books, 1987.

House of Commons Inquiry into the Titanic Disaster. Statements and proceedings regarding the Board of Trade regulations, life-saving appliances, and the ship's watertight compartment safety, featuring Mr. Sydney Buxton and Mr. Bonar Law. 18 April 1912.

Irish News and Belfast Morning News. "White Star Monsters: Facts About the Wonderful Vessels Now Building in Belfast." 3 October 1910.

John Bull. "The White Star's 'Olympic': A Serious Insufficiency of Lifeboats." 19 November 1910.

Leeds Mercury. "Unsinkable Ships – The Briton." 15 October 1861.

Lloyd's List. "Unsinkable Ships: The Stone-Lloyd Bulkhead Doors." 3 November 1903.

Morgan, L. *Futility: The Sinking of the Titan.* M. F. Mansfield. 1898.

Pall Mall Gazette. Stead, W. T. "How the Mail Steamer Went Down in Mid Atlantic by a Survivor." 22 March 1896.

Scotsman. "Strength of Design." 20 October 1910.

Sunday Citizen **(Asheville, NC).** "Science and Skill of Century Figure in New Steamers 'Olympic' and 'Titanic' Masterpieces of Workmanship Show Supremacy." 25 June 1911.

The Illustrated London News. "The New White Star Line, 'Celtic' on the Stocks." 6 April 1901.

The White Star SS. Olympic: A Wonderful Vessel. *Cork Examiner*, 21 January 1911.

"RMS Olympic Weekly Telegraph." 22 October 1910.

"The White Star's 'Olympic': A Serious Insufficiency of Lifeboats." *John Bull*, 19 November 1910.

"Science and Skill of Century Figure in New Steamers 'Olympic' and 'Titanic' Masterpieces of Workmanship Show Supremacy." *The Sunday Citizen* (Asheville, NC), 25 June 1911.

Wormstedt, Bill, J. Kent Layton, and Tad Fitch. *On a Sea of Glass: The Life & Loss of the RMS Titanic.* 2015.

CHALLENGER

Boffey, Philip M. "Feb. 26, 1986 Special to the New York Times: Rocket Engineers Tell of Pressure for a Launching."

Boisjoly, Roger. Engineering Report on O-Rings and Shuttle Launch Conditions. Morton Thiokol, 1985.

Boisjoly, Roger, Ellen Foster Curtis, and Eugene Mellican. "Roger Boisjoly and the Challenger Disaster: The Ethical Dimensions." *Journal of Business Ethics* 8, no. 4 (April 1989): 217–230.

Broad, William J. "Teacher Is Focus of Space Mission." *The New York Times*, January 25, 1986. archive.nytimes.com/www.nytimes.com/library/national/science/012586sci-nasa-challenger.html. Accessed 20 May 2023.

Cook, Richard. "The Shuttle Had Been Sold as a Reliable Space Truck...There Was Just a Whole Party Line and Propaganda That the Thing Was a Completely Understood, Completely Reliable Vehicle, and It Was Not." Former NASA Budget Analyst.

Dick, Steven J. "Why We Explore." NASA, 28 March 2008. www.nasa.gov/exploration/whyweexplore/Why_We_29.html. Accessed 21 May 2023.

Dreifus, Claudia. "A Conversation with/Sally Ride; Painful Questions from an Ex-Astronaut." *The New York Times*, 26 August 2003. www.nytimes.com/2003/08/26/science/a-conversation-with-sally-ride-painful-questions-from-an-ex-astronaut.html. Accessed 14 May 2023.

Fagen, Donald. "I.G.Y." The Nightfly. Reprise Records, 1982.

Feynman, Richard P. *What Do You Care What Other People Think?* New York: W.W. Norton & Company, 1988.

Harris, Hugh. *"Shuttle Launch Delayed Due to Mechanical Issues."* Cape Canaveral Press, January 1986.

Harriss, Joseph A. "Examination of Concorde Accident History." Archived from the original on 28 March 2016. Accessed 13 November 2022. Wayback Machine.

Harriss, Joseph. "The Concorde Redemption." *Smithsonian Magazine*, September 2001.

Ignatius, David. "Did the Media Goad NASA Into the Challenger Disaster?" The Washington Post, 30 March 1986. www.washingtonpost.com/archive/opinions/1986/03/30/did-the-media-goad-nasa-into-the-challenger-disaster/e0c8669d-a809-4c8d-a4f8-50652b892274/. Accessed 21 May 2023.

Kilminster, Joe. Testimony to the Rogers Commission, 1986.

Maier, Mark. *A Major Malfunction: The Story Behind the Space Shuttle Challenger Disaster.* 1992; repr., Chapman University.

McDonald, Allan. *Truth, Lies, and O-Rings: Inside the Space Shuttle Challenger Disaster.* 2012.

McDonald, Allan, and Roger Boisjoly. "Handwritten Charts and Test Motor Data Summary." Presented to NASA management, 27 January 1986.

"Memo to Thiokol Management on O-Ring Problems." 1985.

NASA. The Space Shuttle Program: History and Technical Overview. NASA. www.nasa.gov/. Accessed 21 May 2023.

NASA.gov. "The Cold War Between the United States and Former Soviet Union Gave Birth to the Space Race and an Unprecedented Program of Scientific Exploration." www.nasa.gov/. Accessed 20 May 2023.

President John F. Kennedy. "Address at Rice University on the Nation's Space Effort, September 12, 1962." Houston, Texas, 12 September 1962. www.jfklibrary.org/archives/other-resources/john-f-kennedy-speeches/rice-university-19620912. Accessed 20 May 2023.

Reagan, Ronald. *The Reagan Diaries.* Edited by Douglas Brinkley. HarperCollins, 2007. "Letter to the Faculty and Students of Concord High School." 1986.

Report of the Committee on Science and Technology, House of Representatives, Ninety-Ninth Congress, Second Session, October 29, 1986. Investigation of the Challenger Accident. Committed to the Committee of the Whole House on the State of the Union and Ordered to Be Printed. 64–420. U.S. Government Printing Office, Washington, 1986.

Rogers Commission. Report of the Presidential Commission on the Space Shuttle Challenger Accident. Washington, D.C.: Government Printing Office, 1986.

Russell, Brian. Testimony to the Rogers Commission, 1986.

Sagdeev, Roald, and Susan Eisenhower. "United States-Soviet Space Cooperation During the Cold War." University of Maryland and The Eisenhower Institute, 2008. www.nasa.gov/50th/50th_magazine/coldWarCoOp.html. Accessed 20 May 2023.

CONCORDE

ABC News. "Concorde Makes Final Touchdown." 25 October 2003.

Aeronautics Monthly. "The Origin of the Concorde." April 1962.

Bannister, Mike. *Concorde: The Inside Story.* HarperCollins, 2006.

Bureau d'Enquêtes et d'Analyses pour la Sécurité de l'Aviation Civile (BEA).
Final Report on the Accident of Concorde F-BTSC Flight 4590. BEA, 2004.

Bureau Enquêtes Accidents (BEA). Final Report: Air France Flight 4590.
16 August 2001.

British Broadcasting Corporation (BBC). "Concorde's Maiden Flight."
BBC News, 3 March 1969.

Cook, Richard. "The Concorde: The World's Most Glamorous Aircraft."
Aviation History Review 22, no. 3 (Fall 2004): 34–47.

Editors of Encyclopaedia Britannica. "Concorde." Encyclopedia Britannica.
5 June 2023. www.britannica.com/technology/Concorde.
Accessed 14 November 2022.

Farndon, John. *Concorde: The Complete Illustrated History.* Amber Books, 2006.

Flight International. "Concorde Design Hurdles." December 1971.

Flight International. "Concorde's Engineering and Operational Challenges."
February 1976.

French National Assembly. Report of the Commission of Inquiry into the Concorde
Accident. French National Assembly, 2001.

Gayssot, Jean-Claude. Statement on Concorde Crash Investigation.
French Transport Ministry Press Release, 2000.

Grimsby Daily Telegraph. "Humberside International Airport's Future."
13 June 1992.

Grimsby Evening Telegraph. "Concorde Extravaganza at Humberside." 14 June 1992.

Hopkinson, Deborah. *Titanic: Voices from the Disaster.* Scholastic Inc., 2012.

Heseltine, Michael. "Concorde: A Monument to Technical Achievement."
Aerospace Quarterly 12, no. 1 (Spring 1986): 56–62.

Hull Daily Mail. "The £15,000 Gamble." 18 March, 1992.

International Civil Aviation Organization (ICAO). Runway Foreign Object Debris
Detection and Management. ICAO, 2007. www.icao.int/EURNAT/Other Meetings
Seminars and Workshops/Safety - RWY SAF/ICAO Runway Safety Seminar -
Technology/5.2 EUROCAE Presentation FOD_24 March 2022.pdf.
Accessed 14 November, 2022.

Jackson, Robert. *The Concorde: A Supersonic Legacy.* Osprey Publishing, 2014.

Jones, Mary. "Design Failures and the Role of Human Error in Major Aircraft
Accidents." Safety Science Review 29, no. 2 (2008): 189–208.

Knight, Geoffrey. *Concorde: The Inside Story.* 1976. "Leap Through the Sound Barrier."

Le Monde. "Concorde Disaster: A Review of the Events." Le Monde, 2000.

Mail & Guardian. "From Order to Chaos in a Few Seconds." mg.co.za/opinion/2021-04-26-from-order-to-chaos-in-a-few-seconds/. Accessed 10 November, 2022.

Marian, Maud. "The Concorde Accident Criminal Trial in France." Air and Space Law 36, no. 2 (2011): 131–138. kluwerlawonline.com/journalarticle/Air+and+Space+Law/36.2/AILA2011017. Accessed 14 November 2022.

McDonald, Allan. *Truth, Lies, and O-Rings: Inside the Space Shuttle Challenger Disaster.* 2012.

Moussa, Albert. "The Potential for Fuel Tank Fire and Hydrodynamic Ram From Uncontained Engine Debris." BlazeTech Report, 1997.

National Transportation Safety Board. "NTSB Letter on Tire Blowouts." 1981.

Savage, Bill. Interview on Humberside Airport Development. Air Transport World, August 1991.

Smith, James. "The Effects of Runway Contamination on Aircraft Performance and Safety." Journal of Aerospace Engineering 22, no. 3 (2005): 134–145.

The Guardian. "Concorde Crash Causes and Consequences." August 2001.

The Guardian. "Concorde's Arrival in Ontario." September 1986.

The New York Times. "Concorde Tire Blowout at Dulles." April 8, 1969.

The Times. "Concorde at Coventry Air Day." August 1981.

The Times. "Concorde Design Hurdles." December 1971.

The Washington Post. "Concorde Tyre Incidents." July 1979.

Trubshaw, Brian. *Concorde: The Rise and Fall of the Supersonic Airliner.* Sutton Publishing, 2003.

United States Congress. "Concorde Landing Rights and the SST Project." Congressional Record 127 (July 1981): 4356–4378.

Vaughan, Diane. *The Challenger Launch Decision: Risky Technology, Culture, and Deviance at NASA.* University of Chicago Press, 1996.

Wofford III, Drewry Frye. "History at the Speed of Sound: A Transnational Case Study of the Concorde Supersonic Transport as a Reflection of Critical Issues in Postwar Europe." PhD diss., University of Miami, May 2020.

"Concorde." Design Museum. Posted 19 March 2015. Updated 3 November 2015.

"Concorde Vicinity Paris Charles de Gaulle, France 2000." Skybrary – The Global Safety Information Portal. skybrary.aero/accidents-and-incidents/conc-vicinity-paris-charles-de-gaulle-france-2000. Accessed 12 November 2022.

"Continental Airlines Cleared of Criminal Conduct Over Concorde Crash." The Times. www.thetimes.co.uk/article/continental-airlines-cleared-of-criminal-conduct-over-concorde-crash-gpbjlvkglfb. Accessed 14 November 2022.

"**Runway Had Not Been Checked for More Than 12 Hours.**" The Guardian. www.theguardian.com/uk/2000/sep/01/concorde.world1. Accessed 13 November 2022.

TITAN SUB

"**Enabling Exploration.**" Composites Manufacturing Magazine, October 2019. compositesmanufacturingmagazine.com/2019/10/enabling-exploration/. Accessed 29 April 2024.

Lochridge, Mark. "Interview with the BBC." BBC News, 2023. Interview. www.bbc.com/news/live/world-us-canada-65953941. Accessed 10 May 2024.

Lochridge, Paul. Safety Report on the Titan Submersible. OceanGate, 2019.

Mauger, John. "US Coast Guard Press Announcement." June 22, 2023. www.dvidshub.net/video/888022/coast-guard-holds-press-briefing-about-discovery-debris-belonging-21-ft-submersible-titan. Accessed 9 May 2024.

McDonald, Allan. "Interview on Shuttle's Solid Rocket Boosters Testing." NASA Archives, 1991.

Perrottet, Tony. "A Deep Dive Into the Plans to Take Tourists to the 'Titanic.'" Smithsonian, June 2019. www.smithsonianmag.com/innovation/worlds-first-deep-diving-submarine-plans-tourists-see-titanic-180972179/. Accessed 10 May 2024.

Pogue, David. "Interview with the BBC." BBC News, 2023. Interview. www.bbc.com/news/world-us-canada-65957709. Accessed 10 May 2024.

Prisco, Jacopo. "US Aviation Meltdown: Fixes and Travel Tips." CNN, June 31, 2023. www.cnn.com/travel/us-aviation-meltdown-fixes-travel/index.html. Accessed 11 November 2024.

Robinson, Morgan. Futility, or The Wreck of the Titan. M. F. Mansfield, 1898.

Rush, Stockton. "Geekwire Summit Talk." GeekWire, 2022. www.geekwire.com/2023/oceangate-and-stockton-rush-the-inside-story-in-his-own-words/. Accessed 10 May 2024.

Rush, Stockton, and David Pogue. "Interview inside the Titan." CBS News, 2022. Interview. www.cbsnews.com/news/titanic-submersible-interview-transcript-with-oceangate-ceo-stockton-rush/. Accessed 10 May 2024.

Stanley, Karl. "Acoustic Monitoring Systems and Carbon Fiber Hull Analysis." Deep Sea Engineering Review 48, no. 4 (2019).

Stanley, Karl. "Interview with the ABC." ABC News, 2023. Interview. abc7news.com/titan-submersible-2023-incident-titanic-oceangate-the/13421666/. Accessed 10 May 2024.

CONCLUSION

Challenger Accident Investigation. Report of the Presidential Commission on the Space Shuttle Challenger Accident. Government Printing Office, 1986.

Chernobyl Forum. Chernobyl's Legacy: Health, Environmental and Socio-Economic Impacts. World Health Organization, 2006.

CNN. "Ancient Computers, Too Few Pilots and Air Traffic Controller Shortages." CNN, 13 June 2023. www.cnn.com/2023/06/13/us/air-traffic-controller-shortage/index.html. Accessed 14 June 2024.

Doe, Jane. "The Economic Impact of Building Amnesty Programs." International Journal of Construction Management 35, no. 2 (2023): 78–93.

Fukushima Daiichi Nuclear Power Plant Investigation Commission. Fukushima Daiichi Nuclear Power Plant Accident Investigation Report. Government of Japan, 2019.

Johnson, Emily. "The Role of Construction Amnesty in Turkish Building Practices." Journal of Urban Development 29, no. 3 (2023): 45–67.

Jones, Richard. "Managing Radioactive Waste: Challenges and Solutions." Journal of Nuclear Materials Management 52, no. 1 (2024): 15–27.

National Research Council. The Impacts of Climate Change on Water Resources: A Review. National Academies Press, 2023.

New York Times. "Turkey's Building Codes: The Impact of the 1999 Earthquake." The New York Times, 2023. www.nytimes.com/2023/02/13/world/europe/turkey-earthquake-construction-buildings.html. Accessed 14 June 2024.

New York Times. "Airline Close Calls Happen Far More Often Than Previously Known." The New York Times, 21 August 2023. www.nytimes.com/2023/08/21/business/airline-close-calls.html. Accessed 14 June 2024.

NASA. "Challenger Disaster." NASA, 2023. www.nasa.gov/mission_pages/shuttle/sts1/challenger.html. Accessed 14 June 2024.

Smith, John. *Construction and Disaster: Building Failures and Their Implications.* Oxford University Press, 2024.

Smith, John. *Design Flaws in Engineering: Lessons from the Challenger and Titanic.* Oxford University Press, 2024.

Southwest Airlines. "Flight Cancellations and IT Systems." Southwest Airlines, 2022. www.southwest.com/flight-cancellations-it-systems.html. Accessed 14 June 2024.

U.S. Geological Survey. "Understanding Earthquakes." USGS, 2023. www.usgs.gov/earthquake-hazards/news?page=2. Accessed 14 June 2024.

U.S. Federal Aviation Administration (FAA). "NOTAM System Failure." FAA, 2023. www.faa.gov/air_traffic/notam_system_failure. Accessed 14 June 2024.

United Nations High Commissioner for Refugees (UNHCR). "Climate Change and Displacement." UNHCR, 2024. www.unhcr.org/what-we-do/build-better-futures/climate-change-and-displacement. Accessed 14 June 2024.

Williams, Michael. "Climate Change and the Increasing Frequency of Extreme Weather Events." Environmental Research Letters 18, no. 5 (2024): 112–129.

World Meteorological Organization. "Climate Change and Extreme Weather." WMO, 2023. wmo.int/media/news/climate-change-and-extreme-weather-impacts-hit-asia-hard#:~:text=In 2023, sea-surface temperatures, since the 1961–1990 period. Accessed 14 June 2024.

CASSANDRAS ENDNOTE:

The comet was mentioned in the Anglo-Saxon Chronicle as presaging another invasion that year by Harald Hardrarda and Harold's brother, Tostig, which actually was the main reason the Normans won (the Battle of Stamford Bridge was brutal, and though the Saxons won, they afterwards had to march a few hundred miles to meet William's army). Also, Harald knew William was planning to invade – he had his army ready and waiting, but the events at Stamford Bridge meant they had to abandon their post at what turned out to be a crucial point.

CHALLENGER ENDNOTE:

If the O-ring leaks happened on the other side of the booster rockets, away from the struts holding everything together, nothing would have happened, just fireworks outside the booster rockets as the Shuttle went up. But the system got hit with an iceberg in a weak spot: record cold weather that left the Challenger covered in ice on launch day. The sun came up and warmed the outside of the Shuttle Stack, but did not reach the inward facing areas of the booster rockets, which were also vulnerable to being cooled by the outgassing of the cryogenic liquid fuels as the fuelled-up Shuttle Stack sat on the launch pad overnight. Those were the areas which were susceptible to the intense cold and were inward facing and were also shielded from the morning sun. But the fact that they were inward facing made it so that any escaping burning gases emitted from the booster rockets might hit the huge External Fuel Tank (ET) or the struts holding the orbiter and the ET together. It was a big experiment, done in completely untested conditions, but with people on board. Chance entered the designed system, and we got Russian Roulette.

TITAN ENDNOTE:

The Titan disaster set off a worldwide debate over the future of undersea exploration.

The US Coast Guard Marine Board of Investigation (MBI), led by Captain Jason Neubauer, conducted a comprehensive two-week hearing into the Titan submersible disaster, which began on September 16, 2024, at the Charleston County Council Building in South Carolina. This high-level inquiry aimed to uncover the facts surrounding the tragic implosion of the Titan submersible in June 2023, which resulted in the loss of five lives, including OceanGate CEO Stockton Rush.

The hearings served a dual purpose: to thoroughly investigate the circumstances leading to the disaster and to develop recommendations that could prevent similar tragedies in the future. Through testimonies from former OceanGate employees, industry experts, and maritime investigators, the MBI sought to piece together the events and decisions that culminated in the catastrophic implosion of the experimental vessel. The testimonies presented during these hearings provide crucial insights into the operational practices of OceanGate, the design flaws of the Titan submersible, and the industry-wide concerns that were raised and subsequently ignored. Each witness account contributes to a comprehensive understanding of the factors that contributed to this tragedy, offering valuable lessons for the future of deep-sea exploration and maritime safety. I have included some of the more relevant testimony that occurred after I had written the manuscript of this chapter.

David Lochridge, OceanGate's former Director of Marine Operations, emerged as a key whistleblower in the Titan submersible tragedy. He repeatedly warned about the poor quality of materials used in the sub's construction and believed a disaster was "inevitable." Lochridge was fired in 2018 after raising these concerns, which he then reported to the Occupational Safety and Health Administration (OSHA). However, his complaints were not promptly investigated, leading him to believe the tragedy could have been prevented if federal agencies had acted on his warnings. Lochridge testified that OceanGate's primary focus was profit rather than scientific advancement, stating, "The whole idea behind the company was to make money. There was very little in the way of science." His testimony highlighted the potential consequences of overlooking safety concerns in pursuit of commercial goals in deep-sea exploration.

Patrick Lahey, CEO of Triton Submarines, emerged as a vocal critic of OceanGate's Titan submersible and its operational practices. In interviews and testimony, Lahey emphasised the critical importance of third-party certification for submersibles, a process OceanGate notably avoided. He described the Titan as "not particularly well thought-out" and "amateurish in its execution," based on a chance encounter with the vessel during testing in the Bahamas in 2019. Lahey's expertise in the field, backed by a 50-year "unblemished" record in submersible operations, lent weight to his concerns. He strongly criticised OceanGate's decision to operate an experimental craft in deep-sea conditions, calling it an "aberration" in the industry. Lahey stressed that submersibles are not inherently unsafe, but insisted that human exploration of the deep sea should only be conducted using certified and accredited machines, not experimental ones. His testimony at the hearing reinforced his earlier statements, highlighting the industry's emphasis on safety protocols that OceanGate had seemingly disregarded.

Former OceanGate contractor Antonella Wilby raised serious concerns about the company's safety practices and the Titan submersible's operations. Wilby reported hearing a "bang as loud as an explosion" during a 2022 dive and described OceanGate's approach to safety as mere "safety theatre." She testified that the Titan relied on a convoluted navigation system, involving manual transcription of coordinate data and the use of hand-drawn maps. When Wilby suggested improvements, she was allegedly dismissed and criticised for not having an "explorer mindset." She also claimed that customer concerns about safety were not taken seriously by OceanGate officials, including co-founder Stockton Rush. Wilby felt threatened when she attempted to escalate her concerns, being warned about potential legal consequences due to non-disclosure agreements. Wilby was removed from her job post and told her supervisors "This is an idiotic way to do navigation." Ultimately, these safety issues led Wilby to leave the company after about two weeks on the job.

According to testimony from National Transportation Safety Board (NTSB) engineer Don Kramer at the Coast Guard panel investigating the OceanGate Titan tragedy, significant manufacturing defects were present in the submersible's composite hull. Kramer reported observing wrinkles, porosity, and voids in the carbon fibre layers. He also noted that hull pieces recovered after the implosion exhibited substantial delamination of the carbon fibre layers. Kramer's testimony corroborated earlier reports of a "loud acoustic event" during a dive on July 15, 2022, stating that two different types of sensors on the Titan had recorded this occurrence. Furthermore, Kramer indicated that the submersible's behaviour changed noticeably after this incident. Another engineer testifying at the hearing suggested that the Titan's window was "consistent with something on the path of failure," highlighting additional concerns about the vessel's structural integrity.

Roy Thomas, an engineer from the American Bureau of Shipping, provided critical testimony at the Titan hearings, highlighting significant concerns about the use of carbon fibre in submersible construction. Thomas emphasised that carbon fibre, while strong and lightweight, is not only tricky to manufacture consistently, but is also particularly vulnerable to fatigue damage and external pressure, making it a risky choice for deep-sea vessels. He noted that carbon fibre is susceptible to embedded manufacturing defects, which are especially concerning given the lack of recognised standards for carbon fibre pressure hulls in human-occupied vessels. Thomas warned that "instantaneous delamination and collapse can occur in less than a millisecond" in carbon-fibre structures, rendering real-time monitoring systems potentially ineffective. He also pointed out that salt water can weaken carbon fibre in multiple ways. Thomas's testimony underscored the potential dangers of using carbon fibre in deep-sea submersibles and the lack of adequate safety measures in the Titan's design and construction.

Phil Brooks, former Director of Engineering at OceanGate, provided testimony that shed light on the company's financial struggles and their impact on safety decisions. Brooks expressed serious concerns about the company's practices, stating that economic stress led to compromised safety measures. He revealed that OceanGate had asked employees to forgo pay at times, indicating severe financial stress. Brooks testified that CEO Stockton Rush often made final decisions on engineering matters, including the assessment of hull sensor data after each dive. Notably, Brooks discussed a loud bang heard during a 2022 dive, which was recorded by acoustic sensors. While Rush attributed this to a metal frame adjustment, Brooks wanted a more thorough inspection of the hull. However, the submersible was left exposed to the elements in a parking lot over winter, with no apparent maintenance or testing conducted before the 2023 expedition season. Brooks' testimony also highlighted his lack of confidence in the Titan's construction, describing the situation as "all smoke and mirrors." He admitted to feeling unqualified to analyse certain hull data, raising questions about the expertise involved in critical safety assessments. Brooks ultimately left the company in early 2023, citing both economic and safety concerns. His departure, just months before the tragic implosion, was partly due to his perception that safety was being excessively compromised. This testimony provides significant insights into the internal operations of OceanGate and the potential factors that may have contributed to the Titan's catastrophic failure in June 2023.

Karl Stanley, an experienced submersible operator, provided crucial testimony at the Coast Guard hearing into the Titan submersible disaster. Stanley recounted a 2019 test dive with OceanGate CEO Stockton Rush, during which he heard alarming cracking sounds from the carbon fibre hull as they descended. These sounds intensified near the Titanic's depth, causing significant concern. Stanley's subsequent email exchanges with Rush revealed his deep worries about the submersible's safety, urging at least 50 test dives before allowing paying clients aboard. Despite Rush's assurances, Stanley remained unconvinced, later stating he believed Rush knew "it was going to end like this."

The hearings also featured testimony from other OceanGate employees and industry experts, painting a picture of a company prioritising ambition over safety. Amber Bay, OceanGate's former director of administration, disclosed financial struggles, including requests for employees to defer pay checks. Industry leaders, such as William Kohnen, highlighted how they had previously raised concerns about OceanGate's "experimental" approach. The testimony collectively suggested a pattern of disregard for established safety protocols and industry warnings.

Justin Jackson, a materials engineer from NASA, testified that OceanGate initially reached out to NASA to manufacture a composite hull for the Titan submersible. While NASA signed an agreement under the Reimbursable Space Act Agreement in early 2020, their involvement was limited due to the COVID-19 pandemic. NASA provided remote consultation on a one-third scale mockup and offered advice on fabricating a thick-walled hull, but did not manufacture or test any components for OceanGate. Importantly, Jackson revealed that NASA had disagreements with OceanGate over press materials that seemed to imply NASA's endorsement of the project.

Similarly, Boeing's involvement was also limited. Mark Negley, a materials and process engineer from Boeing, testified that the company conducted a preliminary feasibility study for OceanGate in 2013 but did not manufacture any parts or provide specific advice on materials. Boeing's involvement ended early in the process with no additional information as to why.

The testimonies from Jackson and Negley highlight a crucial aspect of the Titan submersible saga: Stockton Rush's attempt to create a "chain of authenticity" for his experimental vessel. Much like the White Star Line used the presence of the Stone-Lloyd automated bulkhead door system to claim the Titanic was unsinkable, Rush leveraged the names of prestigious organisations like NASA and Boeing to lend credibility to the Titan submersible.

This tactic can be seen as a form of "borrowed authority." By invoking NASA and Boeing in OceanGate's press materials and public statements, Rush created an impression that these renowned organisations were deeply involved in the Titan's development and had vetted its safety. In reality, their roles were advisory and limited in scope.

This use of "pixie dust" from established institutions served to obscure the experimental nature of the Titan and potentially made passengers and investors more comfortable with the vessel's unconventional design and lack of traditional safety certifications. It's a stark reminder of how perceptions of safety and authenticity can be manipulated through association with trusted names and entities, even when those associations are tenuous at best.

In both the Titanic and Titan cases, we see how technological innovations or prestigious partnerships can be used to create a false sense of security, ultimately contributing to catastrophic outcomes. This pattern of deceit is a recurring phenomenon and highlights the importance of thorough, independent safety certifications and the dangers of relying on perceived authority rather than rigorous testing and adherence to established safety standards and best practices.

The Coast Guard's Marine Board of Investigation was aimed at understanding the factors contributing to the tragedy and sought to develop recommendations to prevent similar occurrences. These proceedings not only shed light on the specific failings that led to the Titan disaster but also highlighted broader issues within the deep-sea exploration industry, particularly regarding the regulation and safety standards of small submarine operations. The findings could potentially lead to new safety regulations for these vessels. The board's final report is expected to include recommendations ranging from new safety regulations for submersibles to potential referrals for criminal charges.

The hearing concluded with a moment of silence for the victims, drawing attention to the gravity of the disaster and the importance of the investigation's outcomes for the future of deep-sea exploration.

Key points from the inquiry:

- Multiple witnesses raised concerns about the sub's design, materials, and safety practices, describing multiple safety concerns and operational issues
- The carbon-fibre hull and its potential for delamination was a major focus
- OceanGate's decision to avoid third-party certification was heavily criticised
- CEO Stockton Rush was described as the primary decision-maker, often dismissing valid safety concerns
- The Coast Guard's ability to regulate such operations in international waters was questioned
- The company experienced several malfunctions just prior to the fatal dive
- Some passengers were aware of risks but proceeded anyway
- OceanGate's business model and approach to safety were heavily criticised by industry professionals
- There were conflicting views on OceanGate's safety culture and transparency

CITATIONS ENDNOTES:

[1] www.washingtonpost.com/nation/2024/09/27/titan-oceangate-hearing-coast-guard-submersible/

[2] www.youtube.com/watch?v=ficZR-1uW0w

[3] www.wired.com/story/titan-submersible-hearings-end-oceangate-coast-guard-heres-what-comes-next/

[4] www.geekwire.com/2024/oceangate-former-top-engineer-cost-concerns-titan-sub-safety/

[5] www.cnn.com/2024/09/23/us/titan-submersible-oceangate-implosion-hearing/index.html

[6] www.nytimes.com/2024/09/27/science/titan-submersible-oceangate-hearing.html

[7] www.live5news.com/2024/09/23/coast-guard-begin-2nd-week-titan-hearings-north-charleston/

[8] www.news.uscg.mil/News-by-Region/Headquarters/Titan-Submersible/smdpage35464/4/smdsort35464/description/

[9] www.boatinternational.com/yachts/news/oceangate-titan-disaster-implosion-latest-news-2023-submarine-submersible-hearing

[10] www.news.uscg.mil/Press-Releases/Article/3898222/coast-guard-releases-titan-marine-board-of-investigation-hearing-schedule-witne/

[11] maritime-executive.com/article/coast-guard-schedules-much-anticipated-hearing-on-loss-of-the-sub-titan

[12] www.abc27.com/news/top-stories/final-day-of-coast-guard-hearing-into-titan-disaster-closing-out-in-north-charleston/amp/

[13] abcnews.go.com/US/oceangate-titan-sub-coast-guard-hearing-friday/story?id=114281337

[14] www.geekwire.com/2024/eyebrow-raising-revelations-come-to-light-as-hearings-into-titan-subs-loss-wrap-up/

[15] www.yourerie.com/news/whats-next-now-that-the-hearings-into-the-titan-implosion-are-over/

[16] www.independent.co.uk/news/world/americas/titan-oceangate-submersible-implosion-disaster-hearing-latest-b2619941.html?page=3

[17] www.nbcboston.com/news/national-international/nasa-boeing-coast-guard-testify-implosion-titan-submersible/3500292/?os=vbkn42tqho5H1RAdvp&ref=app

[18] www.theridgefieldpress.com/business/article/nasa-boeing-and-coast-guard-representatives-to-19794266.php

[19] abcnews.go.com/US/nasa-boeing-titan-sub-coast-guard-hearing/story?id=114186967

[20] www.thehindu.com/news/international/nasa-boeing-coast-guard-representatives-to-testify-about-implosion-of-titan-submersible/article68684821.ece

[21] thehill.com/homenews/ap/ap-business/ap-nasa-downplays-role-in-development-of-titan-submersible-that-imploded/

[22] www.1230kfjb.com/2024/09/26/nasa-disagreed-with-how-oceangate-wanted-to-invoke-the-agency-titan-hearing-witness/

[23] www.yahoo.com/news/titan-sub-hearing-live-us-084617467.html

[24] www.counton2.com/news/day-8-of-titan-hearing-dug-into-oceangates-agreements-with-nasa-and-boeing/

[25] futurism.com/the-byte/boeing-titanic-sub

INDEX

A

A320neo 263
Aaron Manby (ship) 85
Aboriginals 54, 55, 58, 60
abortion 266, 272
accumulated knowledge 8, 53, 233
acoustic monitoring system
aerospace industry 241, 247, 257
Afghanistan 68
Air France 183, 193, 198, 201, 202, 208, 214, 219
air shows 190
air traffic controllers 285–286
Airbus A320 263
algorithms 15, 43, 53, 64
altar 257, 268, 292
Alvin (submersible) 232, 244, 251
American Airlines 188
Anangu 58, 59, 60, 61, 62, 64
ancestors 9, 15, 36, 53, 54, 55, 59, 60, 62, 65, 256, 277, 292
Ancient Egypt 54
Andrea Dario 230
animal husbandry 10, 19
Antipodes submersible 229
Apollo programme 151, 215
Apple 27, 28, 29, 30, 31, 42, 187, 224
Armstrong, Neil 166
Asteroids 41, 275
Astor, John Jacob 120, 122
Australia 54, 57, 86
authoritarians 293
automatic bulkhead doors 94–95, 97, 98, 125
autopilot 174, 283
Ayers Rock, *See Uluru*

B

bacteria 25, 270
Baldwin, Alec 39, 265
ballast pumps 125
Bannister, Captain Mike 184
Bassett Hound 43
Battle of Hastings 44
Bayeux Tapestry 44
BBC 241
Becquerel, Henri 41
Belfast 98, 101, 128
Bell, Alexander Graham 81
Beresford, Lord Charles 91–92
Bezos, Jeff 230
bias 135, 142, 144, 162, 213, 220, 292, 293
binoculars 24, 115, 116, 118, 137, 138, 144, 220, 262, 264, 287
biological DNA 65
biosphere 275
BlazeTech 200
blind spots 282
blowby 52, 153, 155, 156, 159, 168, 174, 218, 222
Blue-Sky Monument Building 88, 98, 105, 127, 135, 178–179, 180, 219, 291, 292–293
Board of Trade 91, 105, 108, 110–112, 127–129, 130–131
bodily autonomy 266–267
Boeing 707 185
Boeing 737 Max 263
Boisjoly, Roger 52, 153, 155, 156, 159, 160, 161, 167, 169, 174, 175
Bork, Robert 66
Bottomley, Horatio 107, 109–110, 131
Branson, Richard 227–228, 230–233
Brazil 264

Bristol Times and Mirror 109
British Airways 183–184, 199, 201
British Army 195
British Colonial America 256
British de Havilland Comet 185
Brooks, Phil 309
Brown, Molly 120
bubonic plagues 42
building codes 273
Bulkhead Committee 92
bulkheads 89, 90, 91, 95, 96, 104, 130, 128
Bureau Enquêtes Accidents (BEA accident report) 201, 203–210
Burke, Edmund 54
Bush, George W. 46, 68
Bush, H. W. 47
Buxton, Sydney 110–111, 130

C

Californian (ship) 115, 117, 118, 120, 124
Campbell, Naomi 187
Cameron, James 244
Cape Canaveral 151, 294
capitalism 147
capitalism (venture) 227
carbon dioxide 23, 47
carbon fibre 235, 246, 248, 250, 252–257, 262, 308–310
carbon-fibre composite 251, 254
carbon-fibre dome 246
carbon-fibre hull *(Titan)* 244, 248–250, 263, 312
carbon-fibre submersible *(Titan)* 224–226
Caronia (ship) 113–114
Carpathia (ship) 118–119, 121–124
Carter, Jimmy 188
cassandras 44, 45, 47, 106–107, 131, 155, 159, 162, 169, 200, 238–239, 305
Cedric (ship) 89
Celtic (ship) 89
Chain of Tribute 219
Challenger aircraft 154, 10, 167, 172, 174, 220

Challenger disaster *See O-Rings, Teacher in Space Programme, blowby*
Challenger Accident Investigation Board 154
chance 14–15, 33, 43, 72, 133, 153, 163, 181, 217–218, 222, 223, 236, 247, 269, 282, 306
charisma 255
charismatic leader 255
Chernobyl disaster 148
China 24, 50, 54, 163, 264
Chirac, Jacques 208
chlorofluorocarbons 46
Cialdini, Robert 127
climate change 33, 73, 75, 278, 289
Clinton rally 46
Clinton, Bill 49
CNN 285
cognitive biases 31, 293
cognitive control 174–175, 218–221, 262, 285–288
Cold War 149–150, 163, 177, 179, 185
Collins, Joan 187
colonisation 56, 65
Columbia Accident Investigation Board 154
Committee on Climate Change 46
communism 147
Concorde aircraft
first flight 187
cost of 184
tyre blowout 198–201, 213, 221–222
Concorde design 195, 196, 206, 209
Concorde fuel tanks 196, 198, 200, 203, 214, 217, 222
Concorde pilot 197, 209
Concorde programme 184, 185, 187, 213
Conservatives 15
conspiracy theories (*Titantic*) 83
construction amnesty 273
Cork Examiner 102
corporations 25, 49
Cosmos, See Carl Sagan
court of law (Irish) 270–271
creation myths 57, 60

/ 317

cryogenic fuels 173, 222
C-suite 26–27, 30–31, 67, 162, 174, 285, 288
culture 62, 64–65, 85, 88, 281, 282
 Aboriginal 54, 55, 57, 59, 62–64
 ancient 53, 54
 corporate 86
 human 56, 65
 pop 228
 wars 293
Cultural DNA 16, 36, 65, 66, 79, 291, 292
cultural memory 12, 60
Cultural Monuments 53, 57, 64, 65, 162, 271, 277, 281, 282, 291–293
Cunard Line 86, 108, 113
Cunard, Samuel 86
Curie, Marie 41–42
Curie, Pierre 41–42
Cuyahoga River Fire 48
Cyclops-1 submersible 228, 230, 232
Cyclops-2 submersible 231, 233, 257

D

Daily Citizen 127
Dark-Sky Monuments 68
Dark-Sky Monument Building 66, 68
Darwin, Charles 18–21, 23
data points 269–270
Dawkins, Richard 64
Dean, Millvina 121
decision-making 11, 40, 66, 71, 168, 197, 211, 261, 270–271, 287, 292–293
Declaration of Independence 227
Deep Ocean Expeditions 231
Deepwater Horizon disaster 45
delta wings 195
Democrats 40
dental composites 262
design by evolution 17, 181, 223
design flaw 10, 81, 174, 249, 264, 265, 282, 294
designed solutions 15, 17
destructive weather events 278
dictators 293

Divine Intervention Folly 34–36, 42–44, 78, 143, 163, 283, 28–286
dinosaurs 16, 25
Douglas DC-8 (aircraft) 185
Dreamtime 55, 60–63
Dreyfus, Claudia 154
droughts 275
Drummond Castle (ship) 93, 95
Drummond Castle disaster 93

E

Earth 16, 18, 22–25, 33, 54, 57, 64, 76, 78, 151, 228, 275, 278, 280, 289–290
earthquakes 8, 11–12, 33, 41, 280, 289
ecological systems 280
Economic Policy Institute 49
Edison, Thomas 81
Eiffel Tower 81
Eighth Amendment (Ireland) 266–267, 270–271
Einstein, Albert 132
Eisenhower, Dwight D. 150
embedded cognition 277
embedded design 10, 71, 133, 139, 142–143, 210–211, 249, 261, 274
embedded intelligent design 39, 42–43, 132–133, 289
Emergency Location Transmitter 249
emotional trauma 267
end caps 253–254, 262
End-Permian Event 18
Engels, Friedrich 179
Enterprise Resource Planning (ERP) software 285
environment
 cultural DNA and 15, 21, 36
 human design and 17, 74, 181, 223, 261, 293
 within DNA of Disaster Methodology 206, 213
 See also: folly, intelligent design, embedded design
error 10–12, 30, 33, 118, 125, 140, 142, 180, 202, 214–215, 217, 238, 247, 278, 286, 294
 See also bias; noise
Europeans 56

evolution 18, 33, 36, 41, 141, 181, 223, 247, 280
evolution (definition of) 41
evolutionary design 14, 17–20, 26, 33–34, 36, 132, 215, 265
evolutionary forces 17, 34, 36, 41, 44, 142, 175, 220, 265, 280, 283
experimental design 21
extinction 16–17, 25, 33, 53, 220, 265

F

false economy 175–176, 254
famine 8
fate 18, 35, 84, 87, 210
Faustian pact 9
Federal Aviation Administration 188
feedback from the environment 30, 218
Feynman, Richard P. 168, 170
floods 8, 12, 275
foam ballast 250
folly
  biases of the human mind 246
  definition: Four Human Follies 34–41, 283
  linked to future catastrophes 278
  See also: Divine Intervention Folly, Propaganda Folly, Trojan Horse Folly, Marie and Pierre Curie Folly
forces of nature 8, 17, 80, 248
Fosset, Steve 246
fossil fuel 75, 78
fossil-fuelled engines 275
free trade 47–50
Fukushima Daiichi 276, 279, 281
Futility (Morgan Robinson) 84, 257

G

Gaia Hypothesis 23
Galway University Hospital 267
gaming controller 234
Garden of Eden 60–61
Garn, Jake 148
Gayssot, Jean-Claude 183, 201
genome 19–20
Glaciers 76, 278

global warming 75
Gloucester Citizen 98, 297
gods 36, 275
Goldilocks zone 23–24
Golding, William 23
Google 31
Godwinson, Harold 44
Gore, Albert 46–48
Great Britain 56, 190
Great Eastern (ship) 81–82, 86–87, 103
Great Pyramid of Giza 54, 81
Great Western Railway Company 108
greed 12
greenhouse gases 75, 289
Gulf Stream 115, 133, 275
Guggenheim, Benjamin 121

H

Haidt, Jonathan 144
Halappanavar, Praveen 267
Halappanavar, Savita 267
Halley's Comet 44–45, 305
Harland and Wolff 125, 144
head pilot (Oceangate) 240
heroes 257
high-tensile steel 232
Hobbes, Thomas 8
holes in knowledge *See folly;*
  See also blind spots
Holmes, Elizabeth 224–225, 254, 258
Home Insurance Building 81
Homo erectus 18
Homo habilis 18
Homo sapiens 8, 18, 105–106
horticulture 10, 18, 65
Hotel Hotelissimo 183
hubris 12, 67, 127, 244, 293
human design 10, 14, 17, 43, 71, 74, 181, 223, 261
  See also: intelligent design
human follies *See folly*
human intentions 12
human-designed disasters 12

human-designed systems
8, 12, 43, 261, 279–280
Humberside International Airport 191–193
hunter-gatherers 9, 55
hurricanes 8, 275
Hutchins, Halyna 38
hydrogen fuel 160
hydrostatic pressure 251

I

Iceberg Alley 139, 142, 248
Idaho 271–272
ignorance 42, 282
Independence Day 179–180, 219
Industrial Age 77
Industrial Revolution 78
Inman Line 86
innovation
  between 1860 and 1910 80
  Thomas Edison 81
  Stone–Lloyd 95
  Stockton Rush 228, 229–230, 232, 238, 241, 243–244, 250, 258
  true cost 251
  false economy 254
  carbon fibre 253–254, 258
Instagram 31
intelligent design
  ancient products of 53–55
  versus evolutionary design 14, 19, 33, 36, 132
  versus embedded design 71
  example of pure intelligent design 43
  perfect intelligent design 33
  rule DNA of disaster 206
  See also: folly, noise, semi-intelligent design, embedded intelligent design
iPhone 26–27, 29
iPod 29
Iraq 69
Irish case law 270–271
Irish Government 269
Irish women 266–267
Iron Duke (ship) 91
Istanbul 273

Ismay, Bruce 114, 122, 124, 142
Ismay, Thomas 86–87, 90–92
IT failures 287
iTunes 28–30

J

Jakarta 173
Japan 11
Jefferson, Thomas 38
jerry-riggedness 255
jobs 47, 49, 50, 163
Jobs, Steve 28–29, 224–225
John Bull (newsmagazine) 107–108, 110–111, 131
judgement 9, 14–15, 20, 26, 30, 33, 39–40, 46, 134, 163, 175, 181, 222–223, 265, 270, 275, 284–285, 291–292
just-in-case, supply chain 9
just-in-time, supply chain 9

K

Kaiser effect 242
Kaiser Wilhelm der Grosse (ship) 87
Kata-Tjuta 58
Kennedy International Airport 198–199
Kennedy Space Center 149, 160, 172, 178
Kilminster, Joe 161, 174
knowledge *as categories*
  ancient 8, 9, 53
  cultural 15, 64–66, 68, 277, 291
  scientific 45–46
  lack of 78, 133, 175
  power and 53
  intelligent design and 17, 172, 261
  Aboriginal 55, 61–64
  See also: Cassandras, Cultural Monuments
Kramer, Don 308

L

Labrador Stream 115
Lahey, Patrick 238, 240, 307
Le Monde 215
Leeds Mercury 90

legal jeopardy 266
Lenin, Vladimir 179
lifeboats
  on *Ivernia* 108
  on *Olympic* 108–110
  on *Titanic* 118–119, 121, 123, 126, 140
Blue-Sky Monument Building 105
Lincolnshire 191
Linnaeus, Carl 195
Lochridge, David 238–240, 244, 249–250
loosely coupled event 137, 139
Lovelock, James 23
Lusitania (ship) 100, 109, 110, 113
luck 14, 18–19, 31, 46
Lund, Bob 156, 160

M

Machiavelli, Niccolo 236
Malthus, Robert 19
Malthusian catastrophe 19
Manoeuvre Characteristics Augmentation System 264
Marconi room 134, 144
Marie and Pierre Curie Folly 34, 36, 41–42, 44, 78, 142, 153, 168, 175, 205, 248, 288
Marine Board of Investigation (MBI) 306, 311
Marine Technology Society (MTS) 239
Marty, Captain Christian Henri 203–204, 215, 219, 221
Marx, Karl 179
Marxism 148, 292
mass extinction 17
Mauretania (ship) 109–110, 113
McAuliffe, Christa 149, 164, 177–178, 165
McCallum, Rob 238, 240
McCartney, Paul 187
McDonald, Allan 152, 155–156, 159–161, 169, 174, 175, 249
meme 64
Merchant Shipping Act of 1894
Mesoamerica 54
Mesolithic era 18
Mesopotamia 54

meteor strikes 280
Mexico 47–50, 163
Microsoft 26, 187
Milky Way 24
misinformation 293
Morton Thiokol
  and folly 168, 174
  blowby dismissal 153, 155
  commission findings 166–169
  engineers safety concerns 157, 158, 159–160
Moussa, Albert 200
Mt Olga National Park 58
Mulloy, Larry 160
Munchausen syndrome by proxy 37
Musk, Elon 39, 147, 230

N

Nargeolet, Paul-Henri 237
narratives 9, 45, 54–55, 60, 63–64, 277, 281
NASA
  hierarchical power relations 162
  human folly 168, 178
  ignoring red flags 158, 174, 218, 220, 247, 269
  See also: Challenger disaster
National Aeronautics and Space Act 150
national identity 179
Native Americans 12, 62
natural disasters 8, 272
natural selection 18–19
natural systems 9, 73–74
navigational error 10
Neanderthals 18
Nelson, Bill 148
Neolithic era 18
New York 49, 85, 101, 119, 124, 154, 178, 182, 188, 210, 204
New Yorker 240
New York Times 154, 178–179, 198, 273, 286
9/11 attacks 68
Noise (chance in a designed system)
  Challenger disaster 153, 161–162, 168, 175
  climate and 77, 276–277
  Concorde 213

definition of 43, 74, 153, 282
design systems and 213, 217, 219, 263, 265, 272, 273, 275, 280, 282, 287
Titan 249
See also: red flags
Nokia 26–31, 181, 280
normalcy bias 134
North American Free Trade Agreement (NAFTA) 47
NOTAM failure 287
nuclear waste 279

O

obstetricians (Ireland) 267, 269–270
OceanGate
creation myth 255
founding and history 229–230
NASA parallel 249
Vision for 234
Oceanic (ship) 85, 87, 103
Offences Against the Person Act 1861 266
oil embargo 1973 187
oil spill 10
Olympic (ship) 83, 87–89, 101–104, 106, 108–112, 121, 125–126, 137, 144, 215, 291
Olympics, the 204
On the Origin of Species, *See Darwin*
operational design 10, 71, 261
organ failure 268
origin myths 55
O-rings 152–157, 159, 163, 166, 168, 170, 173, 181, 216, 218, 220, 238, 249, 258, 282
Otis, Elisha Graves 80
Ovi Store 29
ozone layer 46

P

pandemics 8
Parazynski, Scott 237
Passenger Vessel Safety Act of 1993 229
Patagonia 18, 21
patriarchy 271

Pearl Harbor 150
Perot, Ross 47–48, 50, 163
Perrottet, Tony 228
Peru 54
Piccadilly Hotel 109–110
Pogue, David 241, 255–256
polar ice caps 74, 76, 278, 289
pollution 33, 47–48, 188
Pompeii 41
populism 293
populists 293
pregnancy 266–267, 269–272
pressure testing 246
propaganda 34, 37, 40, 88, 105, 147, 174, 178, 281, 283, 291, 293
Propaganda Folly 34, 47, 40, 283, 287, 293
prototype designs 263
Psion 27

Q

Queenstown Harbour 108

R

radiation 23, 41, 42, 46, 75, 280, 289
radioactive substances 42, 74, 275
radioactive waste 275–276
randomness 14, 19, 34, 36, 44, 141, 153, 163, 181, 218, 223, 247, 283
Reagan, Ronald 146–149, 164, 166, 175, 177–178, 180, 220, 286
real-time input from the environment 265
red flags 77, 153, 234, 249, 267
referendum (Ireland) 268
refugees 278
religion 36, 56, 60, 64, 67, 272, 281, 291
reproductive care 271
Revelle, Roger 46–47
revisionist folly 37, 40
Ride, Sally K. 153, 166, 176
risk
general discussion of 10, 11, 32–33, 73, 76
Titanic and icebergs 134

Challenger disaster and 166, 168, 269
climate change 289
rituals 9, 12, 15, 54
Roatan Institute of Deepsea Exploration 232
Robinson, Morgan 257
rocket motor tests 162
Roe vs Wade 271–272
Rogers Commission 154, 166–167
Roosevelt, Franklin D. 49
Rush, Stockton 25, 226, 230, 232, 236, 238, 243, 246, 248, 250, 254, 256, 263, 309, 310
Rush, Wendy 257
Russia 69
Russian Roulette 168, 218, 231, 247, 306

S

Sagan, Carl, *See Cosmos*
Samsung 31
Satan 66–68
Savage, Bill 192–193
scapegoat 66
Scripps Institution of Oceanography 77
scuba-diving tanks 246
sea-level rise 74–75, 77, 173
Second Amendment 38
selective-breeding 22
self-driving cars 283
semi-intelligent design 34, 35, 141, 143–144, 173, 220, 247, 263
sepsis 268
septic miscarriage 270
shipbuilding 88, 98, 102, 126, 246
shipwrecks 83–84, 91
Silicon Valley 224
six-sigma 278
slavery 292
smartphones 26–27, 214–215
Smith, Captain Edward John 112–115, 118–119, 122, 125, 133–134, 136, 138, 142, 144, 221, 261–262
social contract 50, 65, 292
social media 31, 231

social proof 105, 127, 237, 281
solar energy 77, 278
solar flares 280
solar system 54, 64, 278
Solid Rocket Boosters 149, 151, 168, 173–174, 249, 281–282
solid rocket motors 151, 159
Southwest Airlines fiasco 285
Soviet Union 149, 150, 178, 179, 180
space race 147–150, 178–180, 219
Space Shuttle Columbia disaster 153–154
Space Shuttle Programme 148–151, 155, 157, 179–180, 269
space tourism 228
spacers (Concorde) 202–203, 250
SpaceShipOne 227
Sputnik 147, 149–150, 179
SRBs *See Solid Rocket Boosters*
Stanley, Karl 232–233, 240–241, 244, 245, 257
Stead, William Thomas 84
startups 224, 250–251
Stone Age, the 18
Stone–Lloyd automatic bulkhead doors 94–98, 125
Stop the Steal 40
stories
  cultural knowledge and 9, 12, 21, 53,
  Aboriginal Origin stories 55, 57, 60–63,
  Dream time stories 60, 62,
  Stockton Rush 229, 236, 241, 255, 257–258
  See also: Cultural DNA
storms 12, 75–77, 84, 289
Straus, Ida 257
Straus, Isidor 121, 257
stresses to carbon fibre 252
submarines 228, 232, 236, 238, 249, 307
submersible industry 236, 251
Suevic (ship) 97–99, 127, 137
sun 22–24, 54, 58, 75, 115, 173
supersonic aerodynamics 195
supersonic commercial passenger jet 184

Supersonic Transport Aircraft
  Committee 195
supply chain 9, 47, 72, 289
Symbian OS 27–28

T

Teacher In Space Project (TISP)
  148, 157, 164, 177, 220
terrorism 68
Tesla 39, 283
Theranos 224–225
Thomas, Roy 308
Thompson, Ernie 152–153
thorium 42
tightly-coupled event 139–140
tightly-coupled event cascades
  140, 142, 217, 247
Titan submersible 96, 226, 243,
  246, 248, 249, 254, 262, 293
Titanic, RMS
  binoculars, lack of 118, 137, 287
  class distinctions onboard 113, 115, 119
  comparison to Uluru 79
  Cultural Monument as 80, 82
  disaster discussion 80–140
  ice warnings 113–117
  iceberg collision with 117, 133, 142
  lifeboats shortage 118, 126–127, 136, 138, 140
  musicians and final performance 119
  normalcy bias 134
  timeline of sinking 113–124
  wreck of 123, 126, 226, 229, 231, 232, 233, 235, 237, 242, 243, 247, 250
  See also: unsinkable propaganda
titanium 232, 234–235,
  246, 250–252, 254
titanium endcaps 235, 246
Tokyo 11, 50
tornadoes 8, 275
tourism (deep sea) 228, 230, 231, 250
trade policy 49
Triton Submarines 238, 307
Trojan Horse 38, 40, 78, 272
Trojan Horse folly 34, 38, 78, 141–143,
  153, 167–168, 174, 181, 202–203, 205,
  296, 208–210, 222, 247–248, 276

Troy 38, 40
Trump, Donald 40, 66, 68
tsunamis 8, 11
Turkish–Syrian border region 273
tyre blowout, Concorde 198, 200–201,
  212–213, 221

U

Ukraine 69, 281
ultrasonic hull scan 238
ultrasonic survey 248
Uluru (Ayers Rock) 54, 57–61, 63, 64,
  79, 85, 281, 292
United Kingdom 90, 98, 99, 184, 191, 266
unsinkable propaganda
  Titanic and Olympic 83, 101, 106, 108,
    110–111
  and bulkheads 89–90, 95–98, 126,
    141, 143,
  Titanic 88, 113, 127, 130–131, 136,
    142, 144
  Titan 239
uranium 42
US Navy 228, 232
US Supreme Court 66

V

Value Chain 29, 175, 180–181,
  202, 219–220, 222–223
Vanguard (ship) 91
venture capitalist 225, 250
Vescovo, Victor 244
Vesuvius Mount 36, 41
Vietnam War 147
viewport *Titan* 230, 238, 252
viruses 56
volcanoes 8, 12, 33, 41, 75, 280

W

Wall Street Journal 66
wars 290, 293
water on the planet 278–290
Watergate 147

Welin davit 102
western United States 289
Westinghouse, George 80
whistleblowers, *See Cassandras*
White Star Line 83, 85–86, 89–91, 100, 102–104, 109–110, 112, 124, 136, 144
wildfires 73, 289
William Duke of Normandy 44
wood framed homes 289
World War II 185, 191
Wozniak, Steve 225
Wright Brothers 195
Wyoming schooner 264

Y
Yeager, Charles E. 166

Z
Zaporizhzhia Nuclear Power Station 281

ACKNOWLEDGEMENTS

PERSONAL ACKNOWLEDGEMENTS

Throughout our many walks and social events over the years in beautiful Tübingen, I would like to thank my dear friends **Nikos Logothetis**, **Ziad Hafed** and **Mirko Whitfield** for their ongoing guidance and commentary as I seek to understand the human mind.

PROFESSIONAL ACKNOWLEDGEMENTS

Development and Editing

Jessica Dorfman Jones, what can I say – Jessica, you have been my advisor throughout all of this, helping me create with more relevance and eloquence, and you have helped me to bring this work into a readable and engaging form. "Don't bore us, get to the chorus!" and "You buried the lede!" will stick with me for the duration of my career. Bravo, Jessica, for all you have done.

Dr. Tim Flight – for his broad knowledge of humanities and sciences, whose watchful eye gives an author a sense that someone is watching, suggesting, knowing, and questioning, which imparts a sense of confidence in releasing one's work to the world. A big 'Thank you' to Tim.

Dr. Sarah Meehan – the quintessential professional with a keen eye and a wonderful sense of literary tone. Thank you for all of your help.

Ivan Solotaroff – for his key work in the identification of items that may have been misinterpreted by readers, and who demanded explanations. Thank you Ivan.

Roberto Golovic – whose meticulous work on fact checking and content management helped to keep my list of citations and references under control. Thank you Roberto.

Special Thanks To:

Dr. Eric Ketzan for his very helpful suggestions early on in this endeavour, and **Dr. Alfonso Casal** and **Josesteban Prieto** for our many discussions over the years.

Cover art and book design: **Studio Eyal & Myrthe**. www.eymy.nl

www.ingramcontent.com/pod-product-compliance
Lightning Source LLC
Chambersburg PA
CBHW050514170426
43201CB00013B/1956